THE DEVIL WE KNOW

Also by Robert Baer

THE DEVIL WE KNOW

DEALING WITH
THE NEW IRANIAN SUPERPOWER

ROBERT BAER

BROADWAY PAPERBACKS • NEW YORK

Copyright © 2008 by Robert B. Baer

Published in the United States by Broadway Paperbacks, an imprint of the
Crown Publishing Group, a division of Random House, Inc., New York.

www.crownpublishing.com

Broadway Paperbacks and its logo, a letter B bisected at the diagonal, are
registered trademarks of Random House, Inc.

Originally published in hardcover in the United States by Crown Publishers,
an imprint of the Crown Publishing Group, a division of
Random House, Inc., New York, in 2008.

Library of Congress Cataloging-in-Publication Data

Baer, Robert.
The devil we know : dealing with the new Iranian superpower / Robert Baer.
p.   cm.
1. Iran—Politics and government—1997–   2. Iran—Foreign relations—
21st century.   3. Iran—Strategic aspects.   4. Persian Gulf region—
Politics and government—21st century.   I. Title.
DS318.9.B34 2008
955.05'4—dc22   2008025466

ISBN 978-0-307-40867-9

DESIGN BY LEONARD W. HENDERSON

MAP BY MAPPING SPECIALISTS

First Paperback Edition

146028962

CONTENTS

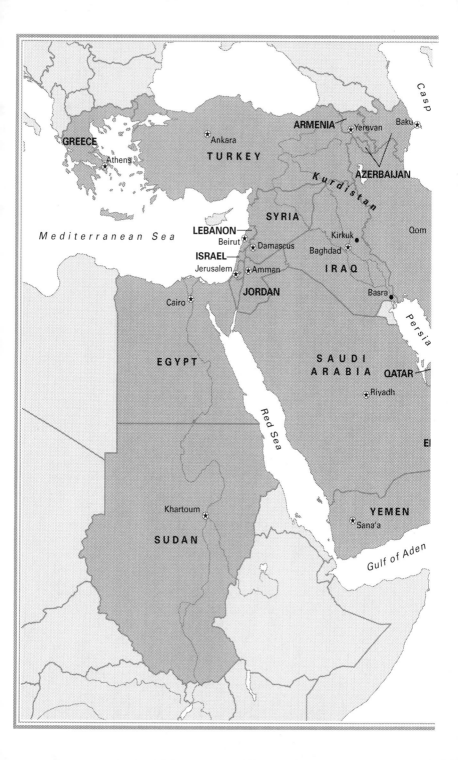

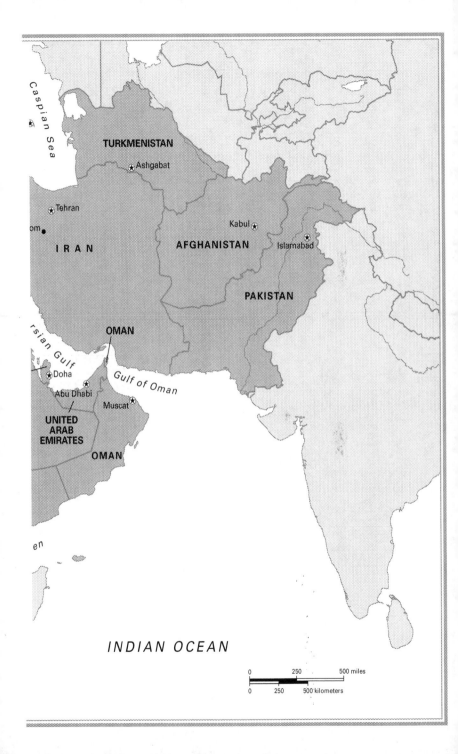

PROLOGUE

I first visited Iran in October 1978, only months before Ayatollah Khomeini would return from exile and take power. I was twenty-four, on my way to my first CIA posting, in India, and had only the vaguest ideas about the Middle East.

The kamikaze taxi driver who drove me into Tehran from the airport that night taught me my first lesson: Iranians can't drive. The way he swooped and darted between the army patrols, I was convinced he was trying to draw fire. And was it legal to drive on the side of the road to get around traffic? My one-week stopover in Tehran did little to clear things up. I left not having the slightest idea what Khomeini would do with the mess when it was his. As I'd find out much later, Khomeini didn't know either.

Less than four years later, Iran was at war with the United States. On Tehran's part it was undeclared; on Washington's, it was ignored. In the middle of the Cold War, who had time for Tehran's idiosyncratic, possibly insane mullahs?

I served on the front lines of that war, declared or undeclared. I lost colleagues at the American embassy in Beirut, which Iran truck-bombed in April 1983. I lost Iranian friends assassinated by the regime. Like many, I was convinced that Iran's revolution would drown in its own blood, the revolutionary zeal draining out just as it had with other violent rebellions in Islam. This seemed all but certain during the Iran-Iraq War, when Khomeini stubbornly refused to settle with Saddam Hussein, sacrificing hundreds of thousands of Iranians for no other reason than that he believed God was on his side. But Khomeini's regime survived, providing another lesson I needed to learn before Iran would come into focus for me.

At the end of the Iran-Iraq War, not only did Iran still have fight in it, it was a lot smarter. Iran and its proxy in Lebanon, Hezbollah, found out they could win by discarding terrorism for a radically new form of guerrilla warfare: roadside bombs, sophisticated precision-guided rockets, and the ultimate smart bomb, the suicide bomber. These are the same weapons and tactics that now have us stalemated in Iraq and Afghanistan. And along the way Iran just as certainly acquired an appetite for hegemony, a belief that it's powerful enough to challenge the United States for dominance of the Persian Gulf—not just control of Iraq but of the Gulf's oil, which is 55 percent of the world's reserves.

This isn't a war the United States has years to prepare for. It's half-fought and already half-won—by Iran. The sooner we understand the Iranian paradox—who they are, what they want, how they want to both humble us and work with us—the sooner we'll understand how to come to terms with the new Iranian superpower.

Twenty-six years after that first visit, I was in Tehran again. This time I was making a documentary with Britain's Channel 4 and an Irish production company. In April 2005, I attended the Liberation of Khorramshahr celebration held at Ayatollah Khomeini's mausoleum not far from Tehran. Outside after the ceremony, I caught up with Iran's hard-line chief of staff. I asked him what the importance of martyrdom was for Iran's armed forces.

He was surprised to be questioned by an American, especially in a place foreigners rarely visit. But he answered anyhow.

"In all religions martyrdom exists," he told me. "Even in Ireland there are martyrs. Anyone who lives and fights for peace, unity, human rights is a martyr. And if his blood is shed, he is considered a martyr. In Islam, martyrdom is the reward for holy war—and whoever is with pure motive and knowingly gives his life, he sees the face of God. He will be received by the angels, who will take him to his paradise."

Of course. This could have been lifted right out of the Koran, the same religious propaganda we've been subjected to for so long. But what did it mean in practical terms to America? I asked.

"America should have understood by now that day by day they have to listen more carefully," he said. "They should know that no army can stand in the way of martyrdom. The Islamic revolution has reached a point where it has access to modern weapons and the experience to plan and carry out its strategy. America should understand that if it takes on Iran today, it will lose its position of strength."

I knew Iran well enough now to know what its chief of staff was getting at. Iran has convinced itself it is America's equal, a statist military power capable of thwarting American power in the Gulf. Iran believes that the new form of warfare it developed in Lebanon can fight a conventional army to a standstill. Iran also believes it is now a global power, inasmuch as its advanced Silkworm missiles positioned along the Persian Gulf can shut off Gulf oil exports in a matter of minutes. The chief of staff's message was clear: The game has changed.

When Americans think about Iran, we see the black-turbaned, long-bearded, scowling Ayatollah Khomeini, a dark specter bent on vengeance. Or we remember young Iranian boys running across Iraqi minefields screaming *allahu akbar,* "God is great." Or the American diplomats in 1979, blindfolded, hands tied behind their backs. It's nearly impossible to get past those images. And Iran's apocalyptic, Holocaust-denying president, Mahmoud Ahmadinejad, hasn't helped.

We have convinced ourselves that Iran is a historical aberration, a medieval throwback harboring an irrational hate for the West. Iranians are "Islamofascists," we've been told, to be lumped in with Osama bin Laden and al Qaeda. And somewhere along the way, we've settled for the easy assumption that the Iranian regime will one day, inevitably, collapse under the weight of the twenty-first century. All we have to do in the meantime is make sure it doesn't get a nuclear bomb, and that its proxy Hezbollah, the Lebanese Shia political and military organization, stops rocketing Israel.

Iran is a closed society and a remote enemy. It's not surprising, then, that the United States missed how Iran has evolved over the last thirty years—how it has modernized, grown up, having abandoned both terrorism and Khomeini's revolution. Iran is still riding the wave of Islamic fundamentalism that's sweeping away the last vestiges of a secular Middle East, but at the same time it's now a rational actor, coldly and methodically pursuing its national interests.

Scratch away the veneer of Islam, and what you find in an Iranian is old-fashioned nationalism—a deep, abiding defiance of colonialism. Keep scratching and what you find at the bottom of Iran's soul is a newfound taste for empire. It runs through Iranian society, even among more secular Iranians. But Iran isn't a new Rome, intent on naked conquest, cultural diffusion, settlements, and religious conversion. What drives Iran to empire is something different. Call it destiny, entitlement, or even manifest destiny: what's critical to understand is that Iran today has an unshakable belief in its right to empire. It means to achieve this through proxy warfare and control over oil supplies.

It's not hard to understand where Iran got the confidence, misplaced or not, that it can beat the West. In Lebanon, from 1982 to 2000, Iran's proxy Hezbollah beat the Israelis on the field of battle, the first time Israel's army had lost since the country's founding in 1948. Israel claims it wasn't defeated militarily in the conflict, that they lost only the will to fight and not the war. But in the 34-day Lebanon war in 2006, the Israeli army was in fact beaten. It retreated from Lebanon with heavy losses and without obtaining a single objective.

Iran's star is rising. And now with a friendly Shia government in

Baghdad, it will rise a lot faster. On the other hand, the old Sunni order—the foundation of American interests in the Middle East—is edging toward collapse. How long can Pakistan and Saudi Arabia hold on? For the first time in the history of Islam, Shia domination of Mecca is not unthinkable. Nor is an Iranian empire in the Middle East. Was Khomeini right after all, that Iran would ultimately defeat America, the Great Satan?

Defining Iran's imperial drive is the subject of this book. The viewpoint is from the periphery, where empires are historically best observed, their character best understood. We better understand Rome's imperial character by looking at Roman Gaul or Spain rather than at the metropolitan center. In the same way, we'll better understand Iran's imperial blueprint by looking at Lebanon, Iraq, and Afghanistan rather than Tehran.

Watching Iran's rise over the last thirty years has been a personal voyage for me. I was fortunate to live on the same periphery I write about—mainly the Arab world. I witnessed firsthand Iran transform itself into a world power, going from a terrorist, revolutionary power to a statist one with imperial ambitions. It is a country that may not be able to challenge the United States for global supremacy, but it is one that can make America's hold on the Middle East untenable.

In the CIA, I was fortunate to observe Iran through a prism of defectors, telephone taps, intercepts, and official Iranian classified documents—communications in which Iranians, expecting privacy, were more likely to be frank, not to mention more careful with facts. But because of the 1947 National Security Act, I am not permitted to name or in any way describe these sources in any detail. Journalists and academics will find this frustrating, and much of the material will be unverifiable and unusable in their own research. This is regrettable but unavoidable.

This is not a book about Iran's people, the way they cope with revolution, their feminist movement, their cuisine, and so on. I touch on Iranian culture only in passing, with the sole purpose of putting Iran's empire by proxy in context. My sole focus is national security: defining Iran's imperial ambitions and its strategy for carrying them out. This is a book about how we deal with a rising Iran—the devil we know.

1

THE IRANIAN PARADOX

One Friday morning in 2005, I attended prayer services at Tehran University. I was traveling with a crew from Britain's Channel 4, and we were treated as VIPs. Security checks were waived and we were given the press booth right next to Ayatollah Kashani, who addressed the faithful for the next two hours. The vast hall was only half full, but Kashani's sermon was long and furious, something straight out of 1979.

Out on the street, a demonstration was forming. There were effigies of President Bush, blood running from his pointed teeth. Across the street, some demonstrators unfurled banners: *Marg bar amerika*—"Death to America."

I walked for a time among the demonstrators. There was one old man who seemed especially passionate about bringing death to America, shaking his fist and shouting. I walked up to him. "Do you mean all Americans?" I asked.

He looked at me curiously. "Where are you from?" he said. I told him I was American. He winked and leaned in closer to me.

"How can I get an American visa?" he asked.

Iran is a country of nuances. Unfortunately, at just the time it most needs to, the United States doesn't see those nuances, or understand Iran for what it is: a country that's deeply pious, yet desperately trying to modernize. Iran's religious parties generally receive only about 10 percent of the vote—considerably less than in Turkey, a member of NATO and an American ally.

Americans see Iran's president and mullahs as relics from a dark age, when in reality they're a driving force behind Iran's modernization. Since the U.S.-led invasions of Afghanistan and Iraq, it's true, there's been a conservative retrenchment, with hard-liners winning the presidency and a majority in parliament. A U-turn like this was all but inevitable with hostile armies on two of Iran's borders. But once the wars are over, Iran will no doubt return to modernizing.

Iranians watch our movies, read our books, listen to our music. They have taken to the Internet and modern technology with an obsession equal to our own. Today Persian is the most common language on the Internet after English and Mandarin Chinese. Iran's president Mahmoud Ahmadinejad writes his own blog.

In some ways, Iran has matched our own modern standards. The country's population growth has plummeted from a high of 3.2 in 1986 to 1.2 in 2001, only slightly higher than America's. Some Iranians still keep an old marriage practice that Sunni Muslims consider morally forbidden: *zawaj al-mita'*—"pleasure marriage," or sanctioned prostitution. The way it works is, a mullah will grant a license for a man and a woman to marry for a set period—two hours, a week, a month. The mullah's only concern is making sure the man pays for the child if the woman becomes pregnant. It's paradoxes like these that make Iran so difficult to grasp.

The signs of change are everywhere. One of the most popular dramas on Iranian state television is about an Iranian diplomat who saves French Jews from the Nazis during World War II. The average age of marriage for an Iranian woman today is twenty-five; during the Shah's last year in power, it was thirteen. And doctors reportedly perform more sex-change operations in Iran than in any other country except Thailand, with the Iranian government even paying up to half the cost for some transsexuals.

If you stroll around north Tehran, the part that runs up into the hills, that's where you're really struck by the contrasts. There are food courts serving Thai and Chinese food, with plastic trays and soft drinks. Young unmarried girls and boys share hookahs at outdoor restaurants, the girls' head covers pushed back, down around the neck. In Iran, unlike in Saudi Arabia, religious police aren't on every corner to enforce the "moral order." And unlike in The Sudan, there are no arrests in Iran for the grave offense of naming a teddy bear "Mohammed."

While I was in Tehran, I was regularly invited to parties; I'd heard rumors they were as hip and wild as anything that goes on in the cosmopolitan Western capitals of the world. But as a former CIA operative involved with the Iranian opposition, I figured I'd already pressed my luck even coming to Iran. What did all this tell me about Iran's imperial grasp? The parties, the love affair with the Internet, the changing sexual mores—they augur a country modernizing, looking beyond its borders.

One piece of Iran that's trying to modernize but can't is the economy. For the life of me, I couldn't find a single good restaurant in Tehran. The restaurants reminded me of those in the Soviet Union: buffets with lousy service. There were more waiters than needed, but all of them stood around, surly, turning away when you wanted something. Kitchens ran out of everything. And breakfasts were peculiar, with mountains of watermelon and boiled eggs and nothing else. Omelets were apparently an outrageous luxury, though with relentless charm and cajoling you might get one.

Another thing that reminded me of the Soviet Union were the soulless, water-streaked cement apartment buildings, office buildings, and hotels. Concierges are invariably polite but hopeless in trying to help you with anything. Phones mostly don't work, and

Internet connections are erratic. To be sure, there are well-heeled Iranian elite reading *Lolita* and dining on nouvelle cuisine, but they keep out of sight.

Tehran's big problem is the internal combustion engine. The Iranian national car, the Peykan, is one of the noisiest, worst-polluting, and least fuel-efficient cars in the world. It was in production for forty years, and many of the cars on Iran's roads predate the 1979 revolution. With gasoline running as low as 7 cents a gallon until recently, though, there wasn't much incentive for change. Even so, in the last three years, 250,000 Iranian cars have been converted to natural gas or hybrids, and today Tehran's smog has cleared up enough to see the snow-covered Elburz Mountains to the north.

When I visited south Tehran's Kumaila Mosque, ground zero of Ayatollah Khomeini's revolution, I noticed the distinct smell of opium smoke drifting through the narrow alleys. This was a conservative neighborhood, the place where the Islamic revolution started, yet there was an incomprehensible tolerance for a vice forbidden almost everywhere else in the world.

And it wasn't as if the Iranian government couldn't close down the opium dens if it wanted to. Iran is a police state. Every day I drove around Tehran, or walked around the streets and bazaars, I was stopped and my papers checked—just because I looked out of place, a foreigner. The tamperproof ID card I was issued by the Ministry of Information was more sophisticated than those you'd find in the United States—a permanent digital record of the ex–CIA agent, now an accredited journalist in Iran.

The contradictions continue. Tehran's Imam Khomeini International Airport is one of the most modern and least traveled in the world—and, I should add, the most polite. On arrival, I handed my passport to an immigration official wearing the hijab, or head covering. When she saw I was American, she said, "I'm so sorry." She entered my name on the flat-screen monitor, then picked up the phone and called someone. A minute later, a man in a suit without a tie appeared behind her. He motioned for me to follow him.

There's no point in pretending I felt anything other than dread. I knew the reputation of the Iranian secret police during both the Shah's regime and the revolution. I remembered how we came across pictures of Iranian dissidents in Tehran's notorious Evin Prison, left in the courtyard in the freezing cold, their legs broken with baseball bats. Or pictures of the CIA's station chief in Beirut after he'd been beaten by Iranian proxies and left to die of pneumonia. Or of Iranian liberals in the late nineties, executed in their homes. Even today, the Iranians still occasionally serve up medieval punishment for crimes, including amputations and public floggings.

And Americans, even after a certain thaw in Iranian-American relations, weren't immune from the Iranian police state. On March 8, 2007, the former FBI agent Robert Levinson flew to the Iranian free-trade zone of Kish Island—and disappeared like a diamond in an inkwell. At this writing, the FBI's best guess is that a rogue element of Iran's intelligence service grabbed him. Not exactly what you'd expect from a modern country. But this is the most important nuance of Iran: It's a country desperately trying to modernize, not one that has already modernized.

I waited nervously until the man in the suit came back. "I'm very sorry," he said, "but we must fingerprint you."

As I followed him to his office, he explained that his ministry had started fingerprinting Americans after the United States instituted the same practice for Iranians visiting the United States. It was a simple matter of reciprocity, equal justice. I had to stop him from apologizing. Iran still had the capacity to surprise me.

A misconception Americans have about Iran is that Iranians hate us and our culture. But that's not true. They simply hate what they consider our occupation of large swaths of the Middle East. I saw this most clearly when making a documentary about suicide bombers in southern Lebanon a couple of years ago. Hezbollah, an Iranian proxy whose name means "party of God" in Arabic, had invited us to film at its martyrs' school in Nabatiyah, to see how their next generation was turning out—Allah's little soldiers.

Nabatiyah itself holds a celebrated place in the history of Lebanon's Shia. On October 16, 1983, on the Muslim observance of Ashura, an Israeli patrol tried to cut through a procession of Shia faithful. Rocks flew, and the Israelis fired back, killing two Lebanese. The incident sparked what came to be known as the Islamic resistance, an insurgency the Israelis couldn't put down no matter what they threw back at it.

Eighteen years of unforgiving war followed, until the Israelis finally pulled their troops out of Lebanon in May 2000. This was a critical turning point, the first time that Israel was forced to cede land under fire. The Middle East suddenly discovered Hezbollah, which emerged stronger than ever, both politically and militarily. For many Arabs, Nabatiyah was Hezbollah's Boston Tea Party; Israel's forced departure from Lebanon was its Waterloo. But Iran knew the fighting wasn't over, and it built the school in Nabatiyah as an incubator for a new generation of suicide bombers, for the next war.

As we pulled up to the three-story school building, perched on a bare hill, I was struck by the eerie silence. The only sound was the mean, thin wind that cut across the jagged limestone escarpment.

Classes were in session, but there was none of the laughing or shouting you'd normally hear at an American school. There were no students out front. No cars or even a bicycle in sight—the students all walk from their homes in Nabatiyah. The grounds were immaculate, from the raked gravel walks to the avocado exterior and the whitewashed classrooms. The school was a model of order and cleanliness. But that's something I'd noticed in the last twenty-five years about Iran and its proxy Hezbollah: they manage to impose order where there was none before.

The principal, in an ash-gray chador and steel-framed glasses, was waiting for us at the front door. The look on her face told me she wasn't happy about our visit, but she didn't have a choice—Hezbollah was now romancing the Western media. It had driven the Israelis out of Lebanon and was in charge now. Sloughing off old skin for new, guerrillas turned statesmen, they were determined to convince the West they'd left their terrorist past behind and were now perfectly comfortable opening up their inner sanctums.

The principal led me up to the second floor and into a classroom. The twenty or so teenagers, all girls, were silent, attentive. The principal told me I should address my questions only to the teacher. I quickly got around to asking her about her special students, the daughters of suicide bombers. There were three in her class.

She said they pay no school fees, they receive gifts every Father's Day, and after graduation their university education is paid for. The other students and the teachers treat them with deep respect as living symbols of martyrdom, sacrifice, and Islam's devotion to justice.

"You have to be proud of your father," the teacher said, looking at a petite girl in the front row, "because he defended the country. Because he is a hero."

The girl, whose father died in an ambush of an Israeli patrol, looked steadily at her teacher, neither smiling nor blushing. Her chador barely covered her raven hair.

Why, I asked the teacher, is martyrdom so important for Shia Islam?

"Because it is at the heart of our religion."

Martyrdom in fact is a canon of Shia Islam, almost as important as the Koran, the mosque, and daily prayer. Hezbollah, like Iran, has turned martyrdom into a state religion. Iran's Martyrs' Foundation, a quasi-governmental institution founded to care for the families of Iranian soldiers who died during the Iran-Iraq War, funds the Nabatiyah school.

But I was more interested in what the girls themselves had to say. "May I ask the students questions?" I asked. The teacher looked at the principal, who shot me a nasty look, but then nodded.

"Who watches American TV?" I asked, addressing the class in Arabic.

Every hand shot up.

"What do you watch?"

One girl giggled. *"Oprah."*

"You're kidding," I said, genuinely surprised at both the answer and the giggle.

At that point the entire class leapt in, in English. "No, no, really!" they said, some of them laughing. "We love *Oprah.*"

And that's another paradox Americans need to understand: While the schoolgirls in Nabatiyah may watch *Oprah* and want iPods and flat-screen TVs, that doesn't mean they want to be like us. They'll never slip into bikinis and flip-flops to go to the beach, or watch our R-rated movies or listen to our garage bands. They take from Western culture and technology what suits them, what fits their beliefs, convictions, and sense of propriety. And nothing more. But what they really don't want forced on them is our politics.

The sooner we understand how a girl from Nabatiyah's martyrs' school can watch *Oprah,* then strap on a suicide bomber's vest and blow herself up in the middle of an Israeli patrol, the better prepared we'll be to face what's coming our way.

Iran is complex enough that even the Iranians themselves have trouble understanding their own country. A conversation I had with one of Ayatollah Khomeini's former aides, a man I will call Amin, illustrated this perfectly.

We met at Amin's bookstore in Paris, where he had emigrated after Khomeini's revolution collapsed. "I sincerely apologize for the cliché, sir," he said, moving a stack of books to see me better, "but Iran is a mosaic. Yes, 'mosaic' is the word I'm looking for."

As an aide to Khomeini, Amin had lived through the lowest point of American-Iranian relations, the 1979 hostage crisis. He later served in the Majlis, Iran's parliament. Since he emigrated, he's had a lot of time to think about Iran and Khomeini's failed revolution.

Amin admits that at times Iran is barely comprehensible even to Iranians. He told me the story of being in Tehran in 1981 when a terrorist group blew up Khomeini's party headquarters, killing four cabinet ministers and leading to fears within the regime that Khomeini's revolution was about to cross over into anarchy. But even though an enormous bomb had just destroyed the building and you could hear sirens screaming through Tehran's streets, no one had the nerve to tell Ayatollah Khomeini what had just happened.

Amin was in the waiting area of Khomeini's office when finally the intercom crackled on an aide's desk, summoning him. The aide tiptoed into Khomeini's office and came back ten seconds later: Khomeini had just heard the news on the BBC's Persian Service— the source of most of his information about his own country. Even though Amin sat in the inner circle, it was difficult to know who really ran the country.

Still, Amin believes the United States misunderstands Iran by an unnecessarily wide mark. On one level, Americans are too distant from the Middle East, too naïve to understand its complexities and history. On another, it's the people who show up in Washington— Iranian and Arab exiles nursing a grudge, with time on their hands and money to pay for a hotel—who influence U.S. policy by default. They color Washington's view of the world, drawing us into foreign adventures we have no business being in.

And then there's just plain shortsightedness, the distractions of modern life getting in the way of our understanding. The world is infinite in detail, and we are finite in our ability to select from it. There are just too many facts, and this is especially true with a country as complex as Iran.

Amin pulled down a UNESCO book on migration to the Iranian capital.

"Look here," he said. "Tehran is a Turkic city. Not Persian. How many Americans understand this?"

Indeed, it comes as a surprise to many Americans that of Iran's 70 million people, just 51 percent are ethnic Persian. The largest minority is of Turkish origin—or Azeris, as they're called in Iran. The rest of the population is a mix of Kurds, Arabs, Baluch, and others.

"C'est un pays sous le voile des apparences," Amin told me—it is a country that hides behind appearances. He went on, "It's not the veil that blinds Iranians. It's the veil that blinds you. Americans see the turban, not the brain." That's another thing Amin learned to do trying to explain Iran to outsiders: reduce complexities to sound bites we're comfortable with.

"You look at the Middle East from the cockpit of a B-52 bomber," he said. "How many Americans realize one of Iran's most sacred martyrs is an American?" Amin was referring to Howard Conklin Baskerville, a missionary schoolteacher in Tabriz, Iran's sixth-largest city. During the constitutional revolution of 1905–1911, Baskerville was shot and killed while leading his Iranian students in an attempt to break the siege of Tabriz. To this day, Iranians put flowers on his grave, honoring him along with the hundreds of thousands of Iranians who died on the front in the Iran-Iraq War.

As I left Amin's bookstore, I couldn't help but think he was on to something. The reason Americans find it nearly impossible to get a grip on Iran, an anachronism with one foot in the twenty-first century, is because it's so damned complicated.

Then again, Iran has done little to explain itself. Iran is a closed society, deeply xenophobic and paranoid. All foreign visitors are seen as potential spies. Iranian leaders don't expose in public Iran's real policies. There's no such thing as investigative journalism. You can only get at the truth in snatches, brief rays of sunlight shining through dark clouds. And this is certainly true when it comes to Iran's pursuit of its core national security interests and quest for empire, subjects Iran never talks about frankly.

The problem is exacerbated, as Amin said, by exiles—usually homesick Iranians who remember an Iran of their dreams. They make themselves indispensable in Washington, in its think tanks, and with Beltway contractors peddling expertise on Iran. But almost invariably the exiles' only service is to promote their own personal interests, which usually come down to changing the regime in Tehran. This is the same malign influence we saw in the fifties when the China lobby convinced us to back Chiang Kai-shek, or today with the Cuban lobby blocking reconciliation with Castro's Cuba. Iraq, though, is the real parable for exiles suckering Washington into a debacle.

Iraqi exile Ahmed Chalabi has been publicly flayed for having prodded and misled the United States into invading Iraq, and for lying about weapons of mass destruction and the reception American troops would get in Iraq. But Chalabi's most damaging deception may prove to be his dismissing Iran as a threat to Iraq. I got a glimpse of this in a conversation with a former deputy assistant secretary of defense under Reagan named Doug Feith.

I went to see Feith in the summer of 2000, just about the time George W. Bush had won the Republican nomination for president, to talk about Iran. Feith was upbeat. He knew that if Bush won the White House, he could pretty much pick any job he wanted. He was in private law practice then, but he was a star in the Republican foreign policy brain trust.

Before we met, I had been certain Feith would understand the threat Iran posed to Iraq. When he was in the Reagan administration, he surely had read the intelligence reports that Iran was behind the bombings of the U.S. embassy in Beirut in April 1983 and the Marine barracks in October 1983. Feith also had lived through Iran-Contra and should have remembered how exiles and middlemen manipulated policy to their own ends, ending up deceiving both sides—Iran and the United States.

But as we sat at opposite ends of the couch in his office, Feith wanted to talk about Iraq, not Iran. Could the Iraqi exiles overthrow Saddam Hussein? Or more to the point, did Ahmed Chalabi and the Iraqi National Congress stand a chance of getting rid of him? Feith thought that Chalabi could, given a little help.

Listening to Feith, I wondered why he wasn't more skeptical of Chalabi, a lifelong exile who hadn't seen Baghdad since he was a child. More to the point, I wondered why Feith wasn't more suspicious about Chalabi's ties to Iran. In the nineties, Chalabi had traveled through Tehran to get into Kurdish northern Iraq. He also had unexplained ties to Iran's hard-line Islamic Revolutionary Guard Corps, one reason the Clinton administration dropped contact with him.

I pointed this out to Feith, telling him how in 1994 and 1995, Chalabi had turned over Iraqi National Congress houses and cars to Iranian intelligence, which then used them to stage the assassinations of Iranian dissidents living in the part of Iraq Saddam controlled. Didn't this sound suspicious to Feith? And that wasn't to mention Iran's long-term interests in Iraq, with or without Chalabi. I also wondered why Feith couldn't draw the obvious parallels between Iraq and Lebanon, which Iran was then effectively annexing.

The longer Feith didn't respond, the more I wondered whether he thought I was making all this up, trying for some inexplicable reason to undermine Chalabi. I told Feith that if George Bush won the presidency, he'd be in a position to confirm everything I'd just told him.

At that, Feith stood abruptly and thanked me for my visit.

"Ahmed Chalabi will be a wonderful leader of Iraq," he said firmly, before showing me out and closing the door behind me.

• • •

This is a book about Iran, and Iraq at this point may seem like an unnecessary diversion. But in fact, the one certainty about the Iraq War is that the United States will see Iran's imperial ambitions played out more clearly there than in Tehran. If it's in Iran's interests to have chaos in Iraq, then chaos there will be. If Iran intends to draw the United States into a quagmire, a quagmire is what we'll get. Our war with Iran will be fought in Iraq, through proxies, on the periphery of Iran's empire. How could we have missed this so badly?

Ahmed Chalabi certainly deserves his share of the blame for misleading Washington about Iran. In a tightly held paper meant only for the Iraq hawks in Washington, Chalabi had this to say about the Shia uprising in southern Iraq at the end of the 1991 Gulf War:

> The insurrection in the south that followed the uprising continues to simmer. The failure of the Islamic groups supported by Iran to wrest control from Saddam in the south has served to diminish any support or hope that the local population had in them. Their behavior during the Intifadah is increasingly believed to have been the cause of its failure.

In other words, according to Chalabi, Iran's proxies were a compromised and spent force. They—and Iran—had no future in Iraq, with or without Saddam. This, of course, could not have been more wrong. The same Shia groups Chalabi so easily dismissed would decisively win the parliamentary elections in 2005. They're now the legitimate government of Iraq.

Chalabi's motives should have been transparent. He obviously had no interest in raising the alarm about Iran and its designs on Iraq. Why give the Bush administration second thoughts about invading? Chalabi's only objective was to remove Saddam Hussein; he'd take his chances with Iran after he got home to Iraq. This was a gamble, no doubt. But it was better than finishing life as a parlor exile in London.

Chalabi knew he could get away with misleading Americans on Iran because we know so little about the country. It was a child's game, playing off American ignorance, reciting a few facts sugared with clichés. Add to the mix Chalabi's beautiful English and you get a glimpse at how he was able to blind Washington to Iran.

Iran myopia is a national ailment in the United States. In his 1008-page memoir, *My Life,* Bill Clinton devoted a total of four sentences to Iran. And in three preinvasion opinion pieces titled "Thinking About Iraq," *New York Times* columnist Thomas Friedman's argument for the war boiled down to this: We needed to remove Saddam in order to plant democracy in the Middle East and force it to join the twenty-first century. Friedman's argument was that "freedom, modern education and women's empowerment" were the cure for whatever ailed Iraq and the rest of the Middle East. But not a word about Iran. Friedman, too, fell for Chalabi's pretty narrative, apparently not foreseeing the certainty that Iran would meddle in Iraq as soon as Saddam's police state was dismantled.

Chalabi returned to Iraq in April 2003—not as its triumphant new leader, as Feith had assured me he'd be, but riding in the back of an American military cargo plane. His political fortunes hit a low point in 2004, when the Coalition Provisional Authority (CPA) accused him of leaking secrets to Iran. A pro-Iranian member of the CPA appointed him deputy prime minister as a consolation prize, but it was a position with virtually no power. Chalabi had fallen hard—and he knew why. He wasn't one of Iran's chosen proxies.

Chalabi lost his gamble. But then again, he'd bet with someone else's money. And through the stress of it all, he still got to vacation in Iran.

Washington was taken by surprise when Iran swept in to fill the vacuum in Iraq. But it shouldn't have been. If the United States had listened to its enemies—Iranian proxies who'd fought other wars for Iran, on other peripheries of Iran's growing empire—it might have understood the problems of occupying Iraq.

In February 2003, a little less than a month before Americans invaded Iraq, a contact in Hezbollah called me, gleefully announcing that the Iraqi-born members of Hezbollah were packing up to go home. Many of them hadn't been back since 1980, when Saddam expelled them to Iran and Lebanon.

"What are they going to do?" I asked, purposely sounding naïve.

"Organize Iraqi Hezbollah, of course. Take over Iraq."

"But how many of them are there?"

"I don't know. Two or three hundred."

"Is that enough?"

"It was in Lebanon, no?" he said as he hung up the phone.

I was afraid he wasn't far from wrong. Iran had incited a revolution in Lebanon building on a core of only a few hundred proxy fighters and co-opted clerics, who eventually turned half the country into an Iranian outpost.

Iran knew that with Saddam gone, secular Iraq was dead, making the Iraqi Shia ripe for the picking to fight a holy war against Western occupation. The Iraqi Shia would reject occupation just as surely as the Lebanese had rejected it in 1982. And Iran also knew Lebanon would be the strategic blueprint for its war of liberation: Iran would dominate Iraq not by invading it outright, but rather through proxies, spreading religious conviction, and employing the new form of guerrilla warfare it had learned in Lebanon.

Granted, Iraq is not Lebanon. In some ways, the country of Iraq was permanently shattered by the Mongol invasion in 1258. The Ottoman Empire reconstituted Iraq into three provinces, but only under the force of arms. And Saddam held the country together only with extreme brutality.

Iraq's soft center, like that of Lebanon in the eighties, is what gives Iran the confidence the Lebanon model is transferable. Even the most nationalist and fractious Iraqi Shia can be manipulated, bribed, and cowed. So, inasmuch as the future in the Middle East can ever be predicted, with time and money Iran stands a good chance of dominating in Iraq. Iran will make the Iraqis understand Iran is a country too powerful to resist, all too easy to go along with.

What Washington missed, and what Chalabi didn't want us to know, was that Iran understands how to manage chaos—that it knew exactly how to benefit from the U.S.-led destruction of the Iraqi army and state. I suspect Chalabi knew what was coming. His political education was in Lebanon; he saw firsthand what Iran could accomplish when there was an absence of central authority.

I was never privy to what Chalabi was telling the White House, the neocons, and journalists, but I'm almost certain he didn't point out that if there was one watermark running through the contemporary Middle East it was political Islam, a current the Iranians long ago learned to turn to their benefit. He also almost certainly didn't point out that a well-organized and well-funded surrogate force, driven by belief, could—and would—easily fill the vacuum in Iraq.

The Iranians know exactly what they have to do in Iraq. They wrote the template in Lebanon, where they learned how to manage chaos, to create order where there was none before. And they know there's nothing the United States can do to stop them from doing the same in Iraq. The U.S. ambassador in Baghdad, Ryan Crocker, called it Iran's "Lebanization" of Iraq.

The question of who lost Iraq isn't just water under the bridge. The truth is, nothing has changed since the Iraqi invasion. The Americans still do not understand Iran's strategy—what it wants in Iraq and how it intends to get it. We still do not understand the nature of proxy warfare, and how Iran can get its way through manipulating proxies. We still reduce the threat of Iran to weapons of mass destruction—to a nuclear bomb—but it has started to dawn on those who deal in facts that in Iran we face a problem that demands a second look.

Hopeful signs of this came when Washington's Iranian policy seemed to turn on a dime in December 2007, after the director of national intelligence issued a judgment, the National Intelligence Estimate (NIE), stating that Iran had suspended its efforts to make a nuclear bomb. The NIE didn't say it in so many words, but the implication was that Iran isn't in a hurry to get a bomb. Nuclear weapons, then, are not vital to Iran's national security. At the same time, the NIE did not diminish the threat Iran poses to U.S. interests in the region.

One Bush foreign policy adviser, a longtime Iranian specialist with whom I'd worked in the past, told me that he despaired of Washington ever really understanding the problem Iran poses for the United States. He said American understanding of Iran today is worse than it was under Ronald Reagan, George H. W. Bush, or Bill Clinton.

"[Washington officials] have no idea about the role the Iranians were playing in the eighties, the damage they did to our interests in the Middle East," he told me. "Today, all across the government, you have young men and women who know about Iran from college textbooks. They've absorbed a conceptual framework about the country that doesn't even come close to matching reality."

And our understanding of Iran wasn't that good to begin with, as he reminded me. In one incident in the eighties, it was discovered that an American who'd been held hostage for a time by an Iranian-controlled group had traces of arsenic in his fingernails. Washington's conclusion was that the Iranians were poisoning the hostages. Never mind that hostages were a valuable commodity that the Iranians would give up only for a price. Or that if they really wanted to kill them, they'd shoot or hang them in front of a camera, as they'd done with an American colonel working for the UN. The Americans couldn't understand, my friend at the White House said, that in the Middle East, small amounts of arsenic are a home remedy for stomach bugs.

I could hear the resignation in his voice: the bureaucracy, the press, and academia would never catch up to reality in time for us to change course. It was inevitable we would commit over and over the same blunders that got us into the current Iraq quagmire.

We didn't talk about confidence men like Chalabi. We didn't need to. We both knew that exiles were still taking us on another bumpy ride, and Iran would be handed victory after victory. Even today, Iranian exiles showing up in Washington say Iran is teetering on the edge—that it will collapse with a real show of force. If we just stay the course in Iraq, squeeze Iran in Lebanon, get rid of the regime in Damascus, they say, we'll win. They still can't conceive that we lost in Iraq, or understand what we lost.

Losing Iraq—letting it fall into Iran's orbit—marked the first time in history Mesopotamia was ceded to a hostile power without a real fight. It's the first time the Shia have ruled an Arab country since the Fatimids in Egypt in the twelfth century. It's also the first time in modern history that an Arab country has been wiped off the map. How could something like this, a God-sent opportunity for Iran, not provoke serious change in the Middle East? The fact that the United States was the agent of this change, in a voluntary war, is tantamount to Rome's willingly ceding the Mediterranean to Carthage, or Britain's ceding the English Channel to Nazi Germany. The stakes in Iraq are just as high.

Iran will attempt to take control of Iraq's oil, which as of December 2007 was 2.3 million barrels a day. In the first days of the war, Iranian surrogates immediately started to steal hundreds of thousands of barrels. No one knows the exact figure, because the Iranian-allied oil minister refuses to provide an accounting. But Iran's grip on Iraqi oil only promises to tighten with its plans for a strategic petroleum alliance with Iraq.

The American backers of the war claimed that with massive investment Iraq's production could be taken to 6 million barrels a day. If they're right, and if Iran proceeds with its de facto annexation of

Iraq and its oil, the combination of Iran's current production of 4.21 million barrels a day with Iraq's 6 million would put Iran within range of becoming the world's largest producer, ahead of Saudi Arabia.

Under a scenario like this, Iran calls the shots in world oil markets, deciding levels of production that lower or raise world prices, which also aids Iran's ongoing campaign to decouple oil from the dollar. If oil markets again tighten, it could fall within Iran's reach to set the global price of oil. If Iran were to force a cutback of, let's say, 5 million barrels a day, Americans could end up paying $10 a gallon for gasoline. If the cutback was compounded with an assault on the dollar, it would start something very much like a depression in the United States.

Nightmare scenarios like this rarely come to pass. Historically, commodity markets have been too fractured, too large, and too subject to economic swings to allow one country to set oil prices. But with oil at $147 a barrel in July 2008, with Iran seeking to take control of Iraq's production and intimidating the Gulf Arabs with its eye on their 50 percent of the world's proven reserves, Iran is not all that far from establishing the oil monopoly it seeks.

Saudi Arabia, for one, takes the Iranian nightmare scenario seriously—the scenario Ahmed Chalabi never talked to Doug Feith about. The Saudis are terrified the United States will abandon Iraq, and Iraq's chaos will then spill into Saudi Arabia. They're also terrified about an Iranian invasion. And they know that American staying power in the Gulf is fading by the day. What's to keep the American people from returning to isolationism and leaving the Gulf? If and when the Americans do go, the Saudis are convinced the entire Gulf will fall to Iran.

In the meantime, the Saudis have two choices: They can goad the United States into a war against Iran, or more likely, they can raise a white flag and hope Iran will be satisfied with dominion over the Gulf rather than occupation when the United States does leave. For the first time in its history, Saudi Arabia in 2007 invited an Iranian president to come to Mecca to perform the hajj. As soon as things in Iraq started to go badly in 2004, and Iran's role became clear, the Saudi interior minister started flying to Tehran almost weekly, assuring the Iranians they would never join in an attack against Iran. At the same time, Saudi Arabia is buying all the arms it can, hoping against hope that they will serve as a deterrent against Iran.

Iran's rise couldn't have come at a worse time for Gulf Arabs. The Saudis would never talk about it in public, but they certainly understand that the Sunni Arab order in the twentieth century has failed. The Sunnis have lost four wars against Israel—in 1948, 1967, 1973, and, indirectly, in 1982. Saddam Hussein, the "shield of the Arabs," or more accurately the "shield of the Sunni Gulf Arabs," lost every war he fought: the 1980–88 Iran-Iraq War, the 1990–91 Gulf War, and now the Iraq War. The Saudis also know that Arab nationalism— a mask for the Sunni order—has also failed. It failed to unite the Arabs. It failed to take an inch of land back from Israel. And it failed to attract support among the Arabs.

A 2008 Zogby poll showed that among Arabs, the three most popular leaders in the Middle East are non-Sunnis: the Shia Hezbollah leader, Hassan Nasrallah; the Alawite president of Syria, Bashar al-Assad; and the Shia Iranian president, Mahmoud Ahmadinejad. And a 2008 poll conducted by the Anwar Sadat Chair for Peace and Development at the University of Maryland revealed that support for Nasrallah is growing. Sunni Islam is founded on victory and power, which are now fast slipping from Sunni hands into the hands of the Shia.

It's Iran's arc that terrifies the Saudis. They haven't missed the fact that over the last three decades Iran has quietly transformed itself from an irritating but essentially harmless revolutionary power into a pragmatic, calculating one that intends to undermine the old Sunni order. The Saudis have watched as Iran left its revolutionary tactics behind and became a skilled player in the game of nations, a country that understands how to exploit political vacuums and appeal to the poor and dispossessed. Who can stop it now?

Whatever the rest of the Arabs thought about Saddam, they in fact looked at Iraq as their protector from Persian invasion. And though no one said it aloud, they also saw Iraq's Sunni-led army as the thin membrane holding back a resurgent Shia Islam. Iraq's army, once the fourth-largest fighting force in the world, was better equipped than most European ones. For years, the Iraqi army kept Iran from invading the Arab Gulf states, America's closest allies in the Middle East.

For eight years, Iran tried, and failed, to defeat Iraq. Then, in the span of just over two weeks between March 20 and April 9, 2003, American Apache helicopters, F-16s, and Hellfire missiles obliterated the Iraqi army, unintentionally handing Iran a victory it could never have achieved on its own. The United States was the instrument of its own defeat in the Middle East. By decimating Iraq's army, we opened the door for Iran to dominate Iraq and its oil through its Iraqi proxies, allies, persuasion, and threat—a process that is now well under way.

Destroying Iraq was the greatest strategic blunder this country has made in its history. Unless we change course, there's every reason to believe the Iraq War will end up changing the United States more than it will ever change Iraq.

2

How Iran Beat America

Iraq is lost. Iran won it.

To be sure, American and British armies won the campaign, routing what was once a truly formidable army. We accomplished what Iran failed to do over eight years of warfare, while suffering remarkably light casualties. The allies' onslaught left Iraq's cities standing, its infrastructure in place. There were relatively few Iraqi civilian casualties. It helped, of course, that the Iraqis didn't put up a real fight, but still, this was one of the most rapid, successful military campaigns in the last hundred years. And it was all the more remarkable a victory because, unlike in the Gulf War of 1991, the Iraqis were fighting for their own country.

But as history has told us often enough, military victory does not necessarily translate into political victory. As it turned out, Iraq was a mirage, a country that had been Balkanized long before the first coalition soldier set foot in it. The Kurds were independent in all but name and had no intention, under any conditions, of again answering to a Sunni, or, for that matter, Shia central authority in Baghdad. The attitude of Iraqi Shia was similar: they would never again agree to be ruled by a Sunni. As for the Sunnis, they wanted nothing less than the old order back, with or without Saddam.

Saddam had been holding on by only a thread. As the insurgency started, supporters of the war argued that the only problem was that there hadn't been enough coalition troops at the beginning to hold Iraq together during those crucial first months. But how do you hold a nation together when there wasn't one to start with? The Israelis had thirty years and more than enough troops to occupy and rebuild the West Bank and Gaza into a nation, but that failed as well.

Even before the guns went silent, Washington became increasingly alarmed at how easily and quickly Iranians crossed the border into Iraq. The Iranians took command of their Iraqi proxies—the same Iraqis who had lived in exile in Iran for almost the last twenty-five years. Iranian clerics showed up in Shia mosques around Iraq, claiming Najaf, Shia Islam's holiest shrine city, and condemning American imperialism from the pulpit. Any Iraqi with aspirations of political power made the overland trek to Tehran to offer an oath of fealty to Iran.

No Iranian regular troops entered Iraq, because they didn't need to—Iran needed only proxies, money, and commerce. Iran didn't publicly acknowledge what it was doing and made no declarations of victory. For form's sake, Iran did demand the United States end its occupation. But it didn't press the point.

In fact, there was suspicion among Iran hands in Washington that Iran was happy the United States was bogged down in Iraq. The on-and-off insurgency and uncontrollable corruption undermined the legitimacy of the occupation, and also made Washington dependent on Iranian neutrality. Iran was delighted when its Shia allies won parliament, of course—Iran benefits from a gloss of legitimacy as much as the United States does—but Tehran knew this was one milestone among many on the road to pulling Iraq into its sphere of influence.

The Iranians are patient. They think in centuries, eras—unlike the Americans, who think in fiscal years. In Iraq, the Iranians will map progress over the next thirty years, not timed for the next Majlis or presidential election. If Iraq remains an ungovernable country for the next decade, debilitated by corruption and civil war, that's enough to prove Iran's point: American imperialism doesn't work. All Iran has to do in Iraq is turn up the pressure when America's attention strays, then turn it down when they see they've twisted the lion's tail a little too hard. The Iranians know we'll leave sooner or later.

"The Iranians have us on a slow boil," as a former colleague assigned to Baghdad in 2004 put it to me.

Iran senses that with Iraq failing, it's on an equal footing with the United States in the Gulf. Along with that, there's a growing confidence in Tehran today that the United States will finally have to come around to recognizing Iran's true stature in the world as the only important player in the Middle East—a superpower, even. Iran is confident that America will have to accept the inevitable, that we've been wasting our time with the Gulf Arabs, and that we have to come to terms with Iran.

Between March 20 and April 9, 2003, allied forces obliterated the state of Iraq, a nation that will never be put back together in any form resembling the old Iraq. What the war planners didn't understand was that Iraq was an army rather than a country. In destroying the Iraqi army, the allies destroyed Iraq.

Driving into Baghdad days after allied forces took the city, I saw how technology accomplished what Iran had failed to in eight years of warfare. The backbone of Saddam's army, T-72 main battle tanks, lay strewn around the city—burned-out hulks. One tank I saw was wedged in a small alley between a couple of two-story buildings, where the driver had obviously parked it hoping to hide it from American Cobra helicopters and Hellfire missiles. It did no good— there was a neat hole in the tank's glacis, a bull's-eye. Other tanks had sought protection under trees and bridges, but they too had been hit. There was no place to hide from the technology of a modern army.

Another thing I learned firsthand was that allied forces had unchallenged control of Iraq's airwaves, the brain of any modern army. Or, as the U.S. military puts it, the allies established from the war's outset complete "information dominance." Iraqi phones were either knocked off the air or intercepted, leaving Iraqi leadership with only commercial satellite phones for communicating. And those also were compromised, as I found out.

Before the war started, I had planned to stay with a Sunni tribal chief near Ramadi, an old friend. But it was too early in the war to cross the border from Jordan—fortunately for me, as it turned out. The tribal chief's house, the house I was supposed to stay in, was hit by six U.S. cruise missiles. A call had apparently been made on a Thuraya satellite phone from near the house. The military suspected it was made by Saddam. Why he was there was another story, but the point was, he had effectively lost contact with his forces the moment the war started. Saddam's only link with the outside world was the equivalent of the corner pay phone.

The allied victory was total. And now, with Saddam Hussein's regime gone, two truths were immediately evident. First, the new occupiers would never be able to force Iraqis to live together within the same borders. Second, without the T-72 tanks whose burned-out hulks I'd seen in and around Baghdad, neither would whatever Iraqi regime replaced Saddam's. The coalition understood too late that for Saddam, the tanks were an instrument of internal repression rather than a national army to defend against external enemies. It overlooked the fact that in March 1991, when the Shia revolted in the south, it was these same T-72s—and helicopters—that kept Saddam from falling.

The only real way to hold Iraq together was through the same kind of brutality Saddam had employed. Was the United States really ready to do that? In 1995, Saddam's son-in-law Husayn Kamil defected with his brother to Jordan. He then proposed the United States overthrow Saddam and install him in Saddam's place. As a qualification, he bragged that one way he intimidated Shia villagers was by making them drink gasoline, then firing a tracer bullet through their stomachs, causing them to explode. No, the United States never envisaged and would never consider using the level of violence needed to hold Iraq together. And the Iranians knew this before the war started.

Without any Iraqi secret police—or really any police at all—Iranians went where they wanted and did what they liked. The borders were wide open, and they could bring anything they wanted into Iraq. The Iranians didn't wear uniforms, and many spoke native Iraqi Arabic, so they could move around the country unnoticed. They were welcomed with open arms by the Iraqi Shia.

And it wasn't just in the Shia shrine cities like Karbala and Najaf that Iran was taking over through proxies. The Iranians quickly infiltrated the newly formed Iraqi security service and the army too. Members of groups that had been based in Iran during the eighties and nineties, such as the Supreme Council of the Islamic Revolution in Iraq (SCIRI) and the Da'wa Party, were placed in key positions, awaiting Iranian orders. Iranian-affiliated militias assumed security for Shia neighborhoods in Baghdad, including Baghdad's vast Shia slum of Sadr City. Iran's proxies were so confident of their place in Iraq, they still carried their Iranian identification cards.

Iran also proved adept at co-opting the most militant Iraqi nationalists—those led by Muqtada al-Sadr. Though a devout Shia, Muqtada had never been a friend of Iran. The scion of one of Shia Islam's most revered clerical families, Sadr is the son-in-law of Muhammad Baqir al-Sadr, the founder of Iraq's Da'wa Party. More important, he is the son of Muhammad Sadiq al-Sadr, a populist and revered ayatollah who Saddam assassinated in 1999, along with two of Muqtada's brothers. Sadr City is named after Muqtada's father.

After the invasion in 2003, Muqtada attempted to build on his father's popularity by trying to stir up class war and issuing an ultimatum that the coalition forces leave Iraq. In 2004, Muqtada's militia, the Mahdi Army, fought the coalition for several months. They were defeated, and Muqtada went on the run—although he wasn't happy about it—to Iran.

There's no evidence that Iran incited the 2004 fighting, and Iran was more often at odds with Muqtada than not—but the Iranians were certainly more than happy to offer him a hand, in the form of money and arms, knowing that one day they would be in a position to co-opt Muqtada's movement. This wouldn't be difficult, because Muqtada and his army were broke.

At the start of the 2003 invasion, Iran gave responsibility for Muqtada and its other Iraqi proxies to Iran's Revolutionary Guards, if for no other reason than that the Guards were ruthless and knew what they were doing, having meddled in Iraq and Lebanon for the last twenty-five years.

The Revolutionary Guards—or as it's known by its full name, the Islamic Revolutionary Guard Corps (IRGC)—was born in blood. Founded by Ayatollah Khomeini in 1979 to solidify control over Iran, the Revolutionary Guards started as a brutal vigilante outfit, torturing or assassinating anyone suspected of opposing the revolution.

When the Iran-Iraq War started, the Revolutionary Guards were integrated into the military and sent to the front, where they learned to fight in a conventional war. During the war, the Guards benefited from the Darwin effect: the smart ones went home, leaving behind on the battlefield the ones who had only zealotry going for them. Today, almost entirely integrated into Iran's regular armed forces, with their own air force, navy, and rocket forces, the Revolutionary Guards are Iran's special forces. They number about 125,000.

Although on paper they're part of Iran's sovereign armed forces, the Revolutionary Guards are, in a sense, a state within a state. They own more than a hundred companies and control as much as $12 billion, possibly more, in assets. They have their own arms-procurement network, their own prisons. They have powers of arrest. The Revolutionary Guards are an exclusive fraternity, almost a rite of passage for Iranian men with political ambitions. President Ahmadinejad is a former Revolutionary Guard, as is a majority of the Iranian cabinet. Former Revolutionary Guard officers hold a plurality of the 290 seats in parliament.

I had my run-ins with the Revolutionary Guards in Lebanon in the eighties, and more recently in Tehran when I tried to make a visit to the U.S. embassy, which the Revolutionary Guards still occupy. I found them to be a dour bunch, without the least sense of humor or willingness to engage a foreigner. I had a hard time reconciling the fact that a large percentage of them had voted for Iran's reformist president Muhammad Khatami in 2001—another Iranian paradox I decided to let pass.

What particularly concerned the allies in Iraq was when the Quds or Jerusalem Force, the intelligence arm of the Revolutionary Guards, started showing up in Iraq, contacting their agents in the Iraqi Shia militias, Da'wa, SCIRI, and commanders in the Mahdi Army. Originally known as the *birun marzi* ("outside the borders"), the "liberation movements," or Department 9000, the Revolutionary Guards finally settled on calling them the Quds Force, or Jerusalem Force. (*Quds* in Arabic means Jerusalem, a promise that one day the Revolutionary Guards would liberate Jerusalem from the Jewish colonizers and destroy Israel.)

The Jerusalem Force has a long history of backing coups, assassinating dissidents, and kidnapping foreigners. It was behind the two U.S. embassy truck bombings in Beirut, the 1983 Marine barracks bombing, and most of the foreign hostage-taking in Lebanon during the eighties and early nineties. And now the American military has accused it of supplying to the insurgency in Iraq sophisticated curved platter charges, or "explosive formed projectiles" (EFPs), which can put a hole in the armor of a tank. At this writing, it

hasn't been proved that the Jerusalem Force is in fact giving the insurgency EFPs, but then again, it has a history of knowing how to
hide its hand.

Whether it's supplying the EFPs or not, the Jerusalem Force has a
well-deserved reputation for having been the most organized, disciplined, and violent terrorist organization in the world, arguably
more so than even al Qaeda. When President Bush designated the
Revolutionary Guards a terrorist organization in August 2007, he was
referring to the Jerusalem Force's past. All of which makes the administration's 180-degree turnaround four months later the more
telling. It's evidence of how very tenuous our hold on Iraq has
become, and of the compromises the United States is prepared to
make in order not to lose it completely.

In December 2007, the U.S. State Department's senior official for
Iraq, David Satterfield, gave an on-the-record interview in which he
said the decline in attacks on American forces in Iraq "has to be
attributed to an Iranian policy decision." In thanking Iran for containing the violence in Iraq, Satterfield was thanking by extension
the Jerusalem Force. It would have been unthinkable to have the
Jerusalem Force as our new partners before the invasion of Iraq.

And Satterfield certainly knows what the Jerusalem Force is. Satterfield and I served in Beirut together in the mid-eighties, at a time
when it was established with complete certainty that the Jerusalem
Force was kidnapping many of the American and other Western
hostages. Now, some of those same Jerusalem Force operatives who
were in Lebanon then—ones with American blood on their hands
and indictable in a U.S. court of law—are helping us maintain our
hold on Iraq.

Turning necessity into virtue, the Bush administration has tried
to make the case that the Iranians were intimidated by the show
of force on their borders, in Iraq and Afghanistan. But in the corridors of the National Security Council, the CIA, and the State Department, Middle East watchers realized that when we legitimized Iran's

presence in Iraq—even that single nod by Satterfield in Tehran's direction—Iran was well on its way to forcing U.S. recognition of the flag it had planted in Iraq.

Where were the moderate Iraqi Shia, the ones who were supposed to embrace the occupation and steer a course independent of Iran? How, in 2005, could the Shia vote Iranian allies—two prime ministers from Da'wa—into the Iraqi parliament? Why didn't they vote in Chalabi, or any of the other exiles the United States flew into Iraq in April 2003?

And what about the moderate Shia clergy? The Iraqi Shia were supposed to listen to us, if for no other reason than gratitude for our getting rid of Saddam when Iran couldn't. Why weren't the Iraqis helping us, instead of forcing us to deal with Tehran and the Jerusalem Force?

Part of the answer lies in the fact that the Iraqi army wasn't the only thing we destroyed when we invaded Iraq. We destroyed another institution as important: the moderate Shia clergy.

In late April 2003, as T-72 tanks still smoldered across Iraq, with Saddam Hussein swallowed up somewhere in the desert and the Iraqis waking up from their long nightmare, the city of Karbala prepared to mark Arba'in, the fortieth day of mourning after Ashura, the holiest day in Shia Islam. It was twenty years since the Ashura demonstration in Nabatiyah that set off the Islamic resistance against Israel in Lebanon.

Saddam had kept a tight rein on Ashura observances, afraid they might spark a Shia uprising. In fact, with the Shia at roughly 65 percent of Iraq's population, crushed under centuries of Sunni dominance, this was one of Saddam's biggest fears, right after an Iranian invasion. But now, with no central government in Baghdad, the Shia could celebrate any way they wanted.

By the time I got to Karbala, 60 miles southwest of Baghdad, the city was braced for the arrival of hundreds of thousands of pilgrims arriving from all across Iraq. Green and yellow banners fluttered across the streets. A thick haze from grilling lamb kebabs hung over the open-air markets. City workers watered the streets to keep the dust down.

Families walked around town, the men arm-in-arm and greeting neighbors, women in chadors following a few steps behind. With their dark, indestructible faces, the Shia look different from other Iraqis—1300 years of oppression shows. A couple of cops, still wearing the blue uniform of Saddam's police, kept the peace, which as far as I could see meant chatting with local shopkeepers. No coalition troops were anywhere to be seen.

I had my driver take me five miles south on the Basra road to watch the first groups of pilgrims approach Karbala.

In groups of fifty or so, they spanned the two-lane road. There were people of every age, from swaddled babies to men and women in their eighties. Families sat along the road on blankets, resting, eating slices of watermelon. Many had walked for hundreds of miles, some until their feet were so blistered they had to be trucked the rest of the way. Every mile or so there were mobile medical aid stations to help. Still, no one had any intention of turning back.

Ashura commemorates the murder of Imam Husayn, the grandson of the prophet Muhammad. In A.D. 680, Husayn was on his way to Najaf in answer to an appeal from his followers there to overthrow the ruling Umayyid Caliphate. But no one moved to join Husayn, and when he reached Karbala an Umayyid force intercepted him and his small band. Husayn was beheaded, and his family killed.

Sunnis also observe Ashura, as a day the prophet fasted. But in the Muslim popular consciousness, Ashura is associated with the Shia, marking the centuries of Sunni oppression. Ashura is the day the Shia betrayed the prophet's line, by turning their backs on Husayn, and a believing Shia will spend a lifetime atoning for it. And Ashura is the foundation of another tenet of Shia Islam: martyrdom, the burning, endless readiness for sacrifice. Karbala is Shia Islam's Calvary.

I had no idea what the practice was for a foreigner, an unbeliever, to march in an Ashura procession. I asked a young man walking along if I could join him. He grabbed me by the arm and pulled me into the center of his group.

As we walked he told me he was from Basra, a city 280 miles away. He had come much of the way on foot.

He talked about Iraq's future—a very bright one, as he saw it. Like other Shia, he rejoiced at Saddam's departure. But this was just the beginning. Soon, he said, the Shia would also rejoice at the departure of their deliverers, the Americans and the British.

"And then, Iraq's Shia will at last be free," he said.

I knew what he was getting at: the impossible Shia dream that history one day would reverse itself, that the Shia would unite with Iran and depose the Sunni usurpers. The Shia would then become the guardians of Islam's holiest city, Mecca. This had long seemed a fantasy. But now, why not? No one had expected Saddam would have been gotten rid of so quickly and easily, after all.

I didn't ask him why he wasn't worried Iran would just annex Iraq. The Sunni Iraqis I'd talked to over the last couple days had made up their minds that Iran had already started. After erasing the state of Iraq, they asked me, how would the United States keep Iran out? It was obvious that a National Guardsman from Kansas couldn't do it. He was sent to Iraq to remove a regime, not build a new one.

I wondered, too, if the Shia were going to try something this Ashura. Would they demand their independence? Ashura was often the occasion for some dramatic Shia political pronouncement. Ayatollah Ruhollah Khomeini chose Ashura on June 3, 1963, to denounce the Shah and declare his rule illegitimate. Although Khomeini had spent a lifetime trying to distance himself from popular Shia custom, like Ashura, he knew that in order to attract a wide following he needed to tap the deep emotional wound of Husayn's martyrdom and the battle of Karbala.

Back in Karbala, I asked around to find someone who could explain to me why the city's Ashura was unfurling so smoothly. Ashura demonstrations I'd seen in Lebanon involved young men who pounded their chests and slashed their heads with razor blades. So far there was no sign of this. (It would come later, after I'd left Karbala, to the shock of television viewers in the West.)

A policeman in front of the Imam Husayn Mosque pointed me toward a shabby, four-story cinderblock building across a narrow street from the mosque's main entrance. "The imam will answer all of your questions," he said.

I was shown into a third-floor office with smudged walls and peeling paint. The furniture was filthy. Imam Karbalai appeared five minutes later. His black turban told me he was a *sayyid*—a descendant of the prophet, and of Imam Husayn. His woolen robes were neatly pressed. There was the scent of rosewater about him. He sat on the settee across from me.

"It's delightful to talk to an American," he said, in beautiful classical Arabic, "especially on the occasion of Ashura. Who would have ever thought I would be receiving an American in these happy days?"

We talked a little about the war, how quickly Saddam's army gave up. I commented how with Iraq's borders open, Iranian pilgrims were flooding into the city. You couldn't miss them, particularly the women in their distinctive black *abayas,* chatting in musical Farsi.

"Iranians, of course, are more than welcome," Karbalai said. "Thanks be to Allah's grace, after all of these years, they've come back."

Ever since the Arabs converted Iran to Islam in the seventh century, Iranian pilgrims have been vital for the economies of Iraq's shrine cities such as Karbala. That came to an end at the start of the Iran-Iraq War in 1980, when Saddam closed the border and expelled tens of thousands of Iranians and Iraqis of Iranian origin. Many were pure-blooded Iraqis he just wanted to be rid of.

But now it wasn't just Iranian pilgrims coming across the border. I'd also seen Iranian produce in open-air stalls, everything from pomegranates to pistachios. For Iraq, a country that had been at war for most of the last twenty-five years, teetering on the edge of starvation, opening the border to Iran was a godsend.

I knew nothing about the man sitting in front of me. "Karbalai" means "the man from Karbala." It could have been an assumed name, for all I knew. He could even have been Iranian. Some estimates put Karbala's residents at 75 percent Iranian or Iranian descent.

I noticed that Karbalai never mentioned Baghdad; only Najaf, Karbala, Qum—the Shia shrine cities, a cosmopolitan link older and more enduring than Iraq itself. This wasn't a surprise. A moderate Shia cleric like Karbalai gives temporal political capitals as wide a berth as possible, preferring to tend to the flock instead.

"Who is the mayor of Karbala?" I asked Karbalai.

He tilted back his black-turbaned head and laughed. "I suppose I am," he said. "For now."

According to Karbalai, the American tank column that dashed north through Karbala to Baghdad didn't stop long enough to hand over the keys of the city to anyone. The Americans assumed order would somehow impose itself. And indeed it had, falling into the lap of the man sitting in front of me.

No one had appointed Karbalai. He had, seemingly without dissent, stepped into the power vacuum left by the Americans. The citizens of Karbala accepted his authority as if Allah himself had appointed him.

I couldn't help but be reminded of Lebanon when the Lebanese state collapsed in 1984. Hezbollah filled the void like water finding its own level, and never stopped appropriating sovereign authority until it became a state within a state. In Lebanon, Hezbollah had proved Friedrich Engels right: "The state is not 'abolished'; it withers away."

It was then, listening to Karbalai, that I finally understood that Saddam's Iraq was gone for good. The Sunni were not coming back. The Shia were going to make a go of it on their own, even if it meant dividing up Iraq. Given the opportunity, they'd take the whole country. But the one thing they were absolutely determined to do was never again take orders from a Sunni.

But what was going to fill the vacuum left by Saddam's exit? A Shia Islamic republic? Headed by whom?

It did not seem possible that this very pleasant and sophisticated man's religious authority was enough to withstand the inevitable political storm, one that every Iraqi was expecting. Could his tiny police force, with only their sidearms, stand up to the anarchy of Iraqi politics? Iraq is the toughest, most uncompromising, xenophobic country in the Arab world. Worse, Iraq was afloat in arms— Kalashnikov machine guns and rocket-propelled grenades, the weapons that have made more than one revolution in the Middle East. And what about Karbalai's boss, Ayatollah Sistani? Was he any tougher?

Ayatollah Ali Sistani is very roughly the pope of Shia Islam. This is by virtue of the fact that Sistani has the most followers among Shia Islam's largest subsect, "Twelver Shia," so called because of its tenet that the prophet was followed by twelve divinely chosen successors. About 80 percent of Shia follow Sistani's spiritual guidance. Generally viewed as apolitical, a moderate, and a rival to the Iranian clerics—a "quietist" cleric—he was the man the United States and Britain had pinned their hopes on to line up Iraq's Shia behind the occupation and shepherd them into building a modern, secular, democratic Iraqi state. *Our* ayatollah on *our* white horse.

There's no doubt about Sistani's religious credentials. Born in Mashad, Iran, Sistani, like many Iranian scholars, finished his religious studies in Najaf, Iraq. A brilliant scholar, in 1992 Sistani succeeded Iraq's highest-ranking ayatollah, Abul-Qassim Khoei.

But Sistani's turban always sat uneasily on his head. He represented a threat to Iran's political mullahs, who considered him too moderate, too independent, and too passive. Sistani also disagreed with Tehran about whether clerics should get their hands dirty in day-to-day politics. In contrast to Sistani, Ayatollah Khomeini and his successor, Ayatollah Khamenei, both held that a Shia cleric must govern in a truly righteous Islamic republic—one accountable for both the temporal and spiritual affairs of its citizens.

Moreover, Sistani's popularity and scholarship—in comparison with Sistani, Khamenei is a virtual illiterate in Islamic jurisprudence—was seen as a challenge to Ayatollah Khamenei's authority. Sistani's quietist doctrine also implicitly called into question the legitimacy of the regime in Tehran. According to Sistani's interpretation of Shia Islam, the mullahs could be voted out, if that was the wish of Iranians, and replaced with a secular government.

The fight between Sistani and Tehran came to a head in December 1993, when Shia Islam's most senior ayatollah died. Sistani was clearly the most qualified candidate to succeed him, if the standard was religious scholarship. But Tehran supported a relatively unknown ayatollah instead, an old man practically on his deathbed. And he, unlike Sistani, had no significant popular following. Tehran prevailed; Sistani's vastly larger following counted for nothing.

Tehran's passing over Sistani came close to causing a civil war among Shia. Lebanon's highest-ranking ayatollah supported Sistani's candidacy. But he was forced to keep quiet after the Iranians circulated a rumor that they intended to assassinate him. It was a credible threat—in 1985 the Lebanese ayatollah had been the target of a massive car bombing. Moreover, the Lebanese ayatollah's bodyguards were under the control of Iran's Revolutionary Guards.

In March 2008, I went to visit this ayatollah. His house and office had been destroyed by Israeli air bombardment during the 34-day war of 2006. He himself escaped death when Hezbollah pulled him out of his house the day before it was hit. Immediately after the war, Iran rebuilt his house and office and supplied him with a new security detail, as well as the latest metal detectors, flat-screen closed-circuit TVs, and energy-efficient fluorescent bulbs. He was in an Iranian gilded cage.

As for Sistani, he got the message: Stay out of Tehran's way or else.

But Tehran wasn't Sistani's only problem. Born in Iran, Sistani is a full-blooded Persian. He speaks Arabic with a heavy Persian accent. He cannot understand, let alone speak, colloquial Iraqi Arabic. And from 1980 on, he was under virtual house arrest under Saddam. Having had almost no contact with average Iraqis, Sistani comes across as cloistered, aloof, and elitist—in other words, little better than an exile. He may be more credible than Ahmed Chalabi, but the Iraqis can't help but look at Sistani as a foreigner. Sistani isn't as powerful as the raw number of his followers suggests.

Before the invasion, I managed to meet a few of Sistani's aides in Syria and ask them about what they intended to do after they got home. "We'll see," one of them told me. My impression was that they were anxious about how they would be received in Iraq's shrine cities like Najaf and Karbala. The younger ones hadn't even been born in Iraq. They too were exiles, even more out of touch with Iraq than their boss. And like Sheikh Karbalai, they were not prepared for a civil war.

Other Shia exiled clerics I met over the years were the same. Majid Khoei, the son of the Ayatollah Khoei (whom Sistani replaced in 1992), was one of the more articulate and sophisticated ones. Thoughtful and cosmopolitan, he spoke flawless classical Arabic and fluent English. He was a multi-millionaire, having inherited part of his father's estate, which was estimated to be in the billions. But with no desire to stay in the West, he was determined to return to Iraq—

he had fled in 1991—and follow in the footsteps of his father, who was Iraq's supreme religious leader for decades.

Like the other exiles, Majid lived in the past. He had an outdated view of the place of Iraq's Shia clerics in history, when the Shia clergy delved into politics only during periods of crisis, righting the nation when it was in trouble, in a kind of *noblesse oblige.* Majid was convinced that as soon as Saddam was gone, the clock could be turned back and the Shia clerics would smoothly resume their traditional role in Iraq, taking care of mosques, charities, and schools.

"And what about Iran?" I asked him at a meeting in Paris in December 1990, not long before the Gulf War started.

"The Iraqi Shia would never allow the Iranians to interfere in their country," he told me. The foundation of his argument was that the Persians and the Arabs don't mix. It was a question Majid had thought a lot about; his family was Iranian, though ethnically they were Turks.

I intentionally pressed Majid on Iran, cautioning him to be careful about the Iranians. He was on his way to Tehran the next morning.

"Ya'badu an-nar, al-farsiin," I said, laughing. The Persians worship fire.

The allusion was to a prejudice in the Middle East, especially among Sunni fundamentalists, that the Persians never gave up Zoroastrianism, the ancient Iranian religion that worships fire. In other words, they're not real Muslims. If I'd meant it seriously, Majid might have taken it as an insult. But he understood my intention was only to gently prod him.

Majid coughed up a nervous laugh, no doubt wondering whether it was worth it to give me his frank opinion. He was mostly immune from Iranian political reprisal, thanks to his father's standing, but then again he also knew how unpredictable Iran's security services were.

"Don't worry," he finally said, falling back on his old argument. "Iran will never take Iraq. Ever."

It was only in April 2003, when I read in the newspapers that a Shia mob had hacked and shot Majid to death in the Ali ibn Talib Mosque in Najaf, that I fully realized just how wrong he'd been. It's still not clear whether Majid's murder was ordered by Iran or by Iraqi Shia leader Muqtada al-Sadr, or whether he'd simply been murdered by an enraged mob. Either way, what was clear was that his father's memory didn't matter after all. And neither had the moderate Shia clergy—Najaf was a city Ayatollah Sistani was supposed to have sway over.

The truth is that, as in Lebanon, the Kalashnikov, not the Koran, rules in Iraq. Both Sistani and Majid represented an old Shia aristocracy that never stood a chance in postinvasion Iraq. The country they thought they knew had died under Saddam's brutal regime, the eight-year war with Iran, and thirteen years of a crushing international embargo. It didn't help that the Shia clergy had been in a steep decline under the assault of twentieth-century secularism. But it was the invasion that ripped away the last illusions.

Washington and London had been encouraged when Sistani supported Iraq's constitutional referendum and parliamentary elections. (Then again, Iran and Iran's proxies did the same. With the Shia a majority in Iraq, this wasn't a surprise.) But democracy wasn't what was at stake in Iraq; armed force was. Without a militia, Sistani couldn't control the street. He was unable to stop intra-Shia violence or Shia assassination squads, or influence the Shia government in Baghdad. Several of his assistants were assassinated. And so today—little different from Saddam's era—Sistani rarely leaves his house in Najaf. He is no more capable of controlling Iraq than Karbalai was Karbala.

The trouble in Karbala started in December 2003, when a suicide bomber attacked the Bulgarian base there, killing dozens. On Ashura the next year, nine explosions went off in Karbala, killing

178 and injuring 500. On April 14, 2007, a bomb went off in a bus station near the Imam Husayn Mosque. The shock waves from the blast would have shattered the windows in Karbalai's office, where we'd met.

Americans were not immune from Karbala's violence. In January 2007, Shia militants executed five American soldiers visiting Karbala. Although the U.S. military was convinced Iran was behind it, there was nothing we could do. Iran's proxies now controlled the police—the same police Imam Karbalai had thought were under his control.

Just as Iran knew how to capitalize on chaos, it also knew how to wield a stick. When Iran's proxies started to fight street-by-street for Karbala, Iran stepped in and imposed order. Shia militia commanders were summoned back to Iran and dressed down. The leader of the Mahdi Army, Muqtada al-Sadr, was given refuge in a religious school in Iran until the storm blew over. The head of Iraqi intelligence told me that in a couple instances the Revolutionary Guards themselves arrested renegade commanders.

By 2007, there was little doubt Iran, rather than Sistani, was pulling the strings. It was again Iran that stepped in to calm the situation when fighting broke out between Muqtada al-Sadr and U.S. forces. With Sistani unmasked, Iraq's independent, moderate clergy was shown to be irrelevant. The British, during the Iraqi mandate in the 1920s, used to talk about a Shia cleric's authority "to loose and bind." Now that's an artifact of history, as quaint as afternoon tea and cucumber sandwiches at the Baghdad British residency.

There's a debate today within the U.S. government about how obligated the Shia Iraqi are to Iran. But in my run-ins with the SCIRI and Da'wa, they never bothered to hide their allegiance. They openly acknowledged that they depended on Iran for religious guidance, money, and sanctuary. Even after the invasion, their families would stay in Iran to avoid Iraq's violence.

But Iran's support had come at a price. A contact in Da'wa told me that in 1982, Da'wa was given the choice of either accepting

Ayatollah Khomeini's dictatorship, the "rule of the Islamic jurisprudent," or leaving Iran. There was little choice but to accept. When I
met representatives of the SCIRI in northern Iraq, they were accompanied by their Iranian handlers—a reminder to me that the SCIRI
answered to Iran. The Shia who assumed police powers in Iraq, then,
were Iranian proxies.

Why do we care if Iran is hijacking Shia Islam and the shrine cities
in Iraq?

For a start, Iraq gives Iran a platform to recruit new legions of believers in its quest for empire. But just as important, with Najaf and
Sistani under Iranian control, the world's Shia now will have only
Iran and its shrine city of Qum to look to for spiritual guidance. The rivalry between Iraq's Najaf and Iran's Qum had been
the guarantor of an independent Shia clergy. But now the spiritual
counterweight to the authoritarian clerics who run Iran is gone,
along with the Iraqi army.

Losing Karbala to Iran was a catastrophe few predicted. Just as few
predicted the consequences of destroying the Iraqi army.

There will be no de jure Iranian takeover of Iraq. No Iranian flag
will fly over the Green Zone. Iranian troops will not occupy Iraqi
cities, and there will be no declarations of victory. Iran will be happy
to pull the strings behind the curtain, ruling through proxies, allies,
and economic ties that bind. Iran will dominate Iraq, piece by piece.

As I've said, it will start with oil, the lifeblood of Iraq. Even though
Iraq's southern petroleum-export facilities are nominally held by
British forces, Iranian proxies have systematically looted them. Some
estimates put the amount of theft as high as 600,000 barrels a day—
nearly a third of Iraq's production. The crude reportedly was barged
to the United Arab Emirates, refined, and sent to Iran to meet its
gasoline shortages.

Iran will continue to eviscerate Iraq's independent Shia clergy. It
will buy off Sistani's followers, appropriate his tithes, and undermine

the seminary in Najaf. If it needs to, it will assassinate Sistani or any other cleric who challenges Tehran. Iraqis already believe that Iranian intelligence has bought houses around Sistani's for that eventuality.

Iran will not delve too deeply into Iraqi politics, or promote one faction over another. As Iran learned in Lebanon, pitting Shia against Shia doesn't serve Iran's interests. Iran found it was more effective to steer a careful course between Hezbollah and more secular Shia groups. Iran will play off differences between Iraq's major Shia parties, gradually imposing its own order through money and arms. It will push them to undermine the occupation but rein them in when the situation threatens to turn into a full-fledged war. Iran is a patient, pragmatic player, and it knows exactly where the red lines are, although this scenario won't hold if Iraq slips into an out-and-out civil war where Shia are slaughtered in large numbers. In that case, Iran would find it difficult not to intervene directly.

Iran also has a geopolitical strategy in Iraq: Bleed the United States dry. Iran demands publicly that America withdraw from Iraq. But its real long-term interest in Iraq is to diminish the United States' will to resist Iran's expansion. Iran has a clear interest in keeping our military bogged down in war without end, which drains our treasury and makes Americans reluctant to enter into another conflict in the Middle East.

The Iranians read American newspapers; they understand that Americans are averse to losing soldiers and squandering hundreds of billions on wars in Iraq and Afghanistan—wars with an end we can't define. Iran knows that Iraq will remain a chaotic, corrupted, ungovernable country no matter what the United States does. Iran ignores the false hopes of the Bush administration, like those that accompanied the "surge." Iran will hold back its proxies to make it appear things are getting better, but then let them loose when the United States looks as though it might achieve some passing order.

By bleeding the United States, Iran knows it can keep it from acting against Iran's allies Syria, Hezbollah, or Hamas. More crucially, a United States bogged down in Iraq will not attack Iran.

Second—and again, this is in the long term—Iran intends to use Iraq as a platform for dominating the Persian Gulf. Given the world's addiction to hydrocarbons, the Gulf is a body of water as strategic as the Pacific and Atlantic oceans. Iraq is the first piece in Iran's quest for hegemony, a reminder to the world that the Persian Gulf has that name for a reason.

In this book, I will focus primarily on the single most important American interest in the Middle East: oil. Obviously, there are wider, more complex issues that drive the United States. But oil is the common denominator that all Americans, opponents and supporters of the Iraq War, share. Oil has apparently now become the official justification of the war. In a closed hearing to Congress in April 2008, the U.S. ambassador to Iraq, Ryan Crocker, testified that once Iraqi oil is fully developed, it will be greater than that of Saudi Arabia. Oil, Crocker said, is our *vital* interest in the region: "An unstable Iraq," he said, "equals an unstable region, equals unstable oil prices."

Iran believes that the Iraq debacle will force the United States to finally come around to an inevitable truth: that Iran has an undeniable place in Iraq, the Gulf, and the rest of the Middle East. Open-ended containment of Iran, with an American fleet and army perpetually in the Gulf, is too expensive for the United States to continue indefinitely. And so, for the first time in its undeclared thirty-year war with Iran, the United States will be forced to deal with Iran on an equal basis.

America's invasion of Iraq wasn't supposed to turn out this way. Where did everything go wrong? And how did Iran become so strong, right under our noses—even as we crushed what was once the world's fourth-largest army in two short weeks?

3

THE MASTER PLAN:

HOW IRAN ARRIVED AT ITS SECRET

BLUEPRINT FOR EMPIRE

Something extraordinary occurred in May 2000. For the first time in modern Middle Eastern history a small guerrilla force defeated a committed, Western-equipped-and-trained conventional army. Until its defeat in Lebanon, Israel had never lost a war. This marked the first time Israel ceded land under the force of arms.

Certainly there have been other guerrilla victories in the Middle East—Lawrence of Arabia's legendary Bedouin tribesmen overrunning the Turkish garrison at Aqaba; Yemeni rebels in the sixties beating the Egyptian army. But the Turks at Aqaba were the remnants of a dying Ottoman Empire who didn't have a fight in them. The Egyptian army in Yemen was anything but committed. In neither case were their armies in the same class as Israel's, a juggernaut that had crushed every enemy it ever encountered.

Israel's retreat from Lebanon in 2000 is sometimes compared to America's defeat in Vietnam—a political rather than a military defeat. An optional war that became too expensive. But the comparison doesn't stand. First, the Vietcong were never a threat to America proper, as Hezbollah is to Israel. Second, Lebanon, with its relatively flat, open terrain in the south, should have been ideal for Israeli tanks and its total control of the air. Israel shouldn't have lost to Hezbollah.

The better comparison is Afghanistan, where Muslim guerrilla forces defeated the Russians, small arms overcoming heavy armor. Like the Israelis, the Russians were a modern army and were fighting on the border of their own country. And the long-term consequences for Israel may prove as dire as they were for the Soviet Union. Israel does not have an empire to lose, but it lost something as valuable: its deterrence credibility, the ability to intimidate its enemies to a point where they deem it too costly to attack Israel.

The Winograd Commission Report—the official Israeli investigation into the 34-day war between Israel and Hezbollah in 2006, the second conflict the Israelis lost—laid it out in stark terms: "Israel cannot survive in this region . . . unless people in Israel itself and in its surroundings believe that Israel has the political and military leadership, military capabilities, and social robustness that will allow her to deter those of its neighbors who wish to harm her."

In Arab eyes, Israel is now beatable. It's no longer the giant they thought it was. A dark shadow has been lifted from the imagination of the Arabs.

Iran's 2000 victory in Lebanon was never a foregone conclusion. In fact, almost everyone was convinced the Iranians' stay in Lebanon would be a short and pointless one.

On June 12, 1982, the Iranian Revolutionary Guards who climbed out of the Iran Air 707 at Damascus airport didn't look like liberators. There were only two dozen of them. More would arrive later. But there were never more than five hundred assigned to Lebanon at a time. Anyhow, where were they going to fight? Lebanon was bedlam. There were no battle lines; the roads were clogged with refugees. The main Damascus-Beirut highway was cut. The Israeli army was as ruthless as it was efficient. What could these taciturn, bearded young men in olive drab hope to do?

There also was the question of whether the Lebanese would even accept them as allies. The Lebanese Shia had welcomed the first Israeli troops as liberators, happy to be rid of the Palestinians, who had caused them nothing but misery. Generally, the Lebanese, even the Shia, look at the Iranians as foreigners; Persians are seen as a race almost as different as Eskimos are from Bulgarians. The Lebanese knew how Persians looked down on Arabs, how they considered all Arabs uncivilized nomads.

And then there was the Iran-Iraq War. Even as the Revolutionary Guards were deplaning in Damascus, Ayatollah Khomeini was ordering wave after wave of Iranian martyrs to attack the Iraqi front lines—Persians killing Arabs, reopening ethnic divisions older than history. Although the Revolutionary Guards didn't come to Lebanon to kill Arabs, the Lebanese still had Arab blood running through their veins.

But it wasn't all bad news. The Revolutionary Guards would count on historical ties between Iran and Lebanon's Shia to at least get them a hearing. When the Safavid Dynasty came to power in Iran in 1501 and decided to convert the country from Sunni to Shia Islam, it sent envoys to Lebanon to recruit Shia clerics to teach Iranians the tenets of their sect. Ties between Iran and Lebanon remained unbroken in the intervening years. The Shah supported Lebanese Shia institutions, schools, and charities, and many opponents of the Shah took refuge in Lebanon. Iran's first defense minister under Ayatollah Khomeini was in exile in Lebanon for years, where he had made close, lasting friends among the Shia. And several of the Revolutionary Guards who arrived in Damascus were Arabs from Iran's Khuzestan Province who spoke Arabic fluently.

Still, the Syrian military intelligence officials who watched the Revolutionary Guards drive away in trucks, heading toward a camp on the Lebanese border, were convinced the Iranians were going to be nothing but trouble. They were right, in ways they couldn't yet understand.

During the first few years of the war in Lebanon, there was little the Revolutionary Guards could do other than cause trouble. The Guards truck-bombed the U.S. embassy in April 1983, the U.S. Marine and French barracks in October 1983, and the new U.S. embassy in October 1984. They kidnapped and killed dozens of Westerners. But in the end, all it won them was a reputation as ruthless murderers, spoilers, no different from the other foreign spoilers that came to Lebanon—Nasserists, Ba'this, Syrians, and Palestinians. The Revolutionary Guards had managed to drive out the West. But what good did it do the Lebanese?

No one knows how or when, but along the way Iran's Revolutionary Guards discovered two truths about Lebanon. First, there was a deep vein of nationalism to be tapped. The Lebanese didn't want to be occupied—by Israelis, Syrians, Americans, or anyone else. Even supposedly pro-Syrian groups didn't want Syrian troops quartered in their country. It was a sensitivity Iran would learn to guard against as well as exploit.

Second, the Iranians discovered that there was an endless pool of street and guerrilla fighters, hardened in the crucible of Lebanon's civil war. They were the best fighters in the world. Combine this with Lebanese rejection of occupation, add money and organization, and the Iranians discovered they would have at their service the most lethal guerrilla army in modern history. During Israel's eighteen-year war in Lebanon, until the day Israel brought the last soldier home in May 2000, the Israelis would constantly ask themselves, *Where did these people come from?*

Answer that question and we start to answer what we face today in the Middle East. The Lebanon war is Iran's blueprint for its new empire, fought for and held by proxies: the first Middle Eastern empire since the Ottomans, a superpower, as the Iranians intend to demonstrate to the world. Flush with victory and experience in Lebanon, the Iranians have set their sights on replicating their Lebanon campaign across the Middle East, claiming ever more pieces of it—and oil—for themselves. Gaza, Bahrain, Iraq—Iran will take them all, as long as there are proxies like Hezbollah's soldiers of God, ready to take Iran's money and pick up a Kalashnikov.

The Iranians had no idea that within three years after Israel's withdrawal from Lebanon, the United States would blunder into Iraq, destroy Iran's historical enemy Saddam Hussein, and offer up Iraq on a silver platter. How could the Iranians not see Lebanon when they look at Iraq today?

In October 2000, Ayatollah Khamenei, Ayatollah Khomeini's successor as supreme leader—the only real executive power in Iran—made it clear what the victory in Lebanon meant for Iran. It was during a secret address to Iran's National Security Council. After the usual long preamble, larded with quotations from the Koran, Khamenei looked around the room to make sure everyone was listening.

"Lebanon," he said, pointedly using the Arabic pronunciation *Lubnan*, "is Iran's greatest foreign policy success. We will repeat it across *Dar al-Islam* (the Islamic world) until all of Islam is liberated."

This wasn't the flowery propaganda Iranians were so used to hearing from their leaders. The men sitting around the conference table were already convinced it was within Iran's power, its destiny even, to dominate the Middle East just as it had Lebanon. Most of them had served in Lebanon during Iran's eighteen-year war there. Many of them owed their position to that war. They had tasted victory, and wanted more of it.

And why not topple the vulnerable parts of the Middle East? Iran had already turned Hezbollah into a military force stronger than the Lebanese army. And Hezbollah's political writ was such that it could block the election of a president. Now there was other low-hanging fruit: Kurdistan. Bahrain. Central Asia. And the rim of the Gulf, which is 90 percent Shia—the same place under which the world's oil reserves lie. If the Iranians succeeded in raising armies of proxies in those places, like the one it raised in Lebanon—and who can stop them?—they would control up to 55 percent of the world's proven oil reserves. Iran would have a hydrocarbon empire the likes of which the world has never seen.

Then there's the question of what Iran would do with all that oil. Iran has been at war with the United States for the last thirty years. It was never a classical military confrontation; the Iranians knew they could never win. Still, it was a war. The Iranians understand how vulnerable we are thanks to our addiction to oil. If Iran were to dominate the Persian Gulf, along with its reserves, why not manipulate the price of oil in the interest of empire? When times are good, drive up the price of a barrel to $250. When times are bad, lower it, feed our addiction. Iran doesn't care if Americans pay $15 a gallon at the pump, or heating bills of $2,000 a month, or $5 for a can of Coke. And while they're at it, why not unseat the dollar as the currency the world uses to buy oil?

It all sounds far-fetched. But so was Iran's Revolutionary Guards creating the world's most lethal guerrilla force out of the mess in Lebanon in 1982, and beating the Israelis. With Iran's star on the rise, the worst-case scenario is often the most likely one. The will to empire is powerful, but especially so when there is the means—in this case, domination of the world's hydrocarbon reserves.

Prognostications like these invite the question: What do we do about it? As a start, we overhaul the way we think about Iran and the Middle East—stop taking our wisdom from White House press releases, the op-ed pages of the *Wall Street Journal*, Fox News, and TV pundits with Pentagon contracts. We must accurately define who the enemy is, his tactics, and what he wants. If we continue to fight on blindly in the Middle East, trying to contain Iran, spending trillions of dollars fighting wars without end, we will lose or be forced into a full-fledged war. It would be a war requiring we bring back the draft, settle into thirty years of conflict, and survive on the hope that a million soldiers permanently based in the Persian Gulf will change our luck.

Or we could figure out how to settle with Iran. If we examine Iran's Lebanon war and the army that Iran rode to victory on, we will understand Iran's coming campaigns, how Iran learned the lessons from a failed revolution and transformed itself into a Middle East hegemon. That knowledge will allow us to define our choices.

South Lebanon, June 6, 1982

It went fast. Faster than anyone anticipated.

At 11:05 A.M. the first Israeli tanks rolled across the Hamra bridge. By June 8, the coastal city of Sidon fell. The disorganized and underarmed PLO that occupied southern Lebanon was no match for the Israelis. By June 11, they were at Beirut's edge, ready to invade the Arab world's most modern and sophisticated city, the brightest light in the firmament of the Arab nation.

The Israelis knew the PLO wouldn't put up much of a fight; the PLO wasn't much of an army. Hopelessly divided into two dozen or so corrupt, competing militias, which themselves were divided into factions, the PLO couldn't even coordinate its retreat. And the Israelis knew the Lebanese army wouldn't be an obstacle either. Like Iraq in 2003, Lebanon had stopped being a country in 1975, when the first shot of civil war was fired. The army, as well as the police, fractured along the lines of Lebanon's three major sects—Shia, Sunni, and Christians. The three sects hated one another more than they hated the Israelis. That would change, but in 1982 the only question was how fast Israel's tanks could cover ground.

The PLO didn't so much retreat as scatter like a flock of pigeons hit by lightning. The PLO abandoned Beirut without a fight, fleeing to the Biqa' Valley and to the far north of Lebanon. Yasser Arafat himself retreated through Lebanon's northern port of Tripoli, and would be forced to leave there December 20, 1983, on a Greek ship, to enter into a long, inglorious, and irrelevant exile in Tunisia. Remnants of his forces would remain scattered around Lebanon, but they would never again pose a threat to Israel. Arafat would never return to Lebanon. Only after he signed what many Palestinians and Arabs considered articles of surrender, the 1993 Oslo Accords, did he return to the Palestinian territories to spend his last years under virtual Israeli house arrest. In the meantime, Israel had created the perfect vacuum in Lebanon.

The Reagan administration was elated, at least for the first few months after the Israeli invasion, convinced that Lebanon, now free of the Palestinian terrorists, would go back to being the Switzerland of the Middle East—a Western outpost, a beacon of change. Lebanon would be the first domino in transforming the Middle East into a moderate, democratic, prosperous, pro-American part of the world. Just as the neocons in 2003 would count on Iraq doing the same.

Lebanon also seemed to the Reagan White House a far more solvable problem than the greater Arab-Israeli conflict. Who knew, it might even serve as a back door to peace. The Reagan administration was so confident of the success of Israel's Lebanon war that even before the fighting stopped, it started pushing the Lebanese to recognize Israel.

But there was one thing the Reagan White House and the Israelis overlooked: the generation of tough, young Lebanese street fighters who were more comfortable with a Kalashnikov than a lever in a voting booth. Some had fought with and some against the Palestinians. But it didn't matter. The point was they knew how to fight, and were ready to bleed and die, given a cause. And unlike the Palestinians, the Lebanese weren't going anywhere. They could either fight for their country or surrender. The unexamined assumption of the Israelis and the Reagan administration, that the Lebanese would be happy to turn in their Kalashnikovs for the old Lebanon, overlooked these young men.

In the meantime, the Iranians wasted little time crossing from their camps along the Syrian border into Lebanon. At first they camped in vacant houses just outside Balabakk, in a village called Ra's al-'Ayn. Those first Revolutionary Guard foot soldiers may not have looked as though they were about to change the course of history, but they were a promise of hope. The PLO may have rolled over, and the Israelis may have achieved total victory, but as the Iranians again and again reassured their hosts, they were there to stay. All the Iranians asked for was time.

Balabakk was fine for a start, but what the Iranians really needed was to get a foothold in Beirut, the gateway to the Shia south, where the same Shia who had welcomed the Israeli invaders lived. The Lebanese Shia tolerance for the Israelis wouldn't last long, the Iranians were certain. What tolerance for occupation does? The Iranians would turn the Shia in the south, convince them to fight against the Israelis. But first, Beirut.

The southern suburbs of Beirut are a miserable, dusty warren of one- and two-story cinderblock houses and apartment buildings. The apartment buildings, six and seven stories tall, were illegally built, many close enough to each other that the residents could reach across and touch hands. Telephone and electrical wires ran naked up the stairwells, and there were constant power cuts. The better-off bought 5-kilowatt generators and put them on their balconies; when the power was off, you'd have to shout to be heard over the generators. It was a chaotic, beaten-down slum, very much like Baghdad's Shia slum, Sadr City.

The neighborhood called 'Ayn al-Dilbah was one of the poorest parts of the southern suburbs. Displaced Shia from the south lived there, and Palestinians too poor to live in their own camps, middle-aged men and women dying from tuberculosis and diseases the modern world had long ago stamped out. There were only a couple hours of electricity a day. The houses were crammed so close together that in the summer, you couldn't even feel the breeze off the Mediterranean.

On July 4, 1982, in a one-story house just off the airport road, a rail-thin, clean-shaven young Shia—a boy, really, with eyes the color of honey—sat in a bare room on mats, his legs pulled up underneath him, with two friends. There was no electricity or water—the Israelis had cut them off when they started their siege of Beirut. As he and the other two young men speculated about what would come next, they could hear the Israeli cannons pound Ramlat al-Bayda, a string of luxury apartment buildings along the Mediterranean. They knew it wouldn't be long before the PLO would give up and flee its headquarters in Verdun Street—the headquarters the PLO had operated out of since the early seventies. And then it would be over.

All three young men had fought with the Palestinian resistance group Fatah in their teens, mostly sniping in a poor Christian neighborhood, Sin al-Fil, turning it into a pockmarked wasteland. The young man and his friends knew all about sudden death. They had learned to accept it the way we accept a cold. Approximately 100,000 Lebanese lost their lives in the 1975–90 civil war, a remarkable number considering Lebanon's population is less than 4 million. Looking at the destroyed buildings in Sin al-Fil at the end of the civil war, one had to wonder how anyone had survived the fighting.

These men were prodigies of street warfare: There wasn't an AK-47 they couldn't unjam or field-strip in the dark. They could drop a rocket-propelled grenade through a window at a hundred yards, or crimp a blasting cap with one hand and blindfolded. They knew as much about street fighting as anyone in the world. And now that the PLO was fleeing, they needed a new flag to fight under. They would soon find one. One of them, within a few years, would become the world's most wanted terrorist—the commander of the "A team" of terrorism, as the Bush administration would come to call him.

The three young men didn't care about democracy, or restoring the old Lebanon. They were eaten up by resentment and anger. They were internal exiles, poisoned by poverty and exclusion from the larger Lebanese society.

'Ayn al-Dilbah sits at Beirut airport's edge. The planes landing at Beirut airport pass right overhead, day and night—planes filled with rich Lebanese vacationing in Paris, Rome, and London. Every day the young men had watched the chauffeured Mercedes as they jockeyed in front of the airport to pick up pampered boys and chic women in scant dresses, speaking French, weighed down with duty-free bags of French champagne, Belgian chocolate, and Cuban cigars. They raced past 'Ayn al-Dilbah on the way to their mansions in the hills around Beirut.

To these angry young men, this was a constant reminder that they were second-class citizens—that Lebanon was, and always had been, occupied, by the Ottomans, the French, and now this Western elite that had "let" the Israelis invade their country. The airport was closed now because of the Israeli bombardment, but everything would resume as soon as the Israelis finished their dirty business. Yet that would come to an end if these young men had anything to do with it.

The men were faithful Shia Muslims, but the war they were aching to fight was not a religious one. When they had fought the Maronite Christians, it was not because they were Christians but because they were the proxies of colonizers, the French. And when the Israelis invaded, it wasn't because they were Jewish that the young men hated them. It was because they were colonizers too—proxies of America, as they saw it.

The three young men knew the PLO was finished. Yasser Arafat had failed both the Palestinians and the Lebanese. He was finished too. But that didn't matter; what good was someone with no fight in him? They knew too, firsthand, that the rest of the Palestinians were as corrupt as Lebanon's Westernized elite, the way they passed the days on Beirut's Corniche, smoking hookahs, clubbing at night. They weren't fighters. All the Palestinian leaders cared about was stealing as much money as they could from their Gulf Arab patrons, who were an even more corrupted race. They only gave money to the Palestinians out of guilt.

Either way, the Palestinians, or even the other Arabs, were never going to take back Lebanon, let alone Palestine, from the Israelis. So where were the young men—and the thousands more like them across Lebanon—to turn? Who could organize them to fight back against the latest colonizers? Who would be clever enough to tap this vast, seething, powerful resource to put an end to the colonization of Lebanon?

The honey-eyed young man stood up to leave. He said he was going to walk north and take a service, a shared taxi, to Balabakk to meet a man who went by the name of "Sheikh Hossein." All he knew about Sheikh Hossein was that he was an ethnic Arab, a Shia who was an officer in Iran's Revolutionary Guards. He was making the trip to see for himself whether Sheikh Hossein was serious about fighting Israel and the American and French soldiers who would soon be arriving in Lebanon. He'd find out for himself whether or not Sheikh Hossein would flinch at shedding blood.

Days after the first Revolutionary Guard officers started crossing the border from Syria into the Biqa' Valley in June 1982, a former schoolteacher turned Shia zealot, Husayn al-Musawi, offered himself as the public face of Iran.

"We are the children of Iran!" Musawi announced to the world.

Musawi loved the limelight. He delighted in sending shivers down the backs of the Western media, coming across as half insane. The group he led was called the Islamic Amal, a breakaway faction from Amal, the mainstream Shia political party. But in fact Islamic

Amal was only a false front, little more than a family enterprise. It didn't have enough soldiers to fight the Israelis or anyone else. They were smugglers, hashish farmers, and common criminals. Iran gladly funded them anyway, to draw the attention of Israel and the West away from what the Revolutionary Guards were really doing.

The Iranians were following a long tradition: Persians through history have believed that any serious work is done in the dark. Whenever Iran deviated from this practice, it got into trouble, including in Lebanon.

In July 1982, the Revolutionary Guards hired a gang of Palestinian thugs to kidnap the acting president of the American University of Beirut, in hopes of trading him for the Iranian chargé d'affaires, who had also been kidnapped. Iran would have kept its hand hidden had it not made the mistake of putting its American hostage in the back of a truck, driving him to Damascus, and sending him to Tehran in a cargo plane. The American was held in Tehran's Evin Prison. The United States found out and raised hell with the Syrians, and Iran was forced to release him.

The Iranians would never again make the same mistake. From then on, proxies would take care of the hostage business, as they would terrorism. Which is why no one knew about Sheikh Hossein's invitation to the Lebanese Shia to come to Balabakk, except the courier who delivered it.

Imad Fayez Mughniyah sat down in the chair across from Sheikh Hossein and listened without even nodding, his honey eyes barely blinking. That's the thing most people remembered about Mughniyah, his unnerving stare. A stare that said *I would as soon kill you as shake your hand.*

It was clear what Sheikh Hossein was proposing: a war with the United States and Israel; driving the West out of Lebanon—the Americans, British, French, and Italian troops that were coming to replace the Israelis in Beirut. The Western diplomatic missions and even the press would have to go too, to purge Lebanon of all Western influences. Iran would put an end to colonialism in Lebanon forever. Were Mughniyah and his followers ready, Sheikh Hossein asked. He already knew Mughniyah's answer because he already knew a lot about him.

The war Sheikh Hossein proposed would be fought entirely by Lebanese. The Iranians were there only to provide money and weapons. Mughniyah would receive an officer's commission in the Revolutionary Guards. He would be head of a secret unit called Amin al-Haras—the Security of the Guards. Everything he did, and the names of his fighters, would be a tightly held secret. Only Sheikh Hossein and a handful of Revolutionary Guard officers in Tehran would even know that Mughniyah worked for Iran.

Sheikh Hossein would never call Mughniyah. He would convey orders and money face-to-face, at meetings in Balabakk, where Sheikh Hossein was out of reach of the Israelis and the Americans. Even Iran's host, Syria, wouldn't know about the relationship between Mughniyah and Sheikh Hossein.

In return, Mughniyah would offer the same strict degree of secrecy. He would recruit trusted relatives and fighters from his Fatah days, people who would never betray him. Even between them, there would be no communication by phone. There would be no payroll; all expenses would be handled in cash. In other words, there would be no record at all of a relationship between Mughniyah, the Revolutionary Guards, and the young men shedding the blood. There would be no trail to follow back to Iran; no return address. Mughniyah, the guerrilla, didn't need to be told why. Iran was the rear base. You protect the rear base at all costs.

As Mughniyah got up to leave, Sheikh Hossein remembered one last thing to tell him. He had come up with a name for Mughniyah's group: the Islamic Jihad Organization (IJO).

The Iranians were always in charge of the IJO, using it to establish a beachhead in Lebanon. Every attack, car bombing, kidnapping, and assassination carried out by Mughniyah was approved by the Revolutionary Guards, which in turn was approved by Iran's Supreme Leader, Ayatollah Khomeini, and after Khomeini's death, by his successor, Ayatollah Khamenei.

In almost every other way the Iranians don't behave like us. They are some of the most secretive people in the world. They don't keep bureaucratic records. They don't rationalize their decisions on paper. They don't leak. They don't splash mistakes or scandals on the front pages of their newspapers. They don't hold parliamentary hearings, or allow anyone to write frank memoirs. The Islamic Jihad Organization would soon become the most mysterious, elusive terrorist organization in the world thanks to Iran's ability to hide its hand.

The Iranians calculated well that Husayn al-Musawi and his Islamic Amal would distract us. It was not unlike the French Resistance during World War II: Charles de Gaulle was only the face of it. Killing or capturing him would have made no difference to the resistance cell leaders fighting the Nazis in France. The execution was left to the anonymous captains—men like Sheikh Hossein and Mughniyah who did the real work underground.

Sheikh Hossein was one of the best the Revolutionary Guards had to offer. He understood how to make himself invisible. Although a devout Shia, he avoided large Shia assemblies and the mosque, where he might be recognized or have his picture taken. Indeed, the United States doesn't know of any existing photo of Sheikh Hossein. He was a man who would never be able to understand America's cult of celebrity.

Sheikh Hossein was a brilliant general in a war of proxies, the perfect handler for someone like Mughniyah. From the beginning, he rigorously vetted and tested Mughniyah and his cell. Discipline was crucial. Sheikh Hossein had to know exactly who was picking up a gun in Iran's name. Just as important, no attack could fail. The Islamic Jihad Organization had to appear invincible, striking where and when it wanted. And it made sure that the world knew only what the IJO wanted it to know about its attacks. To this day, we don't know the name of the suicide bomber who drove a van into the Marine barracks in 1983.

And the mirage wasn't just in Lebanon. Iran, too, is a mirage of sorts. President Ahmadinejad is supposedly the executive power in Iran. He's the man Iran puts on CNN, who speaks at the UN and Columbia University, who writes a weekly blog. But little real power resides with Ahmadinejad. Instead, it lies with Ayatollah Khamenei, Iran's security apparatus, the Revolutionary Guards, the army, and other influential ayatollahs.

"Ahmadinejad is just a spokesman for the Revolutionary Guard and the hardcore commanders in the Revolutionary Guard Corps," Hamid Gul, the former head of Pakistani intelligence who has spent years dealing with Iran, told me. "Khamenei is *primus inter pares*—maybe even the final word, depending on the issue."

Iran's executive authority sits not in the office of the president, but in an informal politburo that has no name, whose deliberations are never made public, and whose membership shifts with the currents of regime politics. For example, the reformist president of Iran before Ahmadinejad, Muhammad Khatami, had absolutely no voice in Iran's national security decisions. None of this is new, as Persia has been governed in a secretive way forever, from the Achaemenid Empire (550–330 B.C.) until today.

"Many of the shrewdest and most influential political figures in Iran have intentionally avoided the blinding sunlight of publicity and have sought to exert power in the more shadowy corridors of the political system," Iranian scholar James Bill writes in *The Lion and the Eagle*. "Here they presented no targets to potential enemies and their influence often transcended that of those who have held ministerial positions."

Iran is a culture completely alien to ours, one more reason Americans are confused about the country. Even when it comes to the face of Iran, President Ahmadinejad, we know very little about him. The few hard facts we know are that he was in the Revolutionary Guards and served as Tehran's mayor. He's an apocalyptic Shia who believes in the "end times," but then again, so are many other Iranians. We also know virtually nothing about the commander of the Revolutionary Guards, Muhammad Jaafari. This would be as if Americans had no idea who the chairman of the U.S. Joint Chiefs of Staff was, other than a name and a rank. The Iranians laugh at the idea of our publishing photos of our military commanders playing Pee Wee football in elementary school.

Iran's embrace of secrecy and deception has proven to be extraordinarily useful. In November 1982, an armed force seized the Lebanese government's police barracks in Balabakk. Husayn al-Musawi's group, Islamic Amal, took credit, but in fact it was the Revolutionary Guards who ordered it. Staying behind the silk curtain spared the Iranians worse international condemnation than they were already receiving.

When the Iranians use proxies to seize the Sheikh Abdallah barracks, rocket the Green Zone in Iraq, or invade a sovereign state, they stymie the traditional international response. The West is so used to thinking in legalistic black-and-white it doesn't know how to respond. A state either commits an act of aggression or it doesn't. If a fictitious organization takes credit, even when it's clear Iran is behind it, Iran gets away with saying, "It wasn't us. But let's see what we can do to help." So not only do they get away with it, they also get credit for trying to solve it. In this way, the Iranians have managed to undermine the international state system to a degree the West hasn't experienced since Communism.

One reason this worked was that Tehran had confidence in its civil servants, enough to delegate complete authority. When Sheikh Hossein got on the plane for Damascus, his orders were clear and simple: Turn the fanatics and believers into a force for destruction, and convince the United States and Israel that the war is unwinnable. Sheikh Hossein didn't need to report back to Tehran, write quarterly reports, or chart his progress in graphs. Tehran would hear about his successes on BBC Persian Service.

The Revolutionary Guard headquarters in Tehran gave Sheikh Hossein carte blanche to do whatever he needed to succeed, and all the money he needed. The money passed through the ultrasecret Jerusalem Force.

Even before Sheikh Hossein arrived in Balabakk, he knew he'd be looking for recruits from the PLO, and not just from among Lebanese Shia. The PLO's leadership may have been feckless, but like Mughniyah, its foot soldiers knew how to fight. It also helped that many were believers; in the seventies, the PLO had set up an Islamic wing to accommodate them. One of Sheikh Hossein's first acts was to get his hands on the Islamic wing's membership list.

The timing couldn't have been better for Sheikh Hossein. With the Israelis shelling Beirut, deepening Lebanese and Muslim grievance and humiliation, he knew he could turn it all to Iran's benefit. The argument was easy: The Arab leaders had failed to do anything for Lebanon other than watch the invasion on TV. They hadn't even mounted an oil embargo as they had in 1973. One more Arab failure, no doubt to be followed by more.

Sheikh Hossein reminded the young men who came to see him that the secular Arab states and the PLO had never taken back an inch of land seized by Zionists. Now was the time to forget Persian-Arab enmity and think about what they could do to right history. It was a persuasive argument, and the PLO was unable to put up a good counterargument.

In fact, the PLO was forced to cede the mantle of resistance to Iran. On October 18, 1979, at a meeting between Ayatollah Khomeini and Arafat, Khomeini declared that "the matter of Palestine is an Islamic issue." A month later, on November 18, Arafat issued orders to Palestinian cadres "putting the PLO on alert to protect the Iranian revolution."

The honeymoon between Palestinians and Iranians would end when Arafat backed Saddam Hussein during the Iran-Iraq War, but there was no way to undo the Palestinian-Iranian ties. The PLO cadres now had a new beacon. Over the next three decades, the Palestinians and their Lebanese followers would drift over to Iran, if for no other reason than that Iran was the only state to show itself willing to fight Israel and the United States. Iran's ability to impose order and discipline was something the PLO always lacked.

It's impossible to overstate how important it was that Iran won over these Palestinian and Lebanese resistance fighters. Khomeini had humiliated the United States when Iranian forces toppled the Shah and seized the American embassy in 1979. But in a sense that was a parochial issue, a symbolic act of Iranian defiance that had little to do with the Arabs. At that point, the United States was the Iranian revolutionaries' enemy but not the Arabs' enemy. If Khomeini wanted to expand his revolution beyond Iran's borders, he knew he needed to universalize it—to encompass the Arabs and make common cause with them against their enemy, Israel. The war on Israel would be Khomeini's fulcrum for staking out something bigger than Iran.

Khomeini intended to fire Arab anger as he had that of the Iranians. His message was simple: If Iran could beat the United States—David slay Goliath—then the Arabs could beat Israel.

Another pool Sheikh Hossein recruited from was the Iraqi Da'wa Party. For many Shia, this came as a surprise. The founder of Da'wa was a rival of Ayatollah Khomeini. His writings directly challenged many of Khomeini's own innovations to Shia jurisprudence. The Revolutionary Guards' embrace of the Da'wa, so soon after the revolution, showed a pragmatic streak that would serve them well in the future.

Muhammad Baqir al-Sadr, the founder of Iraqi Da'wa, shared with Khomeini the belief that a regenerated and purified Shia Islam

would liberate the Shia from colonialism and Sunni oppression—
that justice could be obtained in the here-and-now and didn't have
to wait until the afterlife. But Sadr and Khomeini differed over a
major doctrinal tenet: *velayat-e faqih,* the rule of the jurisprudent.
Khomeini believed that a truly Islamic republic had to be ruled by a
cleric with the highest level of scholarship, someone with an unfail-
ing understanding of the Koran, the sayings of the prophet, logic,
and Islamic jurisprudence. Such a man—the representative of God
on Earth—was divinely ordained to hold executive power in an Islamic republic. Sadr, on the other hand, was wary of having clerics
running a state; clerics had enough to do saving the souls of men.

Even when Khomeini was in Najaf, there was a running dispute
between him and Sadr. Sadr was a powerful and charismatic leader,
and an influential writer. And because Sadr, rather than Khomeini,
posed a threat to Saddam Hussein, Sadr's authority was seen as a
challenge to Khomeini's.

In 1980, after Da'wa attempted to assassinate Iraq's foreign minister, Tariq Aziz, Saddam ordered Sadr executed and his followers
arrested. The Da'wa members who could fled to Lebanon and Iran.
Those who ended up in Iran were forced to adopt Khomeini's
velayat-e faqih, abandoning Sadr's more pragmatic political theory.

It came as a surprise, then, when contrary to Khomeini's interpretation of Shia doctrine, the Revolutionary Guards took Da'wa under
their wing—with or without acceptance of *velayat-e faqih.* The Guards
were more interested in Da'wa's capacity to stir up problems in Iraq
than obscure points of theology. In time, the Guards would treat
other Islamic groups the same way—groups such as the Sunni Muslim Brotherhood that shared almost nothing with Khomeini's brand
of Islam. Because in the end, all that mattered to the Revolutionary
Guards was that these groups were prepared to confront their
common enemy at the time, Iraq.

Pragmatism like this is rare in revolutionary movements, especially religious ones. The Spanish Inquisition could never have

embraced the Protestants. The Bolsheviks could never have compromised with the Mensheviks, nor Mao with China's Nationalists. But Iran was more than happy to cross sectarian lines; in lumping Iran into a monolithic "Islamofascism," Western pundits couldn't have it more wrong.

Tour Tehran's Martyrs' Museum and you'll find memorials to every sort of martyr, from Hezbollah to Da'wa, from Egypt's Sunni Muslim Brotherhood to Zoroastrians—and, oddly enough, Iranian Jewish martyrs who died in the Iran-Iraq War. Iran's pragmatic, almost ecumenical approach to anti-imperialism gives it a much wider, much more supple base. The foundation for an empire.

Unlike any other power in the Middle East, Iran learned how to harness the millions upon millions of oppressed. The angry, proud, dispossessed Shia; the frustrated Sunni—anyone with a grudge and a readiness to fight. Iran stole the Promethean Islamic fire when the Sunni couldn't, organizing the faithful into a disciplined military force, unlike anything the world has seen since the Ottomans.

Iran may not have liked Muhammad Baqir al-Sadr, but it understood how his 1980 execution infuriated and galvanized the Shia. In 2005, two years after the United States invaded Iraq, I asked a Hezbollah cleric what it meant to the Lebanese Shia when the Iranians showed up in 1982. His name doesn't matter; he spoke not for himself but as the voice of the party. Which is why his response was so extraordinary.

"The 1979 Islamic Revolution caused an earthquake that shook the Islamic consciousness," the imam said, pulling at his beard. "It was a new dawn."

Khomeini's message alone accomplished that? I asked.

No. "The martyrdom of Muhammad Baqir al-Sadr in Iraq," the imam told me, "is the symbol of the oppression of Shia."

Evoking Sadr's name wasn't what surprised me. It was the fact that it came out of the mouth of a Hezbollah cleric—an Iranian loyalist who should have been regurgitating Khomeini's doctrine. Once again, Iran and its proxies were proving to be far more pragmatic than anyone expected.

It wasn't just Khomeini's revolution that provoked the Shia revival, the Hezbollah imam went on. Muhammad Baqir al-Sadr was the first ayatollah executed in modern times. His execution deeply shocked all Shia, a reminder of the unacceptable oppression they had suffered for 1300 years. Saddam had crossed a line, and Sadr would be avenged.

The imam wanted me to know that Sadr wasn't just another ayatollah. Ever since the disappearance of the legendary Twelfth Imam in the ninth century—the imam who, many Muslims believe, will return to save the world in the end times—the Shia believed there was no point in revolt, in fighting for justice in the here and now. Justice would return only when the Twelfth Imam reappeared.

But Sadr reversed this, arguing that Imam Husayn hadn't died at Karbala in A.D. 680 for nothing. He had fought back. And as Sadr taught it, his defiance—rather than his murder—was the true metaphor for the Shia. Iran was not above co-opting that message as its own. The Iranians cared only that it appealed to the angry and the dispossessed.

When you fly into Tehran's Imam Khomeini International Airport, the thing you can't see but should know is that everything, from the concession stands to the jet fuel supplies, is owned by the Revolutionary Guards. In a famous incident the day before Iran's reformist president, Mohammad Khatami, was to dedicate the new airport, Revolutionary Guard forces simply rolled up in tanks and seized it. Another business, another piece of Iran the Revolutionary Guards own. Ever the pragmatists.

On Iran's face, it's impossible to tell whether religious authorities or the military is in charge. Ask the question on any street in any of the world's major capitals, and you'll hear that Iran is a theocracy, run by religious ideologues. But that view is dated, by twenty-five years. While theology forms a basis for many of Iran's beliefs and policies, the men who hold the power derive it from the military and security services, even if they are themselves clerics. Even before Khomeini's death, Iran stopped being a country run by mullahs and Islamic militias and turned into one run by the "power ministries," as they're called in military dictatorships. Almost within months after Khomeini returned to Tehran in February 1979, he had to quietly concede that he couldn't make Iran a theocracy overnight. It could take decades. Or maybe even centuries.

Still, Khomeini never abandoned his belief that the Koran, properly interpreted, contained all the laws necessary to govern the ideal Islamic society. A *mujtahid,* a Shia jurisprudent, alone could bring justice and God's will to the affairs of man. This wasn't too far from Plato's rule of philosopher king—along with all the idealistic baggage that came with it. The only problem was that once in power, Khomeini could never figure out how to translate that idea into day-to-day politics. He couldn't find the passage from rebellion to governance.

Khomeini openly acknowledged failure when in 1989 he removed Ayatollah Montazeri as his successor. Montazeri was the most learned *mujtahid* after Khomeini, so when Khomeini passed him over, he abolished *velayat-e faqih* in all but name. Khomeini instead named as his successor Ayatollah Khamenei, a man who was not really even qualified to be a *mujtahid.* But Khamenei had the following and political skills to control the Revolutionary Guards and the secret police. So Khomeini, as it turned out, was as pragmatic as Sheikh Hossein.

If there were any doubts about this shift, they were put to rest in 1995 when Ayatollah Khamenei removed Khomeini's son from power and later, it is believed, had him poisoned. Khamenei needed Khomeini's son out of the way, because he was a rival for the loyalty of Iran's security services. Also, Khamenei early on in his rule had arrested the closest advisers of Ayatollah Montazeri, including

Montazeri's son-in-law, who was executed. And Khamenei put Montazeri himself under house arrest. When he needed to, Khamenei made Joseph Stalin look soft.

Iran prevailed in Lebanon not by religious conversion or cultural diffusion but by sheer power—guns and money. It prevailed just as the Soviets had conquered their empire, not through Lenin's words but with the Red Army. The French Revolution succeeded not as a war of ideas but thanks to Napoleon's army. Iran's "ideological" war was, like so many others, won on the field of battle, not from the pulpit.

Americans generally are blind to complexities like these, finding it easier to simply reduce Iran to a theocracy. This is a mistake that has led the United States to appeal for democracy and Western values in order to bring down the Iranian regime—to reveal the mullahs as false prophets. What we miss is that our ideals will never bring down the mullahs, because the mullahs long ago gave up the Koran for the Kalashnikov.

That metaphor may be a slight exaggeration, but still, it helps make the point that the Shia approach the world from a perspective completely alien to ours. They have suffered repression and economic privation for 1300 years; they have been slaughtered at the hands of Sunni; they are too tough, and too bloodied, to be appeased with our faith in nineteenth-century democracy and liberalism. Combine this with their secretiveness, clannish loyalties, and piety, and the courage not to run under fire, and the Shia come close to being an undefeatable foe. The Israelis in Lebanon were fighting not so much an army but a fierce tribe that would rather die than surrender.

Indeed, it is blood ties that have made the Shia so strong. The Shia who live in Beirut's southern suburbs all know one another, with whole families and clans settling in the same block. They know about the birth of a child, a marriage, who's doing well and who's not. They know who the believers are, the alcoholics, the philanderers, who they can trust and who they can't. They know who will fight and who won't. There is no way for outsiders to break down these bonds, not even through one of the most massive aerial bombardments in history, such as the one Israel launched in 2006.

The Shia also don't talk freely. Their sect has a peculiar tenet called *taqqiyah*—permission for a Shia believer to lie in order to protect the faith. This kind of sanctioned deception spills over into every aspect of a Shia's life, in particular when dealing with outsiders. In conversation, or even listening in on a conversation among other Shia, it's nearly impossible to distinguish what's true and what's not. There's an inner meaning to every sentence, one that a Shia will instantly pick up on but a non-Shia can't comprehend. *Taqqiyah* is one reason that American and Israeli intelligence were never able to effectively penetrate Hezbollah.

Even the Iranians were astonished by Hezbollah's ability to keep a secret, a key to fighting any guerrilla war. In 1996, when Hezbollah launched an offensive against the Israelis, the Iranians called Hezbollah's secretary-general Hassan Nasrallah to Tehran. They wanted to be certain that Hezbollah fighters wouldn't reveal Iran's role.

Nasrallah reassured Iran that Hezbollah's cadres would never betray Iran. They would lie, cover up, obfuscate—whatever was necessary—to keep Iran's involvement secret. Hezbollah also knew how to compartmentalize information—its fighters were only told what they needed to know for their missions. So even if they were caught and somehow forced to talk, they knew only about their own cells. In the battle between America's college-educated, Internet-surfing "experts" on Lebanon and Hezbollah's tough, street-smart, loyal fighters, we were hopelessly outmatched. As, apparently, were the Israelis.

Israel's withdrawal from Lebanon in 2000 passed without any serious comment in this country, because it was a war the Americans didn't know. It dragged on for eighteen years, but it wasn't fought on the front pages of newspapers. It was a confusing war. There were no set battles, no major cities that fell. With Iran using proxies, and the fact that there were no victory parades in Tehran, no campaign ribbons, no after-action press briefings, no white flags, it was difficult for Americans to put a face on the war. Even today, the Americans and the Israelis don't know the names of Hezbollah's field commanders. Israel fought and lost to a phantom.

Americans should definitely be scared about Iran and the Middle East, but not for the reasons the Bush administration has put forth. Iran's foot soldiers are no longer terrorists. They're a formidable army, which makes Iran something much more dangerous. And the creation of that army can be told through the story of one man, Imad Mughniyah: a terrorist turned guerrilla fighter.

4

FROM TERRORISM TO
POWER POLITICS:
HOW IRAN BECAME A STATIST POWER

George Orwell would have laughed at the charade, the way
the United States portrays Iran. Black is white, two plus two
equals twenty-two. The way our government declares something as fact, and we just accept it, uncritically and unexamined.

Nearly everything the average American has been told about Iran
is wrong. Iran is not fighting a crusade. It does not want to convert us
to Islam. Iran truly believes that for the last thirty years, it has been
fighting a straightforward war against occupation.

Iran is not a totalitarian state run by "Islamofascists" who believe
they're in some quixotic war with the West and Western civilization.
President Ahmadinejad is not intent on starting World War III; he's a
figurehead no more able to take Iran to war than Joseph McCarthy
was able to take America to war against Communism. Iran's real leaders are rational, pragmatic, and calculating.

We live in the past; Iran lives in the future. We think of Iran as a
terrorist state, and of Hezbollah as a terrorist cult. Yes, Iran seized
our embassy in Tehran in 1979, bombed the U.S. embassy in Beirut

in 1983, and bombed the U.S. Marine barracks there the same year. But that was more than a quarter-century ago.

In the meantime, we've missed what Hezbollah, Iran's proxy in Lebanon, has turned into. Hezbollah fights for an unambiguous national cause. It operates openly on the battlefield, seizes and holds territory, and exerts sovereignty over a civilian population. In other words, Hezbollah fits the definition of a guerrilla force, not a terrorist group.

Americans have missed Iran's critical transition, its metamorphosis from a Shia rebellion and a terrorist state to a classic military power. And absent a bloody confrontation with the United States or Israel, Iran will continue to act in this same pragmatic, calculating way.

Until we're prepared to see facts when it comes to Iran, we'll never understand how to either confront it or settle with it. Nor will we ever understand that "victory" in the Middle East isn't a question of rooting out small terrorist cells, a finite war with finite ends, as Washington would have us believe. In Iran we are fighting a war of conviction, against an enemy with a bottomless pool of potential recruits. If America keeps acting on a flawed understanding of this conflict, it will lose to Iran.

The transformation of Iran's proxy in Lebanon, Hezbollah, from a small terrorist group into a classic guerrilla army didn't happen overnight. It took place over two decades—legacy of the 1982–2000 Lebanon conflict that's still reshaping Middle East dynamics. The transformation can be traced through the career of Imad Faiz Mughniyah, the honey-eyed Lebanese man who went from Fatah street fighter looking for a war, to the world's most wanted terrorist, to military commander, and finally to someone pensioned off in Damascus—all in the space of about ten years. His story serves as both illustration and warning of what we face in Iran.

His birth certificate said he was born in the village of Tayr Dibba, a small Shia village in the hills above Sidon. In fact, he was probably born in Beirut, his father a poor farmer and vegetable salesman who pushed a cart around the dusty squalor of the Shia southern suburbs. His family was well known in the neighborhood of 'Ayn al-Dilbah. Like everyone else who lived there, they were economic refugees.

The Mughniyah family wasn't without name; one distant cousin was a renowned Islamic scholar whose books are still read. At fifteen, angry over Israel's first invasion of Lebanon in 1978, Imad Mughniyah joined Fatah's student cells, a clandestine organization headed by a Lebanese Christian who had converted to Islam. The student cell members were outsiders: Lebanese Shia and Christians, Islamic fanatics, mercenaries, and anyone else ready to take Fatah's money. It was then that Mughniyah started to fight in the Beirut neighborhood of Sin al-Fil, almost as an after-school activity.

Mughniyah attended the American University of Beirut for a year, where he studied business administration. But as a Shia, he knew he could never get a job in Saudi Arabia or anywhere else in the Gulf where the work was. So he dropped out and again picked up his Kalashnikov.

For a young man like Mughniyah, this was a natural step. Lebanon was an emporium of terrorism, a refuge for almost every terrorist group in the world, from the Baader-Meinhoff Gang to the Japanese Red Army. It had also endured unrelieved occupation—by the Ottomans, French, Israelis, Syrians, and Palestinians. Mughniyah was born four years after President Eisenhower sent the U.S. Marines to Lebanon. He was fourteen when the Syrians sent their troops to Lebanon in 1976. But as with Osama bin Laden, the real turning point in his anger came when the Israelis shelled Beirut in 1982— the first time in modern history that foreign invaders destroyed an Arab city.

In the four years Mughniyah fought with Fatah, he made a name for himself as a smart, fearless fighter. By the time he met with Sheikh Hossein and joined the Revolutionary Guards in 1982, he had vaulted to another level altogether. And when he hijacked TWA flight 847 in 1985, Mughniyah became the emblem of Iran's terrorist war in Lebanon—a hero within the ranks of Hezbollah, or at least to the ones who knew about him. Mughniyah wasn't a thoughtful or tutored believer in Islam. Nor did he blindly accept Khomeini's interpretation of Shia Islam. But his ability to make good on his promises was enough for him to become a captain in what the BBC would call "the most effective guerrilla army in the world."

Though there's no conclusive evidence for it, Mughniyah may have been at the center of the most notorious terrorist acts of the 1980s: the April 1983 bombing of the U.S. embassy in Beirut and the October 1983 Marine barracks bombing there. He may have been the man who turned the twentieth century's dream of the car into the nightmare of the car bomb. But it's known that it was Mughniyah who took dozens of foreign hostages in Lebanon, turning it into a country as hostile to the West as Pol Pot's Cambodia. Until his assassination, on February 12, 2008, there was an outstanding arrest warrant for Mughniyah for the TWA-847 hijacking and the subsequent murder of U.S. Navy diver Robert Stethem. Mughniyah's fingerprints were found on the airplane.

But although Mughniyah lived until 2008, his final act of international terrorism came twenty years earlier, with the hijacking of Kuwait Airways flight 422 in April 1988. That hijacking is a metaphor for Iran's evolution from terrorist state to a Middle East superpower. It shows Mughniyah as both terrorist and soon-to-be-military-commander. It also shows the sophistication of a well-planned commando operation, more precise and disciplined than those undertaken by al Qaeda—one reason Mughniyah and Iran's other proxies were more dangerous.

That statement might raise eyebrows, considering the slaughter al Qaeda inflicted on September 11, 2001. But we have to remember that the objective of the 9/11 attacks was simply to kill as many people as possible as a way to horrify the world. As carefully planned as the attacks themselves were, nothing lay behind them but a determination to create anarchy. After all, what did al Qaeda gain from 9/11? Absolutely nothing. No territory, no concessions, no goodwill. What's left of its leadership is living deep in caves just as before, as if the towers never fell.

Iran, on the other hand, even during the bloodiest stage of the revolution, knew what it wanted and what it was doing. It always focused on the objective, to establish a foothold in Lebanon, rather than on the act itself. The Iranians are too smart and too insightful to kill simply for the sake of it, like an insane gunman opening fire in a McDonald's. This is what makes them so much more of a threat: they learn from their mistakes, and adjust tactics and strategy accordingly. And the hijacking of Kuwait Airways 422 marks one such adjustment—one of the Iranians' last attempts to use terror as a means to an end.

The hijacking was Mughniyah's idea. His brother-in-law had been locked up in a Kuwaiti prison for nearly five years, as one of seventeen Da'wa members arrested for attacks on the American and French embassies in Kuwait in December 1983. Those attacks had come at the behest of Iran, which had taken in the Da'wa members after Saddam Hussein expelled them from Iraq.

Mughniyah knew his brother-in-law would die in that Kuwaiti cell if he didn't do something. Along with Iraqi Da'wa, he had already made several attacks on the Kuwaiti regime in an effort to get the men, known as the Da'wa 17, released. But Kuwait always held firm.

By 1988, Mughniyah was frustrated that the Iranian government hadn't done more to free his brother-in-law. To Mughniyah the loyalist, Iran had an obligation to leave no soldier on the field of battle. Moreover, Kuwait had supported Iraq during the Iran-Iraq War, so why should Tehran have any reluctance to do the Kuwaitis harm? With the same single-mindedness and anger that had fueled him this far, Mughniyah badgered the Iranian government to let him hijack a Kuwaiti airliner.

But in Tehran, a shift was under way. There had already been several attempts at freeing the Da'wa 17, none successful. Why would this time be any different? And in a larger sense, why spend all this time fighting the Arabs, when the real enemy—Israel—still occupied Lebanon? The Iran-Iraq War was at last coming to a definitive end, and the time was right for the shift. The pragmatists in Tehran thought it was time for Iran to look at the bigger picture, to become better disciplined and concentrate on Israel.

But Iran wasn't completely finished with its transformation, so in a nod to their tireless fighter Mughniyah, the Iranian government gave him the green light to hijack a Kuwaiti airliner in April 1988. This was one of the last gasps of the zealots, and Iran would begin to regret it even before the hijacking had ended. The outcome would serve only to confirm that Iran's move from terrorist to military struggle would be the right one.

Mughniyah wasted no time once he'd received his permission. On April 5, eight hijackers operating under Mughniyah's orders seized flight KU 422, which was nearing Kuwait after a long flight from Bangkok. Three of the hijackers, armed with hand grenades, entered the cockpit and informed the captain they were taking control of the plane.

The plane first put down in Mashad, Iran, where it remained for several days. The Iranians wouldn't let the hijackers deplane, as they had in the past. This was Mughniyah's first hint things weren't going well.

Mughniyah's hijackers were proficient, professional terrorists. They understood the psychology of hostages—how to keep them quiet, obedient, disoriented, and terrified. From the moment the flight was hijacked in Bangkok, even though Mughniyah himself was not on the plane, his handpicked team demonstrated they were in charge, making decisions that reflected sharp military precision.

Throughout the hijacking, the team stayed hooded. They spoke to one another in classical Arabic, to hide their Lebanese accents.

They swapped clothes. They kept the plane fueled up and the doors roped closed to defeat a rescue attempt. They turned the lights and air conditioning off and on. They prowled the aisles, picking out passengers and shining lights in their faces, making them believe they were about to be executed.

From his base in Beirut, Mughniyah ordered the pilot to fly to the Beirut airport, which Hezbollah controlled. But even as the plane was in midair, someone on the Iranian side began to have second thoughts. The Iranians had given Mughniyah the go-ahead for this hijacking, but several days into it, they wanted no part of having the plane touch down in Lebanon—they didn't want to risk losing the foothold they'd won in that country. The Iranians lied to the Syrians, who had troops around the airport, telling them they had nothing to do with the hijacking.

The plane circled the airport for hours, and Mughniyah realized that Syria and Hezbollah wouldn't let it land. Dramatically, Iran seemed to have reached an ideological turning point right in the middle of its own hijacking.

He directed the hijackers to fly to Larnaca, Cyprus, deciding Cyprus was the next best airport to put down after Beirut. The Cypriots didn't have a particularly good hostage rescue team, and Larnaca International Airport was small, with a view of all directions. But just as important, Mughniyah had a network in Larnaca that would alert him to any suspicious movement of troops preparing for a rescue.

On April 10, as the plane sat on the tarmac in Larnaca, Mughniyah radioed the airplane in the open: "Golden fiat 101 for this 3." The message was indecipherable to anyone listening in, as was the follow-up message: "We 209 true as a sign everything cold sun." The coded communications displayed a level of sophistication not seen before in terrorist acts of this type. In the course of just a few years, Mughniyah had clearly come a very long way from jagged-edged street fighter.

As the days dragged on, however, the Kuwaitis still wouldn't bend, refusing to release Mughniyah's brother-in-law or any other members of the Da'wa 17. Mughniyah's frustration and anger grew. He knew he had to up the stakes—to murder passengers. He issued the order, and the hijackers shot and killed two of them.

It had no effect. The Kuwaitis would not give in. Mughniyah next directed the hijackers to fly the plane to Algeria, where PLO negotiators became involved. Soon enough, it became clear to Mughniyah that nothing would budge the Kuwaitis. Finally, fifteen days after it began, the drama of KU-422 came to an end when the eight hijackers were granted safe passage back to Lebanon in exchange for abandoning the plane and freeing the remaining hostages.

In the end, Mughniyah's hijacking accomplished absolutely nothing, except perhaps to display the level of discipline and skill he and the Iranians had achieved during the Lebanon conflict. Though it was perfectly executed, it still didn't work—one reason it would be one of the last hijackings Iran would back. The times had changed, as had Iran's objectives. It was time for Iran to grow up, get serious in Lebanon, concentrate on capturing ground from the Israelis, and act like the mature power it had become.

But Mughniyah wasn't interested in Iran's transformation, and when the Iranians told him his terrorist days were over, he didn't take it well. He had lived by the sword for too many years; it was all he knew.

For a few years Iran put him on the front against the Israelis. He fought well, leading several ambushes of Israeli patrols. But he never adjusted to his new role, there were dozens of other independent Hezbollah commanders he had to compete with, and he started to fight with his Iranian handlers. By now, like Leon Trotsky after the Russian Revolution, or Robespierre after the French, he was considered irrelevant, even a liability. When the revolutionaries settle into power, the firebrands aren't so useful: Mughniyah was too radical, so the Iranians marginalized him.

There had been no military academies for Mughniyah, no awards or medal ceremonies, no cash bonuses, no photo ops. He lived and operated in the pitch black, with recognition from only a handful of people. Anger alone kept him on the battlefield. But the same anger that had made him such an effective fighter and terrorist had now made him dangerous to Iran.

Mughniyah, like so many other young Lebanese men, was a nihilist: he wanted to bring down the Lebanese temple around him— the constitution, the political parties, the secular political leaders, anything tainted by the West. For a while, that was exactly what Iran wanted too. But because in the late 1980s Iran had made the transition from being a revolutionary troublemaker trying to export a Shia uprising, to statist, Napoleonic-like conquest, the goal was no longer to destroy and sow unrest. It was to impose order, to take ground, to expand. Even Mughniyah understood that his skills were no longer wanted. He was resigned to end his career training a new generation of Iran's foot soldiers.

In 1996, Iran offered Mughniyah his choice of two missions: to collect intelligence, or to train its two client Palestinian groups, Hamas and the Palestinian Islamic Jihad. The Iranians ignored Mughniyah when he asked to carry out attacks against Israel during the Israeli elections. Iran had too much to lose at that point. Hezbollah was in parliament now; the oppressed were in power. Attacks on Israel would have to wait. Mughniyah, the good soldier, had no choice but to salute.

Not everyone adjusted so easily. Mughniyah's brother-in-law, the man he had tried to free with the KU 422 hijacking, eventually escaped from his Kuwait jail and returned to Lebanon. Mughniyah arranged to appoint him to a senior military command in the south. But the brother-in-law went back to his old ways and started kidnapping foreigners—without Iran's permission. He had no idea how much had changed since his imprisonment seven years before. The Iranians released the hostages and removed him from his post.

Later, he complained bitterly to his friends that everything had changed—that Iran had abandoned Khomeini's revolution.

Another Mughniyah lieutenant also couldn't make the adjustment, and when he kidnapped the children of a rich Lebanese businessman, Iran's response was draconian. He was arrested and executed, his past service to Iran forgotten.

The arc Imad Mughniyah traveled is unambiguous—from rootless teenager with a Kalashnikov, fighting for secular Fatah, to Islamic terrorist, then to military commander fighting to liberate Lebanon. He was invaluable to the Iranians because he was inured to the prospect of death, he took orders, and he terrified the West. But it was only his military role Iran wanted him to be remembered for.

After Mughniyah was assassinated in February 2008, the Syrian foreign minister, speaking for the Iranians, said in a press conference, "The fighter Imad Mughniyah was the target of lots of intelligence agencies—he was the backbone of the Islamic resistance." In acknowledging Mughniyah's role as military commander, but not his terrorist role, Syria's foreign minister wanted to put the past behind him and force the world to focus on the military struggle against Israel.

Within Hezbollah, Mughniyah is a legend—Hezbollah's Patrick Henry. After his assassination, Hezbollah put up his poster all over Beirut's Shia southern suburbs. But in a sense, that's all that he was: an iconic figure, a hero of the early days of the resistance, revered but irrelevant to Iran's larger, new conflict. And at the end of the day, he was only one among the thousands of young fighters recruited out of the chaos of Lebanon. Foot soldiers ready to die for Iran and for Allah.

Iran's transformation from terrorist state to classic military power will have a profound long-term effect on the world's geopolitics. It produced historic victories in Lebanon in 2000 and 2006, victories that became Iran's paradigm for expansion. What does it mean for the next ten years? And what can the West do about it? The answer lies in Basra, which is in the middle of a transformation of its own.

The city of Basra offers Iraq's only maritime access and its main oil export route. A half-million barrels of oil a day pass through Basra, heading to offshore oil terminals in the Gulf. Iraq's Shia-dominated south produces 1.9 million barrels a day, accounting for the bulk of the country's production. The south also possesses 71 percent of Iraq's proven oil reserves, and accounts for 95 percent of Iraq's government revenues. Basra is the beating heart of Iraq's economy.

Yet Basra and its surrounding area are not really part of Iraq anymore. Quietly, without firing a single shot, the Iranians have pulled the entire south into their sphere of influence, fully one-third of Iraq. In Basra today, the preferred currency is the Iranian rial. The Iraqi police, the military, and at least one of its intelligence services answer not to Baghdad, but to the Iranian-backed political parties, SCIRI, Da'wa, and other Shia groups under Tehran's control. But it's not just the police; the same Iranian proxies and allies run the universities, the hospitals, and the social welfare organizations. They exert more control over daily life in Basra than the central government does—and clearly more than Britain or the United States.

Iran supplies Basra with refined fuel and nearly every other raw commodity that keeps the city alive. An Iranian-allied faction is in charge of Iraq's oil exports, siphoning off hundreds of thousands of barrels a day to support the faction and its sponsors in Iran. Iran takes a direct role in reviewing lists of foreign companies bidding on Iraq's mega oil fields in the south. In other words, you can't do business in southern Iraq without a green light from Tehran. And no one even bothers to hide Iran's role.

Iraq's Shia oil minister was quoted in the Iranian press as saying there was an agreement between Iran and Iraq to jointly invest in

Iraq's oil fields. Iran specifically demanded a say in the development of Iraq's huge Majnoun field, which contains approximately 30 billion barrels of oil.

As I pointed out earlier in this book, if Iran's dominance in the south holds—and nothing seems likely to turn it back—the almost inevitable implication is that Iran will one day have de facto control of Iraq's oil, giving it considerably more weight in OPEC. If the Majnoun oil field and other untapped Iraqi fields were to be developed, Iran's and Iraq's total production would begin to rival that of Saudi Arabia. And if Iran were able to fulfill its ambition of producing 8 million barrels a day by 2015, its combined total would surpass Saudi Arabia's.

How did Iran manage to annex southern Iraq right under everyone's noses, without a military incursion?

First, Iran applied the lessons it learned in Lebanon, compelling, cajoling, and persuading warring factions that it was in their best interest to follow Tehran's orders. It took nearly fifteen years, but Iran eventually forced Hezbollah and the more secular Amal Party to cooperate. It was also in Lebanon that Iran learned how to corral normally independent Shia clerics by taking control of their bank accounts and charities, systematically destroying Lebanon's moderate, nationalist, independent clerics—anyone who called into question the legitimacy of the mullahs in Tehran.

Second, Iran demonstrates extraordinary patience and long-term vision when moving its pieces on the chessboard. It's able to tolerate chaos for long periods of time, waiting for local players to fail and then come to Iran for help. And by the 2003 Iraq invasion, Iran had truly absorbed the lesson that the Kalashnikov rules—not Adam Smith, Jeffersonian democracy, or even the Koran. Unless it is somehow miraculously contained, Iran will end up fulfilling Ayatollah Khamenei's 2000 promise to repeat in Iraq Iran's victory in Lebanon.

Iran knows it can't simply march its army across the border and impose order in Iraq. It tried that in 1982, laying siege to Basra in its long, ultimately unsuccessful war against Saddam Hussein. Military incursion didn't work then, so why try it again now? Instead, Iran has decided on a soft takeover, offering a gentle hand, tamping down the fighting when it can, taking control of mosques and charities, keeping Iraq supplied with refined oil products, keeping city services running, gradually building up Shia militias for the day they'll expel the new invaders and take Baghdad. Above all, the Iranians know that they cannot appear to be colonialists in Iraq. Better to let the Iraqi Shia arrive at the conclusion that they can't do without Iran.

And Basra certainly did need a strong Iranian hand, as the place was in utter chaos in the first few years after the invasion: car bombings, assassinations, attacks on bars and restaurants. Through the early years of the Western occupation, the situation worsened by the day, but Iran waited patiently rather than taking action, knowing that the chaos by itself would eventually drive out the foreign occupiers, the British army.

Just after the 2003 invasion, British TV audiences had been reassured when they saw their troops patrolling Basra in regimental berets and without armor. This was so different from the heavy-handed Americans, who patrolled Baghdad in tanks. The ready explanation was the British knew what they were doing, having learned about occupation in Northern Ireland. But the calm was not to last.

In the January 2005 elections, the Da'wa and other Islamic parties won 38 out of 41 seats in the Basra provincial elections, as well as 35 of 41 seats in Maysan, another Shia province in the south. The SCIRI and Da'wa had been in exile in Iran for twenty-five years, and for moderate Shia nationalists, their election victory was far from welcome. Soon, factions of the SCIRI and the Mahdi army started to fight for control of Basra. (The SCIRI had renamed itself the Supreme Islamic Iraqi Council to put space between its present incarnation and the years it spent in exile in Iran. But no one was fooled.)

The British forces might have had the upper hand militarily, but they were utterly powerless politically. And as they soon learned, the struggle for Iraq at this stage was not military, it was political.

Britain had lost long before the first British soldier ever set foot in Iraq. Though they did get support from a few Shia tribes, this was no match for the SCIRI and Da'wa. The British soon realized they were helpless against Iran's proxies—they weren't even able to sort out who was who. They were fighting a war they couldn't understand, let alone win.

Unlike Britain, Iran had been preparing for this day since the start of the Iran-Iraq War in September 1980. It fed, clothed, and armed the SCIRI and Da'wa. It filtered out cadres who wouldn't go along with Iran's agenda. Thanks to SCIRI and Da'wa agents in Basra, Iran understood the politics there better than the British ever could. It took only a matter of months for the Iranian proxies to eliminate their—and by extension, Iran's—opposition. The Iranians clearly knew what they were doing.

"The Iranians aren't crazy or naïve enough to send their own secret service agents, nor do they have to," one Shia politician in Basra told the independent International Crisis Group. "Thanks to the parties that used to be exiled in Iran and those that currently dominate the local government, they already have Iraqi accomplices on the ground."

As for the Iraqis in Basra, whether they're completely controlled by Tehran or not, they're pragmatic and take Iranian support when they need it, whether in the form of rations, bandages, ammunition, or anything else. They're coming to learn that they cannot survive without Iran.

And Iran, as it demonstrated in Lebanon, will work with any Shia group that matters, regardless of any differences in ideology. It won't be long before the Iranians in Basra will start corraling the fanatics—the ones who kill women for wearing lipstick—and the criminal groups kidnapping and ransoming for money. It's all the same to the

Iranians, who will work with any armed groups that can impose order and one day force Britain and the United States to leave Iraq. Iran will allow the Iraqi army to take Basra, knowing one day the Iraqi army will answer to Tehran.

Basra in 2007 resembled nothing so much as Beirut in 1982. The shootings, bombings, grotesque corruption, and political and social anarchy weren't identical, but the situations were similar enough to give Iran the confidence it needed to annex Basra.

All this raises a question: If Iran is able to dominate a large chunk of Iraq without ever firing a shot, what can the United States do about it?

We could send tanks into Basra, but what good would that do? We couldn't hope to do what the British failed to do. Just rolling into town with conventional arms and armor would do nothing in terms of winning Basra back politically. And if we were to try to use force, as we did in Fallujah, whom would we fight? We could shell Basra, but we'd only succeed in creating more hatred, just as Israel did in 2006 when it bombed Beirut's Shia southern suburbs.

Even assuming the Americans could temporarily impose order, it would be little more than symbolic. And then who would we turn Basra over to—the Iranian-allied government in Baghdad? The Iraqis will continue to embrace the order Iran brings. Either way, the Iranians win.

Here's a quote from Hezbollah's secretary-general Hassan Nasrallah about Israel's war in Lebanon. Substitute "American forces in Iraq" for "Israel" and you'll have Iran's blueprint for how they intend to beat us in Iraq. "It is impossible for us to fight the Israelis through traditional and classical methods, but rather through a war of attrition, whereby we drain its energy, weaken it, then one day force it to withdraw."

The Iranians know the official estimates of the Iraq War's cost will soon surpass one trillion dollars, and that America will eventually run through its money and political will. But the Iranians would like to keep the United States engaged in Iraq as long as possible, as it serves their long-term interests, giving them more time to consolidate control over the Shia south. In the long term, Iran intends to wear down the United States to the point that it will not want to confront Iran anywhere in the Middle East.

But there's another option for the United States, one that is neither clean nor risk-free: simply getting up and leaving, dropping the Iraqi mess in Iran's lap.

All of a sudden, it would be Iran deciding whether it wanted to be directly responsible for keeping a lid on the anarchy, and whether it wanted to send in its own troops and start killing Iraqis. A direct Iranian role in Iraq would involve Iranians killing Sunni and even Shia, turning the conflict into a civil war. Everything Iran achieved in Lebanon, turning the Shia and the Sunni against Israel and the United States, would be lost. The Iranians would suddenly be the occupiers, and as such would absorb the full political impact of running a foreign country. They'd no longer be able to hide behind their proxies. It is unlikely Iran would do well as pure colonial power, burdened by the inevitable blame that comes with occupation.

Withdrawing is a high-risk gamble, of course—a threat to the Arab peninsula, as the Arabs on their own cannot hold back Iran. But in staying in Iraq indefinitely, the only thing the United States can absolutely count on is going broke.

Removing Saddam in March 2003, destroying Iraq's military, exposing the moderate Shia clerics as powerless, and creating another vacuum for Iran to fill was a colossal blunder. The United States effectively offered up another Arab country to Iran—another jewel in Iran's imperial crown.

Iraq isn't just a quagmire, another Vietnam we can just walk away from without consequence. If we were to withdraw today, what would stop Iran from pushing into Kuwait and Saudi Arabia, starting a Shia insurgency along the rim of the Gulf, which is 90 percent Shia?

Yet if the United States sticks it out and spends twenty or more years holding Iraq together, we'll still have a messy, impermanent solution, one that will quickly fall apart the moment we leave. There are three main reasons why:

First, any government the United States backs in Iraq, no matter if it includes our avowed enemies, will always be viewed as a puppet regime. We are outsiders, and Iraqis, the most xenophobic people in the Middle East, will never see us as otherwise.

Second, Iran's interest in Iraq is considerably stronger and more enduring than America's, its will is stronger, and it will never overcome the temptation to meddle, to undermine us in Iraq. Iran also cannot afford to allow Shia Islam's historical center of learning in Iraq, Najaf, to return to being a moderate rival of the Iranian learning center, Qum. Iran will not abandon its quest for control over Shia Islam, nor allow a quietist form of Shia Islam to challenge the legitimacy of Iran's mullahs.

Third, and most important, Iran has a pragmatic, realistic strategy and the United States doesn't. It knows that in one way or another, every major Shia political party in Iraq will ultimately have to answer to Tehran, whether it's for money, for arms, or just to keep a safe rear base. Iran knows how to use its strengths. Iranians are Muslims, and like the majority of Iraqis, they are Shia. The two countries' histories are intertwined and their bloodlines mixed, as are their economies, which both depend on oil. In other words, Iran is only half-foreign. Iran will always have more pieces to play with than the Americans do.

To Iraqis, Tehran matters. Washington doesn't.

5

LETHAL AND ELUSIVE:

WHY IRAN'S WEAPONS AND TACTICS

MAKE IT UNCONQUERABLE—

EVEN WITHOUT NUKES

The United States cannot stop Iran's rise short of an openended, thirty-year policy of containment or a full-scale war. Alliances, unenforceable sanctions, threats—none have worked so far, nor will they.

But even a war against Iran is not a real option. America can't bomb Iran without starting a war in the Gulf. There aren't enough soldiers to invade Iran, let alone hold it. And that's not to mention that a war would break the bank, turning the United States into a country with a Third World economy.

In May 2008, there were rumors the United States was going to bomb Jerusalem Force training camps in Iran to end the Shia insurgency in Iraq. I asked the former head of Pakistan's Inter-Services Intelligence organization, Hamid Gul, what he thought about the rumors. Gul had spent much of his career trying to contain Iran, both in Pakistan, with its 20 percent Shia population, and in Afghanistan.

"You never slap the king; you kill him," Gul told me.

"You mean the United States has to invade?" I asked.

"Maybe," Gul replied. "But don't forget: You can occupy Iran, but you cannot defeat it."

We both knew that Iran's military wasn't the same one Iraq fought to a standstill in the eighties. Over the course of the Iran-Iraq War, and the eighteen-year conflict in Lebanon, Iran learned how to fight a modern guerrilla war. It learned how to defeat a conventional military, taking and holding ground in the name of a nationalistic cause. But more important, Lebanon was a tactical proving ground for Iran, a place where it learned to combine asymmetrical warfare with both advanced and primitive weapons.

The superiority the United States had in weapons, training, and tactics was effective in fighting a Soviet-trained and -equipped army like Saddam's. But that effectiveness is undercut when confronted by small, highly mobile units armed with rockets, car bombs, and advanced improvised explosive devices that can defeat tanks and evade air superiority. An American conflict with Iran would be met with these deadly tactics—the same tactics the Iranians used to beat the Israelis.

Over the last three decades in Lebanon, the Iranians constantly adapted, innovated, and tested new weapons and tactics. Advanced shaped charges, car bombs, precision-guided rockets, ambushes, swarming, decoys, and underground bunkers halted an Israeli advance into Lebanon in 2006. The sheer number of rockets Hezbollah fired into Israel in 2006 blanked out Israel's defense radar network. And the same tactics lie in wait for the United States should it try to invade Iran. There's a good argument that Iran's modernization of guerrilla warfare is a military development as important as the introduction of the machine gun was to World War I, or the tank to World War II.

In April 2008, a Hezbollah official told me, "We studied the

United States and Israel. We knew they could not sustain many losses, that the drip-drip of casualties would turn the people against the war and they would leave. And that's what we will do for the next war." The United States can send the Marines to Iran's shores, even push on to Tehran, but what would it do after that? A truck bomb here and there, and America could be losing hundreds of soldiers a week. How long would Americans stand for that—three or four C-17s a week full of caskets coming back home?

Just as the Vietcong melted into the jungle, Iran's fighters will melt into the population and into caves. And because they have perfected asymmetric guerrilla tactics in their wars in Iraq and Lebanon, they'd make American occupation a living hell. Iranian "resistance" would always be there, bogging us down forever. We could turn Tehran into a pile of rubble, but we never could really defeat Iran in the sense of controlling it.

In the bloody, eight-year Iran-Iraq War, only one side came away with a battle plan for how to win future such wars. And despite the fact that Iraq had the stronger army, its failure to learn the lessons of asymmetrical warfare would ultimately doom it.

The Iran-Iraq War began on September 22, 1980, with a full-scale Iraqi invasion of Iran. As Iraqi air force planes quickly breached Iran's airspace, Saddam Hussein's troops crossed the border lightly opposed. In the first days of the war it looked as if Ayatollah Khomeini's regime, not even two years old, would collapse.

Saddam had several motivations for invading Iran. But the event that finally provoked him to give the order was what he considered an attack on his regime, Da'wa's assassination attempt on Tariq Aziz. Saddam was convinced that Iran was behind it, and that unless he did something about it, he would be next. He also dreamed of seizing Iranian oil, most of which was in ethnic Arab Khuzestan. Khuzestan's Arabs, he thought, wouldn't be able to resist the call of

Arab nationalism. Finally, he intended to occupy the confluence of the Tigris and Euphrates rivers, arguably the most strategic delta in the world.

Iraqi troops quickly captured the Iranian port city of Khorramshahr, but the Iranians stopped them just short of taking Abadan, Iran's oil-processing center just 10 kilometers away. And despite Saddam's hopes, the Iranian Arabs in Khuzestan stayed loyal to Tehran. By December 1980, two months after the invasion, Saddam's offensive was halted, and by 1981, Iraqi troops were already falling back. In 1982, the Iranians recaptured Khorramshahr.

Saddam tried to sue for peace, but Ayatollah Khomeini thought the Iranians could not only repel the Iraqis but also capture Baghdad, so he ordered the Iranian army to take the offensive. It made only small advances. No one in the Iranian military could convince Khomeini of the futility of the war; he believed that Iraqi Shia, the bulk of Saddam's army, would not fight—that given the chance, they would side with Shia Iran and not a Sunni Arab regime. At the bottom of it all, though, Khomeini believed God was on Iran's side, and that Iran would be graced with certain victory if it just kept fighting.

The blood flowed. Iran fell back on World War I trench warfare tactics, throwing waves of infantry against fixed Iraqi positions. Hundreds and thousands of young Iranian men, many without guns, died for no other purpose than to affirm the mullahs' faith. Iranians answered the call to martyrdom, but rather than fulfilling Khomeini's dream of getting rid of Saddam, their sacrifices turned into pointless death.

Eight years later, after a generation of Iranians had died, Khomeini finally understood that Iran could not win a conventional war against Iraq. The casualties, between one and two million, were staggering. But Iran did come away with a lesson: It could never again fight a war like that one. The next war—and Iran was certain there would be more—would be different.

In the Iran-Iraq War, Iran recognized that it won more engagements through unconventional tactics and asymmetrical warfare than it did through mass, frontal assaults. But more important, the Lebanon War, waged in the same time frame, had emerged as a paradigm. By 1988, the war in Lebanon was in its sixth year, and Iran couldn't miss the fact that the Islamic resistance there, just a couple of thousand guerrillas, had taken relatively more ground than the Iranian army had in the entire Iran-Iraq War. Iran's Lebanese proxies were on to something.

The first thing the Iranians learned from the Lebanon War was that small is better. Large formations in an open terrain are easily detectable from air, either by the Israeli F-16s that made twice-daily passes over Lebanon, by satellites, or by drones with cameras. But Islamic resistance fighters moving in groups of two or three were indistinguishable from farmers. They of course never wore uniforms, so they moved easily among the civilian population. Israeli aerial reconnaissance was virtually worthless.

This lesson was reaffirmed in the 1990–91 Gulf War. Allied precision munitions obliterated Iraq's conventional army in a matter of days. Western technology advances now made troops in the open fatally vulnerable. Again in 2003, Iran could see for itself that even the thickest armor is vulnerable. Immediately after the war's end, Revolutionary Guards were in Baghdad inspecting the damage caused by American armor-piercing Hellfire missiles that destroyed Saddam's T-72 tanks. The lesson: If a piece of equipment is in the open at the start of a war, you might as well consider it lost.

Iran adapted the same technology to build its own advanced antitank weapons. Modern antitank missiles borrow their design from shaped charges, which are explosives molded in a way that concentrates the energy of the blast on the smallest point possible, causing a tank's armor to "spall," or melt, showering the inside of a crew cab. Iran now has an advanced shaped charge that can penetrate armor steel to the depth of ten times the diameter of the round. So tanks have been forced to add layers of armor, and even explosives or sand to the outside of the armor, to dissipate the shaped charge's impact. But this in turn weighs down the tanks, making them less maneuverable. And even with the extra armor, an antitank round still can penetrate a tank's armor at its vulnerable points.

The second thing Iran learned in Lebanon was that Israel can be beaten in a war of attrition. In a full-fledged war, the Arabs might lose ten million men to one million for the Israelis. But can the Israelis afford that? Like the drip-drip of casualties described by the Hezbollah official, this slow attrition, and the associated cost and emotional expense, isn't something the Israelis can accept forever.

Iran also realized that increasing the size of its army wouldn't necessarily give it an advantage. Currently Iran has 325,000 men in uniform; 125,000 Revolutionary Guard troops, which are now more or less integrated into the army; and a million reservists. Iran's army outnumbers any Arab army in the Gulf. But at the same time, Iran understands it's no match, in conventional terms, for two or three U.S. carrier groups in the Gulf and U.S. strategic bombers, cruise missiles, and tactical nuclear warheads. And Iran also doesn't spend much money on its army. In 2006, Iran spent 2.5 percent of its GDP on the military—a fraction of the 10 percent Saudi Arabia spends.

Recognizing these inequities, Iran spent the nineties quietly buying advanced weapons from Russia and China—weapons that would level the playing field but not bankrupt Iran. Every time there was an arms show anywhere in the world, Iranian officers from both the army and the Revolutionary Guards would show up to inspect the latest Russian and Chinese arms. The Iranians never bought anything openly, but instead turned to trusted intermediaries in Russia and Eastern Europe to do the purchasing for them. They wanted to avoid a splash in the press, and they often got better deals that way. Still, Iran couldn't always hide its hand.

For the last ten years the Iranians have had their sights on the Russian S-300 surface-to-air missile defense system, which would give Iran an enormous advantage in controlling the Gulf's airspace. It would prevent a surprise Israeli attack by air, and would make it considerably more costly for the United States to go to war with Iran. The terms of the deal are already set, and now the Russians are just waiting for the right time to let it go through, when Washington is distracted by some unrelated crisis.

In the meantime, the Iranians bought all the weapons they needed to wage an asymmetrical war. In one deal the United States failed to stop, Iran bought highly advanced HMX explosives from Pakistan. In another, it bought a different sophisticated explosive, RDX. Both were ingredients for Iran's rocket production. Some of Iran's most sophisticated new equipment came from rogue states like North Korea. One item Iran bought from that country in large quantities was crystalline graphite, used in rocket nozzles. The sale was made quietly so neither the United States nor Israel could stop it.

For many purchases, Iran used false end-user certificates. In one deal, it bought advanced MiG-29 jets from the former Soviet republic of Moldova, handing over end-user certificates that stated the airplanes were going to the Central Asian republic of Tajikistan. In return for its help, Moldova got $250–$300 million in Iranian light crude. And the Iranians also secretly bought laser-guided missiles from corrupt Russian officials. Wherever there were cheap, sophisticated weapons for sale, the Iranians were there, ready with money.

Many of the advanced airplane parts the Iranians bought went through Swiss firms—entities that were nothing more than shelf companies, each set up for that particular transaction, often with false Russian destinations provided in the paperwork. One Turkish company took Iranian oil in exchange for Iran's purchase of equipment for a Russian-manufactured reactor. China, of course, was more than willing to sell its advanced weapons to Iran for oil and oil concessions. In the mid-nineties it started selling C-801b cruise missiles to Iran—the prototype for the missile that knocked out an Israeli frigate during the 34-day war of 2006.

In another quiet deal, Russia sold Iran 500 T-72 battle tanks—25 percent newly produced T-72s, and the remainder T-72M1 tanks, refurbished according to Iran's specifications. Iran paid $1 million each for the new T-72s, and $315,000 for the refurbished tanks. The high-explosive heat-seeking missiles for the tanks went for $650 a round. Iran couldn't buy enough SA-16 and SA-18 shoulder-fired missiles, missiles it was prepared to hand out to not only its regular troops but its proxies as well. At $40,000–$60,000 per missile, they were wonderful bargains. Had Iran bought similar equipment from a Western country, it would have paid ten to twenty times these amounts.

Everything from Russia came at fire-sale prices. Through the 1990s, the Russian army was broken and its soldiers starving—and Iran had money. There were few consequences for Moscow in making these deals. Arms were bought and shipped sub rosa, from fictional companies with untraceable post office boxes. They were exported from Russia as "civil aviation" equipment. There was nothing the United States could or would do about it; embargoes don't work, especially when the seller is an ally on the brink of collapse.

And the flow of advanced weapons to Iran continues today.

On January 6, 2008, five small boats from Iran's Revolutionary Guards challenged a three-ship U.S. Navy convoy in the Strait of Hormuz. This wasn't supposed to happen. The United States owned the Gulf, not Iran.

The fast boats raced toward the ships, clearly challenging the Americans. Though Iran's boats were a fraction of the size of the American ships, those on board remembered the devastating October 2000 attack on the USS *Cole* in Yemen, which proved that all it takes is one small craft with a bomb to cripple one of the most advanced ships in the U.S. fleet.

This was a mock attack, a not-so-subtle message that Iran hadn't accepted American suzerainty in the Gulf. But more ominously, it was another warning that the United States didn't enjoy the military superiority it thought it did.

President Bush was on his way to the Gulf; the timing of the incident wasn't a coincidence. For a start, the Iranians were warning the Gulf Arabs not to join an American coalition against Iran, which was clearly what was on Bush's mind. In October 2007, Secretary of State Condoleezza Rice had traveled to the Middle East in an attempt to rally "emerging moderate forces" against "the Iranian threat." This was the only thing the Bush administration could think to do in response to Iran's spreading its influence in Iraq.

Iran's choice of Hormuz for the confrontation also wasn't a coincidence. The Iranians wanted to remind Bush of the stakes of any confrontation. The only real egress for Gulf oil, Hormuz is the world's oil spigot. If Iran turns it off, America goes into a depression.

The small-boats incident didn't come out of nowhere. After the U.S. invasion of Iraq and the destruction of its army, there's been increasing euphoria in Tehran that the military balance in the Gulf is finally tipping in Iran's direction. Iran's asymmetrical warfare in Lebanon, which was now about to be applied in Iraq, was finally paying off in larger strategic terms. Iran had made an enormous blunder in the eighties, taking on Iraq head-on. But since then, the Iranians had figured out how to win Iraq—and just maybe the rest of the Gulf as well.

Soon the clock would be turned back to 1763, the year the first British warship passed into the Persian Gulf and Iran formally lost control of it. This was when it just became the Gulf, rather than the Persian Gulf, and the Arabs became subjects of the Crown of England. In the eighteenth century, the Iranian Dynasty was weak because it couldn't fight a modern navy—the British boats could have sunk the Iranian fleet in a day. And today, while the Iranians have no illusions that their navy can sink an American carrier group, they know they can do enough damage to stop the United States from attacking. The tide is turning.

Iran is calculating that the United States will get tired of Iraq, pull out, and let fall the first domino in a Persian reconquest of the Gulf. In December 2007, when Iranian President Ahmadinejad crowed that the National Intelligence Estimate—the document that confirmed Iran had stopped building a nuclear bomb—was a "declaration of surrender," he had the Gulf in mind. The United States couldn't beat Iran in the Gulf and it couldn't stay there forever—and when it left, Iran would fill the void. This is precisely what the Revolutionary Guards have in mind.

The Iranians understand perfectly that the only reason we care about that miserable body of water called the Persian Gulf is that 55 percent of the world's reserves lie beneath its shores and 17 million barrels of crude oil pass daily through the Strait of Hormuz. Given Iranian military dominance in the Gulf, Iran would be delighted to use oil for political dominance as well. So it definitely was no accident that Iran's Revolutionary Guards chose Hormuz to put down a marker, ruin Bush's visit to the Gulf, and remind everyone that worse would come if they weren't careful.

But it wasn't the politics the U.S. Navy was thinking about when the fast boats challenged its ships on January 6. It was the Iranians' military tactics.

According to the *New York Times,* during a classified simulated war game in 2002, the Iranians were able to sink sixteen U.S. Navy ships in the Gulf. Surface-to-sea missiles, the element of surprise, and the tactics in which small, fast, agile boats swarmed the ships were able to defeat the Navy's sophisticated defensive weapons. The Iranian tactics of approaching at high speeds, from multiple directions, left the bigger ships highly vulnerable.

"The sheer numbers involved overloaded their ability, both mentally and electronically, to handle the attack," said a retired Marine officer who participated in the war games. "The whole thing was over in maybe 10 minutes." The American military command was forced to admit that these new Iranian tactics, as simple as they seemed, could seriously challenge our dominance of the Gulf.

"It's clear, strategically, where the Iranian military has gone," Joint Chiefs of Staff Chair Mike Mullen said after the January 2008 encounter. "For the years that this strategic shift toward their small, fast boats has taken place, we've been very focused on that."

Another officer who participated in the 2002 war game said the idea of a "swarming attack" was taken from nature, where insects and small animals—from ants to wolves—can overwhelm a much larger animal using speed and simultaneous attacks. The banding together of many small fighters to defeat a powerful, looming threat— it's a perfect metaphor for the Islamic fight against the Western superpower.

Iran's naval "swarming tactics" follow a trend of using relatively unsophisticated weapons to cause heavy damage. The 9/11 hijackers used ordinary box cutters and civilian airliners to destroy the World Trade Center and attack the Pentagon. The USS *Cole* was attacked by a small launch. In each case, less was more: simple weaponry was used to inflict massive damage of the sort usually caused by bombers or heavy artillery.

Innovative tactics like these are virtually impossible to defend against, showing once again that while the United States could "conquer" Iran by bombing it into submission, it will never be able to hold Iran.

There are other such tactics:

Evading overhead surveillance and aerial bombardment. The Iranians know about our satellites and have buried their rockets, surface-to-air missiles, and even tanks underground and in caves, planning to pull them out minutes before an engagement. During the 2006 Lebanon War, the Israelis were constantly surprised when rockets were fired from areas they had thought were clear of Hezbollah forces. Iranian Silkworm missiles are buried all along Iran's shore on the Gulf, ready to be unearthed and fired at tankers or oil facilities to close Gulf shipping routes, and there's nothing we can do about it.

Secure communications. In early 1979, when Iran's new revolutionary government broke into the Shah's intercept sites along the Caspian Sea, they were amazed to discover how many Soviet communication channels the Shah's secret service had been listening in to. It was a lesson the Iranians never forgot.

In the eighties, the Revolutionary Guards took their communications off the air, both on the Iraq front and in Lebanon. When they did talk on the telephone or walkie-talkies, they coded their conversations, making them indecipherable to anyone listening in. They also never discussed their plans in the open, either on the phone or in large meetings. Everything important was discussed face-to-face or conveyed orally or by hand-carried messages.

In the 2006 war, Hezbollah used sophisticated computer codes and electronic drop sites, defeating Israel's most advanced intercept systems. And today, Hezbollah uses fiber optic cable technology for telephone communications, which can't be intercepted by Israel or the United States. If Iran ever decided to attack the Gulf's oil facilities or the United States in Iraq, we wouldn't know about it until the first shot was fired.

Secrecy. After Imad Mughniyah was assassinated, his family told the press that they'd had no idea he was a senior commander in Hezbollah's military wing. This level of secrecy has made it nearly impossible to place spies inside Hezbollah. To this day, the United States doesn't know who Hezbollah's senior field commanders are.

Hiding in plain sight. Iran learned to disperse its fighting forces throughout the civilian population. Hezbollah, the all-volunteer

Basij military force, and the Jerusalem Force are scattered through-out built-up urban areas, rendering our weapons virtually useless un-less we're prepared to inflict massive civilian casualties. Hezbollah picked up wide popular sympathy across the Middle East when Israel bombed Beirut's southern suburbs, killing civilians. If America was forced to do the same, any chance of spreading a pro-democracy, pro-freedom, populist message would be lost.

Car and truck bombs. Iran turned the car into a weapon as effec-tive as heavy artillery or airpower. There's not a tank in existence today that can't be destroyed by a truck bomb. The immediate conse-quence is that Iranians can stop a conventional army from securing cities or any built-up area with heavy traffic. A couple of years ago, Hezbollah escorted me through its "battlefields"—a tour of charred car hulks and pieces of tanks and armored personnel carriers, all destroyed by car bombs. Even traditional ambushes were initiated by a car bomb to block off the front, followed by an attack at the rear, which boxed the Israelis in. In Baghdad today, the same tactics learned in Lebanon have forced U.S. troops behind blast walls and into heavier and heavier armor, isolating them from the population. Just as the Crusaders were isolated in their castles.

Code-cracking. Hezbollah and Iran learned how to crack Israeli communication codes, perhaps the first time an enemy has been able to do this since Israel's founding in 1948. "We were able to mon-itor Israeli communications," a Hezbollah official has been quoted as saying, "and we used this information to adjust our planning." It is still not known how Hezbollah was able to make advancements in this normally esoteric side of warfare.

Explosives. The Iranians are ingenious in their ability to disguise and ship explosives around the world. In one incident, a shipment of olives destined for the United States was discovered to have C-4 plastic explosives inside, shaped and painted like olives and sealed in cans.

In another incident in November 1989, Spanish police seized the *Cedar*, a commercial cargo ship that was carrying nearly a half-ton of C-4 plastic explosives surreptitiously smuggled on board by Hezbollah operatives. Sealed in 193 tin cans along with 258 20-millisecond-delay electronic detonators, the explosives were of French origin and were probably headed for Western Europe, to be either sold or used for future attacks. It is suspected there were another dozen shipments like it, some undoubtedly headed for the United States.

Although Iran has moved away from terrorism, its explosive caches and skills still make it potentially one of the most dangerous terrorist states in the world. This is a capability Iran would not hesitate to unleash if faced with a major war. There are thousands of Hezbollah cadres around the world, many with European passports, ready to carry out acts of terror on Iran's orders.

Shaped and platter charges. Curiously, it was probably the United States who first convinced Iran of the effectiveness of platter charges. In the early eighties, we taught the Afghan mujahideen to pack their small iron stoves with explosives, with the stove lids acting as projectiles to penetrate light Soviet armor. The Iranians advanced the technology, shaping and milling the projectiles for a vastly more lethal effect. The U.S. military has seen the results of this advancement in both Lebanon and, today, in Iraq. Platter charges, or "explosively formed penetrators" (EFPs), have reportedly put holes in our heavy armor, including Abrams tanks. This was a remarkable battlefield shift; the Abrams tanks were supposed to meet American military needs for decades.

Shaped charges can be concealed in the doors of cars or in the sides of buildings, or simply buried in the road. There is no certain defense against them. If the Iranians were to introduce EFPs in great numbers in Iraq and Afghanistan, our troops would have to retreat to fortified areas and never leave—castles we'd have to resupply by air.

Electronics. When I was in Beirut in the eighties, the United States came across an Iranian explosive "firing train" that showed a sophistication we hadn't suspected the Iranians had.

"It's pretty goddamned amazing," the tech who looked at it told me. "A 567 tone detector . . . in an integrated circuit board that activates a 555 timer IC—only precisely when the relay was open for seven seconds." Don't ask. But the point was that at times Iranian technical skills were as advanced as any.

And Iran's technical sophistication was found in more than just its terrorist devices. Hezbollah learned to thwart Israeli counter-measures such as radio jamming, securing its own communications. Among other things it switched to detonating bombs by light-emitting diodes that are virtually impossible to protect against. With Iran's advancing technology and tactics, the nature of warfare in the Middle East will never be the same.

Iran's transformation to an elite asymmetric war machine certainly got Israel's attention. As the Winograd Commission Report, the official Israeli investigation into the 34-day war of 2006, put it, "A semi-military organization of a few thousand men resisted, for a few weeks, the strongest army in the Middle East, which enjoyed full air superiority and size and technological advantages."

And Iran and Hezbollah are only getting better.

Deterrence credibility. Iran has convinced its enemies that attacking it comes at too high a price. As the rhetoric picked up with the United States in 2007, Iran sent emissaries to all the Gulf states with one simple message: If the United States attacks us, we will destroy your oil facilities.

The Gulf Arabs closely watched the Israeli-Hezbollah war in 2006.

They saw how Israel was unable to protect its cities, how forty-three Israeli civilians were killed, forcing Israel to retreat from Lebanon without achieving any of its stated objectives. What could Iran do to the Arabs, whose military isn't even a shadow of Israel's?

What's particularly odd about Iran's advancement in conventional military tactics is that the West has largely ignored it, choosing instead to focus almost obsessively on whether Iran is developing nuclear weapons. It's more evidence that we are miscalculating the nature of the Iranian threat.

Right now, at least, the Iranians don't need a nuclear bomb. If a war is to be fought in the Gulf, Iraq, or Lebanon, Iran will almost certainly fall back on its asymmetrical tactics and weapons. There are also innumerable drawbacks to rushing the development of a nuclear weapon in today's global atmosphere—and few benefits.

One reason we're obsessed with the idea of Iran's developing nuclear weapons is that we're once again fighting the last war rather than this one. We remember it was Saddam Hussein's chemical weapons that stopped Iran from taking Basra. We're worried that the Syrians intend to put chemical warheads on their Scud missiles and fire them at Tel Aviv. We're blinded by the worst-case scenario, which happens not to be Tehran's preferred scenario.

That's not to say Iran has lost complete interest in a nuke. As early as 1989, a year after the end of the Iran-Iraq War, Iran started buying electromagnetic isotope separators from China, installing them in Karaj, a city just west of Tehran. The Chinese Precision Machining Import/Export Company sold Iran a three-axis turntable, which could be converted for grinding explosive lenses for a nuclear triggering device. Iran also bought bomb technology from the rogue Pakistani nuclear scientist A. Q. Khan. These were all signs that Iran planned to secretly build a bomb. The question was: Why?

First, Iran wanted to counter Pakistan's bomb—the "Sunni" bomb, as it was called—and they also believed Saddam Hussein was building one. Second, Iran wanted to be taken seriously as a major power, in the same way it wanted to control Hormuz and the world's oil.

But at the same time, the Iranians see a nuclear bomb as nice to have but not crucial to their survival. The Iranians are too smart to risk the gains they've made in Iraq and Lebanon by forcing the issue. The National Intelligence Estimate reflected this calculation, offering the estimate that Iran had only suspended its nuclear bomb building, rather than stopping it permanently. The neocons and Bush administration officials challenged the estimate—but to anyone who'd really been paying attention to Iran's actions in the last six or seven years, it shouldn't have come as a surprise at all.

Iran may not yet have nukes, but it has three things that are vastly more important: highly developed asymmetrical fighting skills and weapons; a growing army of hungry, disaffected, street-smart fighters; and an invincible anticolonial message. With that, Iran has set the stage for its push toward empire—a push they've already begun. The next target: Turkey.

6

Seizing the World's Energy Corridors: Why Iran Will Shortly Control the Most Vital Oil and Gas Trade Routes

There was no mistaking it: In the wake of Ayatollah Khomeini's 1979 revolution, Iran attracted legions of angry young Shia from across the Middle East. It didn't matter whether they embraced the revolution in full or not—Iran was happy to have them, especially if they were prepared to fight under Iranian orders. With time, though, Iran started to look across sectarian lines, to the Sunnis—notably, to the Sunni Kurds. By the early nineties, the Iranian revolution had started to look less like a Shia revolution and more like one with universal appeal. Iran's shadow takeover of a small piece of Iraqi Kurdistan in the mid-nineties is a perfect metaphor for Iran's evolving tactics and strategy.

There are two different notions of "Kurdistan" in the Middle East today. First, there's Iraqi Kurdistan, which has been a more or less independent state since the end of the Gulf War in 1991. Since the 2003 invasion, Iraqi Kurdistan has been governed by the Kurdistan

Regional Government, a sovereign government in all but name, although it doesn't print its own currency or legally export its oil.

At the risk of oversimplification, one can say that the Iraqi Kurds only agreed to join the American-created Iraqi government after they were promised the Iraqi presidency. The position, currently filled by Jalal Talabani, a Kurd from a small village in northern Iraq, is largely ceremonial. But after hundreds of years of Sunni Arab and Ottoman subjugation, this acknowledgment of Kurdish ethnicity and equality was enough. And the Kurds also believe that they received an implicit promise to absorb the northern Iraqi city of Kirkuk, along with Kirkuk's million barrels of oil a day.

The other "Kurdistan" is Greater Kurdistan, which loosely refers to ethnic Kurds dispersed among northern Iraq, southeastern Turkey, eastern Syria, and northwestern Iran. The Kurds, an Indo-European people who speak an Iranian language, are estimated to number anywhere from 25 to 35 million. They make up 15–20 percent of Iraq's population, 20 percent of Turkey's, 7 percent of Iran's, and 8 percent of Syria's. As the Kurds will tell you, they are the largest ethnic group without their own country.

While the rest of the world dismissed Greater Kurdistan as strategically insignificant, Iran saw that the Kurds sit astride the most strategic areas of the world—a crossroads between Iraq and Europe, between the Arab peninsula and the Caucasus, between Iran and Europe. Iran also saw the Kurds as a convenient proxy to stir up problems in Turkey, Syria, and Iraq, inciting them when it served Iran's interests. It didn't matter in the least to Tehran that the Kurds were overwhelmingly Sunni, just as long as they were a thorn in their neighbors' side.

Iran's interests in the Kurds are several. Iran would like to position itself as the predominant influence among Kurds—as their protector, even. At the same time, Iran intends to keep a brake on the creation of a greater Kurdish state, which Iranian Kurds would clamor to be a part of. Iran's offer to the Kurds is that it will grant the

Kurds a large degree of suzerainty over their own lives, but it will not tolerate a completely independent Kurdish state—in Iraq, Iran, or anywhere else.

But on a more tactical level, the Iranians see in the Kurds an instrument to undermine their neighbors: if Turkey or Iraq opposes Tehran on some issue vital to Iran, Tehran will fund and arm Kurdish guerrillas in those countries to hit back. It's another side of proxy warfare.

The moment Saddam Hussein lost control of Iraqi Kurdistan at the end of the Gulf War in 1991, Iran sent officers from the Revolutionary Guards into Iraqi Kurdistan. Their first objective was to hunt down Iranian Kurds who had taken refuge there. At the same time, the Guards started to recruit and arm Iraqi Kurds to raise an insurgency against Baghdad.

Recruits against Saddam weren't hard to find. The Kurds historically never wanted to be a part of Arab Iraq, and they had fought the regime off and on for years. But by 1991, ravaged by war, the Kurds were on the edge of starvation. They needed everything, from gasoline to wheat to guns and ammunition. Iran kept its border wide open to Iraq's Kurds—a sign of goodwill the Kurds wouldn't forget.

At some point, the Revolutionary Guards started to fund and arm the Turkish guerrilla group called the Kurdistan Workers' Party, or the PKK. Although the PKK is made up entirely of Kurds with Turkish citizenship, their only sure sanctuary from the Turkish army is the high mountains of Kurdish Iraq. The PKK's goal is to establish a socialist, independent Kurdish state in southeastern Turkey.

Iran's motivations at first weren't completely clear. Did they want to provoke a civil war in Turkey? Or somehow drive a wedge between Turkey and the European Community, by forcing the Turks to clamp down and anger the Kurds' European supporters? It was known that Iran was determined that if Turkey were to have one important alliance, it would be with Iran rather than NATO, which Turkey already belongs to, or the European Union, which Turkey would like to join. Still, funding the PKK seemed an odd way for Iran to win Turkey.

Iran's inroads into Iraqi Kurdistan went largely unnoticed, because it's one of the most desolate, remote parts of the world. With few exceptions, Iraq, Turkey, and Iran banned the press from entering northern Iraq. And there were no air links into Iraqi Kurdistan until after the U.S.-led invasion in 2003. So, as with many vital strategic shifts in the world, Iran managed to impose its will quietly. By the time anyone in the West noticed what Iran was doing, it was too late to do anything about it.

In the mid-1990s, when I was in Iraqi Kurdistan and still working for the CIA, I got a glimpse of how the Iranian takeover worked.

I knew, of course, that Iran had its eye on the Shia-dominated south of Iraq. But Iraqi Kurdistan, in the north, was another story. We had little idea what was going on there, because the only American view was from 25,000 feet—the F-16 jets that enforced the no-fly zone over Kurdistan.

I was there only a week when I started hearing rumors that Iran had annexed a thin slice of Iraqi Kurdistan along the mountainous Iranian border, including the town of Hajj Umran. Frankly, this didn't seem likely. The Kurds who live in those mountains have a reputation for being stubbornly independent, prepared to die to defend their steep, bare defiles. Historically, they had nursed a deep hatred for Persians, a hatred that was only exacerbated by Khomeini's revolution. Taking into account Iran's geopolitical interests, one could understand why Iran would want to control Kurdistan, which was located in a sensitive border area. But why would Sunni Kurds go along with it? Had Iran really succeeded in breaching this sectarian divide—and no one noticed?

When I asked, I was told there were no Iranian troops actually in Kurdistan. Rather, Iran had created a proxy force, Kurdish

Hezbollah, a name borrowed from the more famous Hezbollah in Lebanon. (This is Iran's version of branding.) Iran's intent was to have control over the area without invading it, I was told. The Revolutionary Guards funded and trained Kurdish Hezbollah, and worked side by side with the man who headed it, Adham Barzani, a Sunni Muslim. He was a man worth talking to.

Even today, I laugh when looking back at that trip. It was something out of an Evelyn Waugh novel—this stealth invasion of a land in the back of beyond, the naïve adventurer in his pith helmet unearthing a momentous truth. But then again sometimes that's all spying is about, a windshield tour of someplace the average American would never dare go.

In a bitter early-February cold, two other CIA officers and I set out from Salah ad-Din, a small town in the north we were based in. There was never much traffic on the roads in Iraqi Kurdistan, but that morning we had the road completely to ourselves. It had rained all night, a chilly downpour that kept promising to turn to snow. After a two-hour drive, we descended into a broad valley. Patches of low-lying clouds obscured most of the surrounding mountains, which rose to nearly 4,000 meters. The snow line was just above the valley floor.

I had a sense now of just how cut off northern Iraq was from the rest of the country, and how easily and quickly Saddam must have lost it. He would have had a hard time supplying his troops there, let alone retaking those mountains. I was starting to see how it was possible for Iran to come to quietly dominate this piece of Iraq.

You couldn't miss Adham Barzani's lair, a fortified stone house on an outcrop looking out over the Zagros Mountains where they spill into Iraq. A tangle of barbed wire, trenches, and sandbagged, belt-fed machine guns covered the approach to the house. An antiaircraft gun sat perched on the roof.

Barzani's guards fixed us with a steady stare as we drove up. With their trimmed beards, olive-drab jackets lined with synthetic fur, and scuffed boots, they could have passed as Revolutionary Guards. They had the same messianic look I'd seen in Revolutionary Guards' eyes in Balabakk in the eighties. They were believers who knew the apocalypse was near and felt contempt for us, the unbelievers, who couldn't see it.

One of the gunmen showed us into a room with a half-dozen filthy mattresses on the floor. He watched as we took off our shoes and sat down. Noticing the cold, he went off to find *mazout* for the stove. He came back with a bucket, poured it into the cast-iron stove, and lit a match to get it going. He then turned around and left without saying a word.

Five minutes later, Adham Barzani walked in. Like his soldiers, he was dressed in olive-drab. We shook hands and sat back down. Adham noticed we didn't have the customary green tea and called out for one of the guards to bring us some. It was Ramadan, and Adham was fasting, but that didn't stop him from being a good host.

Adham grinned. He said he'd just had a visit from a couple of Iranians, who knew that we were on the way to see him.

"And how could they possibly have known that?" he said, his smile widening. "You were supposed to be here yesterday, not today."

We both knew who'd told the Iranians about our visit: Masud Barzani, the pro-American head of the Kurdistan Democratic Party and our host in northern Iraq. Masud was Adham's cousin. But that wasn't what led Masud to tip off the Iranians. Like the rest of the Kurds, Masud depended on Iran for refined gasoline, wheat, and anything else the Kurds still needed to stay alive. There was no chance that Masud or his cousin would go behind Iran's back, especially when it came to dealing with the CIA. Today, Masud is the head of the Kurdistan Regional Government.

We continued with small talk. Adham spoke about the fighting going on between the Iranian-backed Kurdish Hezbollah and a Kurdish group headed by Jalal Talabani—the same Jalal Talabani who is now the president of Iraq.

"I didn't start it," Adham said defensively. "Talabani did."

At the time, Talabani was in a hot war with both Barzanis, Masud and Adham. But it was a turf war that had nothing to do with Iran, because when it came to economics, Talabani was as beholden to Iran as the Barzanis were. All these Kurdish groups were, to some degree, dependent on Iran.

We sat sipping our tea, not saying anything. I was deciding how to bring up Iran's designs on Iraqi Kurdistan. It's not the kind of question you ask someone on Iran's payroll, or at least not out of the blue. Instead I offered my usual boilerplate: It would be a good idea if the Kurds stopped fighting one another, I suggested, and turned their guns on the common enemy, Saddam Hussein.

Adham ignored my suggestion. "Why doesn't America stop Muslims from being killed in Bosnia and Chechnya?" he asked. "How can the United States remain silent, a country that is supposed to stand for human rights?"

Naturally, I thought. I wondered if he'd just finished reading an editorial in *Kayhan,* Iran's hard-line, regime-backed newspaper that reminds its readers every morning that Islam is locked in a war for its very existence, that Muslims are oppressed everywhere, and that if the Russians kill a Chechen, they might as well have killed an Iranian.

The unspoken thought that hung in the air was that we didn't have a lot to say to each other. Barzani was relieved when I said I wanted to see the Iranian border before dark. He offered to send an escort with us.

Outside, the marble sky dropped its first snowflakes. A pair of Nissan pickups stood idling, belt-fed machine guns perched over their cabs. The gunners wore bug-eyed goggles and old-fashioned hunting caps with the flaps down but untied. I had to hold back a laugh.

A slight man in a heavy, olive-drab wool coat climbed into the passenger seat next to me. "My name is Dulayr Surkan. I'm an officer in the Sepah." Sepah is short for the Revolutionary Guards. *Okay,* I thought. I had no idea whether Dulayr was an Iraqi or an Iranian Kurd. But the message was clear: The Iranians had their eyes on us.

As we were about to pull away, there was a tap on the window. It was Adham, a plastic bag in his hand—sandwiches for lunch.

"Why not stop in Choman on your way?" he asked. "You can talk to my Shura. I've already arranged it." The Shura is Hezbollah's politburo.

The road north to Choman took us even higher into the mountains. The farther we went up, the more red triangles we saw alongside the road—warnings of buried land mines. Dulayr said some of the heaviest fighting of the Iran-Iraq War had occurred here. Choman had been flattened, as had Hajj Umran. Iranian troops had occupied large parts of the north during much of the war. Saddam hadn't had the troops to dislodge them.

We pulled into a walled compound on the outskirts of Choman, stopping in front of a one-story unfinished cinderblock building. Rebars stuck out of the roof, someone's promise to add a second story one day.

Dulayr jumped out and shook hands with a bearded man standing at the front door. He was wearing a Central Asian *chopan,* a tube-shaped cloak. He pointedly ignored us and led Dulayr into the building.

We filed in after them, into a room with cheap synthetic carpets and recently whitewashed walls. There was no furniture, and we sat down on the floor facing a photograph of Ayatollah Khomeini staring down at us accusingly. This time no one bothered to turn on the heater or bring us tea. In the distance, east of Choman, there was the sound of heavy artillery. Someone outside cleared a .50-caliber machine gun, rattling the windows in their frames.

Ten minutes later, Adham's Shura walked in: six bearded men in their thirties and forties, all wearing black clerical robes. They sat down across from us on the other side of the room. They didn't say a word, waiting for me to start.

Suddenly realizing that Adham hadn't explained to them who we were, for a moment I had no idea what to say. Finally, in the most formal Arabic I could muster, I offered the same boilerplate I'd offered Adham: Let's get rid of Saddam. But even as I said it, I knew I wasn't helping. All six men looked at me blankly, no doubt wondering whether my words contained some coded message. Had we come all the way from America to tell them *that?*

I asked a few questions about the road to Hajj Umran, land mines, the economy. "Good. Thanks be to God," they replied. I ran out of questions, and we were left with an uncomfortable silence. They were as relieved as Adham had been when I thanked them for our talk. But the real eye-opener was still ahead.

After an hour's drive, Dulayr motioned for me to stop in the middle of a couple of dozen mounds of snow, with an occasional brick or two-by-four sticking out. "Welcome to Hajj Umran," Dulayr said.

Iranian artillery barrages during the Iran-Iraq War hadn't left a house standing. The only building in sight was an Iranian blockhouse on the other side of the border, about a hundred yards away. A half-dozen Iranian border guards watched us through binoculars. So, being good tourists, we got out our cameras and started taking pictures of them.

Almost immediately the driver of the escort pickup, walkie-talkie in his hand, came running toward us. He whispered to Dulayr, who turned to me.

"Iran does not allow pictures here," he said, apologetically.

I knew what was going on but still asked, incredulously, "Iran's in charge on this side of the border?"

Dulayr's silence answered my question. Iran, of course, controlled both sides of the border, and the rumors were right: Iran had brought this piece of Iraq under its sway. It didn't matter that there were no Iranian troops inside Kurdistan. Iran didn't need them as long as they had their proxy Adham Barzani watching out for their interests.

The answer to my question of what Iran intended to do with Kurdistan wouldn't come until later, when it was learned that Adham, only months after my visit, had started shipping weapons and ammunition to the PKK—Turkey's Kurdistan Workers' Party. At the time, the PKK was preparing for a new offensive against the Turkish government. Barzani, we knew, was acting on the orders of the Revolutionary Guards. Passing the arms and money through Kurdish Hezbollah provided Iran another layer of deniability.

The question then was: Would Iran get away with it? It was assumed in Washington that the Turks would find out and take some sort of reprisal. Turkey could either close the border with Iran in a diplomatic protest, or turn the tables on Iran by arming Iran's Kurds. On the face of it, it seemed that Iran's backing of Turkey's Sunni Kurds was a risky policy. Wasn't Iran worried about causing the blowback that comes with inciting ethnic and sectarian divisions, Turks versus Kurds? Iran had already had one bad experience with this in the past.

In November 1979, a radical Saudi messianic sect seized Islam's holiest site, the Mecca Mosque, shaking the Muslim world to its core. In the long, bloody siege that followed, the attackers were killed or executed before the Saudis could properly interrogate them. But it's generally accepted that Khomeini's revolution in February 1979 and the takeover of the U.S. embassy in Tehran on November 4, 1979, were the catalyst for the Mecca attack. The attackers were inspired by Iran's revolution, and at the same time they were convinced that because of the weakness of Al Saud, Sunni Islam itself was under threat from the Shia—a prelude to end times. And they believed that true Muslims—Sunnis—had to have undisputed control of Mecca when the apocalypse arrived.

The Sunni reaction to Khomeini wasn't confined to Saudi Arabia. In Pakistan, another Sunni state with a tradition of strong Islamic fundamentalism, the government declared Islamic law, along with steps such as banning liquor in military messes and pouring money into its conservative madrassas, or schools. Things turned violent on November 21, 1979, the day Mecca was seized, when Pakistani students burned the U.S. embassy in Islamabad while the Pakistani government stood by and watched. The students were incited by rumors the United States was somehow behind the Mecca attack. But Khomeini's revolution also played a part, with Pakistan unsure how its own Shia would react to it.

After the Soviet invasion of Afghanistan, in December 1979, Pakistan's insecurities only worsened. Pakistan insisted that American money and arms in Afghanistan be funneled to Sunni Afghan fundamentalists, intending that they serve as a quarantine to keep Khomeini's revolution from infecting Pakistan and its Shia. Pakistan was too absorbed by its war of conviction with Iran to realize it was indiscriminately funding the most radical Sunni fundamentalist movements.

Even today, Pakistan's greatest worry after India is Iran. With 20 percent of Pakistan's population Shia, and the country seemingly ripping apart at the seams, Pakistan's leadership feels that it has no choice but to fall back on political Islam as a last defense. As late as May 2008, the Pakistani government was backing Sunni militants in Taliban-dominated northwest frontier tribal areas to fight against the small Shia enclave Parachinar—a place Pakistan believes Iran is meddling in. Pakistan had to overlook the fact that the money it sent was ending up in the hands of the so-called Taliban *takfiris*.

The Middle East is a world of shifting definitions. But the word *takfiri* generally refers to a Sunni Muslim who looks at the world in black-and-white: there are true believers and then there are nonbelievers, with no shades in between. A *takfiri*'s mission is to re-create the Caliphate according to a literal interpretation of the Koran.

Anyone who is not a true believer is by definition a *kafir*—an atheist—who either submits to second-class citizenship under Islamic rule or is destroyed. Along with convictions like these comes a readiness to slaughter, assassinate, and ethnically cleanse nonbelievers. *Takfiris* are not unlike the Khmer Rouge, the Cambodian Communists who slaughtered a million people to "purify" Cambodia; or the terrorists who truck-bombed the Alfred P. Murrah Building in Oklahoma City. Al Qaeda, the Taliban, and Osama bin Laden often are classified as *takfiris* in the larger definition of the term.

Takfiri demands are impracticable. They propose turning the clock back to seventh-century Arabia, living under nomadic tribal customs that were never meant to adapt to the twenty-first century. The Taliban banned toothpaste, for example, because the prophet didn't use it. Unlike Hezbollah and Iran, the *takfiris* care less about occupying ground and more about overthrowing "apostate regimes" in the Middle East, from Mubarak's Egypt to the Al Saud in Saudi Arabia—a world Islamic revolution. Their failure to establish a lasting *takfiri* government in Afghanistan under the Taliban wasn't a deterrent in the least; divinely ordained revolutions don't worry about small setbacks like this.

In looking at Iran's support to the PKK and the risk Iran took in attempting to undermine a Sunni country, it's important to understand the wider context: Sunnis, in supporting *takfiri* movements, suffer a morbid, existential angst. Saudi Arabia and Pakistan are relatively new nations—Saudi Arabia was formed in 1932, Pakistan in 1947. Both bank on Islam, if for no other reason than to hold their countries together. Unlike Iran, Saudi Arabia and Pakistan almost seem to have been a religion first, upon which they then built their nations.

To a lesser degree, Turks are from the same mold. Today, they're increasingly falling back on Sunni Islam as a bond to overcome their ethnic and sectarian divides. And for the Sunni Turks, like Pakistan and Saudi Arabia, Iran's revolution will always be the joker in the pack: a resurgent, victorious Shia order challenges both Sunni supremacy and its legitimacy.

With Sunni Islam under a worsening threat, *takfiris* lash out blindly and viciously—against Shia, the United States, the West, or anything else they feel threatens their existence. Area weapons, weapons of mass destruction—whether car bombings, massacres, or flying planes into buildings—are directed against civilians. The Sunni *takfiris* react against inanimate objects as well, as when the Taliban blew up two massive Buddha stone carvings near Bamiyan, Afghanistan. The Sunni saw the rise of Ayatollah Khomeini and his Shia followers as the end of their world—an imperative to use any weapon available to stop the fall.

Was Iran worried about a Sunni backlash in Turkey, rousing Turkish *takfiris*? Or that the Turks might back Sunni *takfiris* in Iran? Again, we have no public record of the motives behind Iran's decision. But one thing is clear: By 1996 Iran, thanks to its experience in Lebanon, understood a lot more about managing an insurgency and overcoming sectarian divisions than it did in 1979.

When Iran started arming and supplying Turkey's Kurds, urging them to launch attacks inside Turkey's borders in an attempt to destabilize the government, it underscored Iran's transition to a more calculating, pragmatic power that aggressively pursues its core foreign policy interests. But now it was minus religion and ideology. The Iranians would never admit they had abandoned Khomeini's revolution, but that's what in fact had happened. Funding the Kurdish PKK—a Marxist-Leninist cult with few beliefs in common with Shia Islam—was a radical departure from the early, radical sectarian ideology of revolutionary Iran.

Iran's incursion into Iraqi Kurdistan turned out to be an unqualified success. First, since Iran knew from the Lebanon experience how to hide its hand in a proxy war, Turkey was never able to make a case against Iran. Second, Iran also knew how to keep a tight rein on its proxies, on men like Adham Barzani. And finally, the Iranians knew how to tread lightly in Iraqi Kurdistan. They never attempted to spread Persian culture, garrison Iranian troops there, or convert the Sunni Kurds to Shia Islam. One irony of it all is that today there are hundreds of American missionaries in Iraqi Kurdistan, attempting to convert the Kurds to Christianity. The Kurds ask themselves the question: Who are the religious fundamentalists here, the Americans or the Iranians?

The United States didn't fully grasp Iran's inroads into Kurdistan, partly because it didn't understand Iran's tactics or strategy. Washington still looks at Iran through the prism of World War II. We're comfortable fighting a war of fixed battles, fixed objectives, and easily definable enemies such as Nazi Germany or Saddam's Iraq. Where our vision fades is where the enemy doesn't follow these rules.

When we invaded Afghanistan in October 2001, we went to war against the Taliban and al Qaeda not understanding that they are religious convictions, not countries. Neither Osama bin Laden nor Mullah Omar, the Taliban's leader, can be neatly classified as a head of state, a military commander, or even a religious leader. Unable to define the enemy, the United States declared war on an idea—one that now spans the Afghan and Pakistani border. How do you wage war against an idea, a way of thinking?

America is not only still fighting World War II, it also sees the world through nineteenth-century ideologies of fascism, communism, liberalism, and democracy. Reducing the Taliban to Islamofascists obscures the terms of the conflict. And again, by lumping Iran into that same category, we are seriously mistaken. For a start, unlike Osama bin Laden and the Taliban, Iran manipulates belief, allowing it to adapt and appeal across sectarian and political lines. In contrast, the Taliban and al Qaeda can't cross that divide, because their doctrine forbids them to deal with Muslims like the Shia, who are apostates, according to the *takfiris'* dualistic view of the world.

Iran has also been helped by its hybrid political system, which allows it to manipulate international law. Iran doesn't accept Western definitions of how the world should be organized. The way Iran sees it, Iran didn't sign the Peace of Westphalia, which established the modern nation-state system in 1648, so there's no need for Tehran to pay any attention to it.

Iran's lines of power and authority are almost impossible to follow. They seem to change between morning and night. But again, what's critical to understand is that real executive authority doesn't reside with President Mahmoud Ahmadinejad but rather with Iran's Supreme Leader, Ayatollah Khamenei. Khamenei is part cleric, part mediator, part dictator, part military commander, and part police chief. He governs more like a twelfth-century pope than an American president. But what he definitely is not is a totalitarian fascist like Adolf Hitler.

The Revolutionary Guards, Khamenei's Praetorian Guard, is a hybrid too. Only half integrated into Iran's military, it is a blend of paramilitary force, conventional military, and business conglomerate whose interests are almost impossible to follow for anyone outside the system. It would be incomprehensible to Americans if the Pentagon were to open up a tire factory and go into competition with Goodyear. But that's more or less what the Revolutionary Guards do.

Iran is not a totalitarian state. It has checks and balances, and Khamenei rules by a consensus obscure even to insiders. During the Lebanon hostage crisis, for example, when Iran kidnapped dozens of hostages, it was difficult to tell who was in charge in Tehran. At one point a family friend of Ayatollah Rafsanjani, who served as Iran's president from 1989 to 1997, came to Lebanon to look for his brother, who had been kidnapped in 1982. After failing to negotiate his brother's release, the man started kidnapping Westerners himself, intending to exchange them for his brother. This man didn't belong to any official Iranian government agency; his mosque in Tehran underwrote the kidnappings. But when the Revolutionary Guards complained about him, Rafsanjani told them it was none of their business. No one dared refer the matter to Khomeini, because the man's family was politically important. The man never did get his brother released—as it turned out, he'd been murdered—but the point is that there are nonstate actors in Iran who assume the role of the state. The lines are blurred.

Iran, then, saw no contradiction in confronting Turkey in an underhanded way, ignoring the nation-state system. Undermining Turkey using Sunni Kurds—proxies—was a legitimate tactic as far as Tehran was concerned, just as long as it didn't get caught red-handed. Only Iran's interests mattered, not the West's rule of law. And again, the Iranians asked themselves, why should Iran care about the nation-state system anyway—a system that puts Iran at a clear disadvantage?

Finally, unlike Washington, Iran views its vital interests through the prism of history—history we either never knew or have chosen to ignore. Iranians are still driven by ancient conflicts and grievances, ones dating back to the Achaemenid empire of the fifth and sixth centuries B.C., the Crusades, the Persian-Ottoman wars, and nineteenth- and twentieth-century colonialism. The Iranians remember as if it were yesterday when the Soviet Union used the Iranian Communist Tudeh Party to undermine Iran.

Today's Iran sees the West through the prism of the Crusades, with NATO as the modern-day Crusader alliance and Turkey as NATO's foothold in the Middle East. This perception is only reinforced by the alliance between Turkey and Israel, and the large U.S. military base in Incirlik, Turkey. What's to stop the United States from using Turkey to invade Iran—to launch the kind of modern-day crusade Bush has threatened? Or for that matter, what's to stop the United States from arming Iranian Kurds and using Turkey as a rear base?

Just as the Americans reduce war to a fight against totalitarianism and fascism, the Iranians reduce war to defensive struggles against occupation and colonialism. The Iranian regime, rather than justifying its aggressive foreign policy in terms of spreading the faith or creating an empire, falls back on a claim of righting historical wrongs. This makes it a lot easier to rouse the average Iranian or Hezbollah's faithful. And by defining its wars as defensive, Iran can justify enlisting non-Shia allies, whether they're Sunnis or the Marxist PKK.

It's within this greater historical and geopolitical context—Iran's sense of the drift of history—that Iran decided it could risk a conflict with Turkey.

There's another side to Iran that makes it difficult for Americans to understand the country. Iranians look at geography differently from the way we do. When we look at a map of Iran and Turkey, we see a bold, fixed border separating the two countries. An Iranian may see that same line, but he also sees the Royal Road, the ancient trade route that ran from Iran, across Mesopotamia and Anatolia, to Europe. When he looks at a map of China and Central Asia, he's reminded of the Khorasan Highway, the trade route that linked Persia with the East. These are historic corridors of commerce and corridors of invasion, and today they're corridors of energy.

The Silk Road and the empires along it were arteries of invasion and trade, and the Iranians today look at trade routes to export the Middle East's oil and natural gas. Dominating these trade routes not only means securing energy export routes for Iran's exports, it also means controlling Iran's neighbors. If Saudi Arabia can't export its oil through the Strait of Hormuz, it collapses. If Iran stops gas exports to Turkey, the lights go off in Ankara.

Not surprisingly, Turkey discovered that Iran was arming the PKK.

But the Turks chose to ignore it, deciding they couldn't risk confronting Iran and losing it as a source of gas. Putting its anger aside, Turkey went ahead and signed a 10-billion-cubic-meter natural gas deal with Iran, to extend over twenty-five years. Turkey also signed a parallel deal to buy gas from the former Soviet republic of Turkmenistan, which would transit through Iran. The United States actively opposed the deal, but Turkey turned a deaf ear. Economics trumped politics.

In 2001, again over strong, public U.S. protests, Iran and Turkey signed a deal to invest $3.5 billion in Iran's South Pars megafield. The South Pars/North Dome gas condensate field, which sits in the middle of the Persian Gulf and is shared by Qatar and Iran, is the biggest gas field in the world. With South Pars's 1900 trillion cubic feet of gas, Turkey knew that the field could keep it and Europe warm for the next thirty years.

The United States would counter the South Pars deal by offering Turkey natural gas from Iraq's Anbar Province, but the Turks knew that one way or another gas would have to pass through a route effectively controlled by Iran—through either Syria or Iraqi Kurdistan. If Turkey had to deal with Iranian-allied Kurds, it asked itself, why not just deal with Iran directly?

Nothing the United States said could deter Turkey.

"Iran and Turkey are two friendly countries," Turkey's prime minister said in late 2007, "and Turkey will continue to import gas from Iran."

Turkey's alliance with Israel also apparently didn't figure into Turkey's calculations.

"U.S. and Israeli opposition to importing gas from Iran is not important," the prime minister declared, "because they cannot meet Turkey's need for energy, and Turkey must fulfill its needs from Russia and Iran."

At the end of the day, the raw economic numbers were on Tehran's side rather than Washington's. As the world's second-largest producer of natural gas after Russia, Iran is Turkey's only alternative supplier if relations with Russia go sour. And as the second-largest producer of oil in OPEC, Iran could meet much of Turkey's increased demand for oil over the coming years.

As global energy markets have tightened, it has become evident that Iran doesn't need to invade northern Iraq or Turkey to exert its influence. Iran's gas and oil, and the energy corridors it sits on, are more effective. Iran's bet in Kurdistan paid off, convincing the Iranians more than ever that controlling the world's energy bloodstream is the way to become a superpower.

And now there were other energy corridors to conquer.

Afghanistan has long been a source of instability and strategic interest for Iran. Under both the Shah and Ayatollah Khomeini, Iran demonstrated that it will take almost any measure to keep western Afghanistan out of the hands of its enemies. In 1996, for instance, Iran's National Security Council voted in an emergency meeting to invade Afghanistan and capture Herat to stop the Taliban from marching on Iran's border. Ultimately, the Taliban threat subsided and Iran didn't need to invade, but the vote was evidence of Iran's commitment to keep that part of Afghanistan at least neutral.

NATO's invasion of Afghanistan in October 2001, destroying the Taliban, was a godsend, not unlike the destruction of Saddam's army a year and a half later. Almost as providential, NATO left a vacuum in western Afghanistan, allowing Iran to annex it economically.

Today in Herat, just as in the Iraqi city of Basra, stores are filled with Iranian goods, the gasoline is from Iran, and the preferred currency is the Iranian rial. Iran's inroads into the Herat governate were made easy because the population is 40 percent Shia. Increasingly alarmed by Iran's incursion, NATO engineered the removal of Herat's longtime governor because of his ties to Iran. As a consolation, he was appointed energy minister—which, as it turned out, was a position as important as the Herat governate.

In April 2008, as energy cuts swept Pakistan, a serious debate arose about how to pipe in gas from Central Asia—through Afghanistan or Iran. The Afghan option (TAPI, the Turkmenistan-Afghanistan-Pakistan-India pipeline) and Iran option (IPI, the Iran-Pakistan-India pipeline) would cost roughly the same amount of money. But the route is of lasting strategic importance to Pakistan: Is it better for Pakistan to depend on Afghanistan or Iran for its energy supplies?

Whatever route Pakistan chooses, Iran intends to control it. Iran believes it must. With the *takfiris* wielding ever-stronger influence over a weak government in Islamabad, Iran has to have some source of pressure over Pakistan, a knife at Pakistan's throat. If a hostile, Taliban-like government were to come to power in Islamabad, Tehran would cut off Pakistan's gas, bringing Pakistan to its knees.

Iran would prefer that the Central Asian gas pipeline pass through its own country, but if this can't be arranged, Iran will stop at nothing to maintain de facto control over the Afghan pipeline's route—which fortunately for Iran goes through Herat, a city Tehran owns in all but name.

There are other energy corridors Iran has its eye on. Azerbaijan, with its plentiful oil and its strategic location on the western shore of the Caspian Sea, is the main energy link between Caspian oil and the Mediterranean. One million barrels a day of Azeri crude is exported via a pipeline that crosses Georgia and Turkey.

In April 2008, an official from the National Iranian Oil Company said in a conference that by 2020 Caspian sea oil exports could reach 4.65 million barrels of oil a day, much of it from new fields in Azerbaijan. The Iranian made a point of saying that the export route west through Georgia and Turkey doesn't have the capacity to handle this much oil. He offered Iran as a second route—a pipeline crossing Iran from the Caspian to the Gulf.

"The countries in the region should not ignore Iran as an attractive option," he said, "for access to international markets and a reliable partner."

The Iranian didn't say it, of course, but the Caspian Sea oil producers understand the implicit Iranian threat hanging over their heads: If they ignore Iran's offer, Iran always has the option of sabotage, or fomenting civil unrest to get its way.

Ever since Azerbaijan gained independence after the breakup of the Soviet Union, the Iranians have been meddling there. Azerbaijan is a predominantly Shia country, and as it did in Lebanon and Kurdistan, Iran recruited proxies to spread its influence. It created an Azeri Hezbollah. Iran has yet to attract a wide following there, or anything matching the armed groups it has in other parts of the world—it had to go slowly because of Russian complaints—but the Iranians are confident that, given the need, a handful of proxies could disable Azerbaijan's Turkey-and-Georgia pipeline with a couple of pounds of explosives.

But the real prize among world energy corridors, of course, is the Strait of Hormuz. A narrow waterway connecting the Persian Gulf with the Gulf of Oman, Hormuz is the main export route for Gulf oil. About 20 percent of the world's daily consumption passes through it—approximately 17 million barrels a day. If the Strait of Hormuz were closed, the price of oil would instantly skyrocket to several hundred dollars a barrel.

Hormuz is only 21 miles across at its narrowest point, making the oil tankers that pass through it easy prey for Iran. Iran has tried to close the Strait of Hormuz once before—on April 18, 1988, when the U.S. Navy and Iranian forces fought a skirmish in open waters there. Since then, Iran has issued explicit threats that it will close Hormuz if America goes to war against Iran. In 1988, that was an empty threat. Today, it is no longer.

From the early nineties onward, Iran adopted the tactic of

burying Silkworm missiles along its side of Hormuz. It understood that the Silkworms were a strategic weapon that could close traffic within minutes, in which case the United States—or anyone else in the world—couldn't do much to rescue global oil supplies. Contacts in the Pentagon have told me that it would take at least three days of constant bombing to destroy the Silkworm missiles. And even then that's an optimistic estimate. As Hezbollah proved during the 2006 war in Lebanon, Iran has buried its missiles and rockets deep enough underground that it would be impossible to know whether or not they were all destroyed.

It's not just the energy corridors that Iran intends to put its hands on; it wants the oil under the ground too.

For the moment, Iran is satisfied pilfering 300,000 to 600,000 barrels of oil a day from southern Iraq. But in the long term it wants de jure control over all of Iraq's oil, and it's preparing to build a pipeline from Basra to the Iranian terminal at Abadan. So not only would Iran have a legitimate say in Iraq's oil exports, it would also profit from transit fees.

Iran also has made it clear that it intends to have a decisive voice in Iraq's new upstream production. In February 2008 (as noted), the Iraqi oil minister announced that Iran and Iraq had agreed to form a bilateral commission to review investments in new Iraqi fields. The commission would decide on the development of the immense Maj-noun field in southern Iraq, whose reserves are estimated to be 30 billion barrels.

According to an ExxonMobil official who asked not to be named, the U.S. oil major was caught in the Iranian trap. In late 2007, the Iraqis offered the company an opportunity to bid on several Iraqi fields. ExxonMobil accepted, but just as it was about to send representatives to Baghdad for discussions, the Iraqis advised company officials that they had to consult with Tehran to do the deal. ExxonMobil declined—it had no choice because of UN sanctions on

Iran—but it got the message: Iraq's oil is now in Iran's sphere of influence.

Equally important to Iran, it doesn't want oil from the Iraqi Kurdistan city of Kirkuk, which lifts about one million barrels a day, to come under the control of a sovereign Iraqi Kurdish state. The Iranians are convinced that an Iraqi Kurdish state underwritten by Kirkuk's oil wouldn't be able to resist the temptation to fund Iranian Kurdish separatists.

It looks as if Iran will prevail. In late 2007, the Iraqi oil minister, a Shia close to Tehran, nullified fifteen oil deals signed by the Iraqi Kurdish regional government, underscoring that the Kurds would not be allowed to independently make their own oil deals. "There is an understanding between Tehran, Ankara, Damascus, and Baghdad," he said—a statement that was remarkable not only because it didn't mention the United States or Britain but also because it did name the four countries with large Kurdish populations that oppose an independent Kurdistan.

Not long after that, the Iraqi government's oil-marketing company, SOMO, canceled a major oil supply deal to South Korea. The Kurds were convinced this was also at the behest of Tehran, because the Iranians were angry that a South Korean company had just signed a production-sharing deal in Iraqi Kurdistan.

But controlling energy corridors and stealing Iraq's oil aren't the only ways Iran intends to control the world's oil supply. The Iranians are now reaching for the rest of it—the oil of the Arab Gulf sheikhdoms—in their quest to become the world's first hydrocarbon empire.

7

TOPPLING THE ARAB SHEIKHDOMS: HOW IRAN PLANS TO SEIZE THE PERSIAN GULF'S OIL

Iran dominates a third of Iraq and the bulk of its oil. It is tightening its control over three vital energy corridors: Afghanistan, the Strait of Hormuz, and Kurdistan. If that's not enough to scare anyone who drives to work or heats his house in winter, Persian Gulf oil itself is now within Iran's grasp.

The Gulf Arab sheikhdoms, and the oil that sloshes just under their sands, are vulnerable to military takeover. Iran is the overwhelmingly dominant military force in the Gulf, capable of quickly putting a million men in uniform. The next largest military, Saudi Arabia's, is just a quarter of its size.

Iran's army is combat-hardened, thanks to the 1980–88 Iran-Iraq War; Saudi Arabia's has never fought a war. The Saudis' last engagement was during the 1990–91 Gulf War, when the Saudi soldiers threw down their rifles and ran. If it hadn't been for the U.S. Marines, there would have been nothing standing between the Iraqi army and the Saudi capital of Riyadh. Even today, the only thing that stands between Iran and Riyadh is the United States.

In one scenario, Iran could provoke a war with Saudi Arabia, sending ground troops and paratroopers to take Riyadh within forty-eight hours. And it would take even less time for Iran to seize Saudi Arabia's oil fields, which are particularly vulnerable from the sea. The United States would massively retaliate from the air, and ultimately destroy the Iranian attacking force. But the global consequences would be catastrophic: The Iranians could be counted on to instantly sabotage Saudi oil facilities, taking 9 to 10 million barrels of oil a day—nearly all of Saudi Arabia's production—off world markets, spiking oil prices well beyond global economic tolerances, leading to a worldwide depression. It would take at least two years to bring Saudi production back onstream.

The only real deterrence to an Iranian attack, then, is American ground forces. But the American military is bogged down in Iraq and Afghanistan. There simply aren't an additional 200,000–300,000 troops available to protect Saudi Arabia or its oil fields, at least not without bringing back the draft and taking two years to train and equip the new troops. And even if this were to happen, with the Middle East already costing us trillions, spending trillions more to defend Saudi Arabia would cripple the U.S. economy.

In December 2007, the Congressional Budget Office estimated that the cost of our occupation of Iraq and Afghanistan will reach $2.4 trillion over the next decade. A truly effective containment of Iran—retaking Iraq, disarming Hezbollah in Lebanon, protecting the Gulf Arabs and their oil—could easily double that. We're talking about the money for the baby boomers' retirement, the education of three generations of Americans, the price of converting to alternative energy sources. The United States would be spending the equivalent of what it cost Rome to maintain its empire, or Spain or Britain theirs—empires that financially drained their metropolitan centers and collapsed.

Besides, Iran doesn't actually need to militarily invade Gulf nations to control Gulf oil. The rim of the Persian Gulf, 90 percent Shia, is vulnerable to Iranian meddling. The population of the

United Arab Emirates (UAE), for instance, is only 19 percent Emirati Arab, while non-Emirati Arabs, many of them Shia and ethnic Persians, make up 23 percent. Dubai, the UAE's largest city, also hosts a large number of Iranian residents, who also are susceptible to Iran's influence.

The Gulf Arabs understand their predicament, especially when they remember that in 1971 the Shah of Iran seized three Gulf islands that belonged to the UAE. Iran has shown no inclination to return them—yet another reminder that the Persian Gulf is named that for a reason.

A second Iranian scenario would be to incite demonstrations in Dubai, declare the overthrow of its ruling Al Makhtoum family, call for elections, and have the new "legitimate" government appeal to Iran for help. There would be little the Gulf Arabs could do but stand by and watch. In fact, a takeover of Dubai is not only completely within the realm of possibility; I'd say, should any serious confrontation arise between Iran and the United States, it's a near certainty.

The Makhtoums, like the Saudis, fully grasp the threat. In February 2008 the ruler of Dubai, Muhammad bin Rashid Al Makhtoum, flew to Tehran to reassure the Iranians he would never consider joining any U.S.-led alliance against Iran. It was the first such high-level visit since the fall of the Shah.

"Iran and the United Arab Emirates have historical and strong relations," Rashid said at his press conference in Tehran, "and with my trip to the Islamic Republic of Iran, bilateral relations will rise to new horizons." Considering that Dubai is a constituent member of the UAE and that Iran was still holding on to the three islands it had earlier seized from the UAE, this was tantamount to an unconditional surrender.

In the case of an American retreat from Iraq or even the Gulf, Iran could simply bully the Gulf Arabs into accepting Iranian suzerainty. A few military confrontations on Gulf waters, either accidental or intentional, and the Arabs wouldn't have a choice. Iranian president Ahmadinejad already hinted at Iran's plans in December 2003, when he offered the Arabs a "joint security pact"—the Iranian equivalent of NATO, over which Iran would clearly dominate. Already, Arab Gulf emissaries these days travel to Tehran more often than they do to London or Washington.

If Iran succeeds in taking control of the Persian Gulf, it would not only mark the first time that the waterway hasn't been under Western dominance since the British Navy first sailed into the Gulf in 1763, it would be a massive geopolitical shift, akin to Japan's invading China in 1931 or Russia seizing Eastern Europe at the end of World War II. And considering the West's hydrocarbon addiction, the economic consequences would be catastrophic.

There's something else that makes this dark narrative even darker: In spite of industry and OPEC claims, the Persian Gulf is running out of oil. Its true reserves may be half of what we've been told they are, a radical recalculation that alters all other calculations.

Oil reserve estimates are based on data provided by oil-producing countries and oil companies. They're not independently audited, and the numbers are impossible to corroborate. The higher reserves an OPEC member claims, the higher the OPEC quota it's allotted, and the more oil it's allowed to "lift," or pump out. And of course, the more barrels of oil a company "books," the higher its stock prices—and the higher the bonuses for its executives.

Not surprisingly, it has been well established that both countries and companies systematically overestimate their reserves. Several years ago, Royal Dutch Shell was caught and fined, and its stock was downgraded. Other major oil companies have been luckier. Still, their data is notoriously unreliable.

The more reliable way to calculate reserves is by looking at production data—how much oil is actually lifted from a particular field. Based on inflated industry and company estimates, the remaining proven reserves worldwide amount to 1.255 trillion barrels. But if we go by actual production, according to the respected, independent Energy Watch Group, oil reserves in fact are closer to 854 billion barrels. Energy Watch Group believes that Middle Eastern reserves are overestimated more than most. Officially they're put at 677 billion barrels. But calculated on the basis of production, they're more like 362 billion barrels—a little over half of what is claimed.

The numbers for each country tell the same story. Saudi Arabia, rather than possessing the 286 billion barrels it claims, has only about 181 billion barrels. Iraq claims 99 billion barrels, but in fact has 41 billion. Kuwait claims 51 billion but has closer to 35 billion. As for Iran, it has just 43.5 billion, rather than the 134 billion barrels it claims.

Saudi Arabia's shortfall in reserves is the most alarming. Its mega oil fields are the world's reserve tank, and their true capacity will determine whether we bicycle or drive to work in the decades to come. Saudi Arabia produces roughly 11 million barrels a day, accounting for 19 percent of the world's oil exports. Analysts, going on industry and Saudi calculations, count on Saudi Arabia to boost its production to 15 million barrels a day to meet increasing global demand.

Historically, Saudi Arabia has also been the world's "swing producer." When demand spikes or collapses, Saudi production goes up or down accordingly, smoothing market prices. For instance, during the Gulf War, Saudi Arabia boosted its production by 3.1 million barrels a day, at a time when 5.3 million barrels of Iraqi and Kuwaiti production were off the market. Thanks to this Saudi surge production, world oil prices rose only moderately. Add to this the fact that Saudi oil is some of the world's cheapest to produce—about $1 to $2 a barrel to lift, compared with $11 to $15 a barrel in the Caspian Sea, where the oil lies deeper underground—and there is no doubt that Saudi Arabia and its oil are a pillar of the world's economy, expected to fuel uninterrupted world growth for the next fifty years. Or so we've been led to believe.

There's a growing conviction that Saudi Arabia, more than any producer, is lying about its proven reserves. In one particularly telling study, a computer scientist looked at Saudi Arabia's giant Ghawar field, which stretches for more than 150 miles beneath the desert. Ghawar is the largest oil deposit in the world, producing approximately 5 million barrels a day—almost half of Saudi Arabia's production. Its cumulative production since it was discovered is 55 billion barrels.

The study, taken entirely from public data, looks at the amount of water injected into Ghawar over the years. (Water injection forces oil to the surface.) The only conclusion the scientist was able to arrive at from the amount of water injected is that Ghawar is filled mostly with water. In other words, Ghawar is nearly depleted, the consequence of which is that Saudi production could fall off faster and more steeply than anyone has so far predicted. If the numbers are indeed accurate, no wonder the Saudis lie about their reserves: with no new discoveries of oil to offset Ghawar, $4.00 for a gallon of regular will soon look like a fantastic bargain.

Adding to the skepticism about true Saudi reserves, Saudi production is declining, down a million barrels a day since 2005. The Saudis claim this is because of declining global demand, which of course is nonsense. In 2006, the price of oil went from $60 to $74 a barrel, then to $100 in 2007 and $135 in 2008 (at this writing). OPEC blamed the decline of the dollar for the rise, but that didn't account for all of it. Saudi Arabia either couldn't or wouldn't boost production to smooth out prices. Evidence suggests they couldn't: From 2004 to 2007, the Saudis tripled the number of their oil rigs in an attempt to find new fields. In any event, the days when Saudi Arabia could lift oil for $1 to $2 a barrel are disappearing, and the notion it will take its production up to 15 million barrels a day is a fantasy.

Iran faces an oil depletion as severe as Saudi Arabia's, with an even larger disparity between its real and claimed reserves. In 2005, Iran produced approximately 3.94 million barrels a day. But Iran's sustainable capacity, meaning the amount they can recover from their existing oil fields without damaging them, is only 3.8 million barrels a day—it's running out of oil even faster than Saudi Arabia. Although Iran doesn't rely on one mega field like Ghawar, 60 percent of its production comes from oil fields more than fifty years old. To take just one comparison, in 1974 Iran was producing 6 million barrels a day. Today, with domestic consumption at 1.5 million barrels a day, Iran very well could run out of oil sooner than we expect. It's counting on making up the shortfall by drilling its South Pars mega gas field, but South Pars is still a speculative investment.

Iran also does not produce enough gasoline, thanks to a shortage of refineries and increasing demand. In June 2007, Iran ordered a comprehensive gasoline rationing program—one reason cars there are switching to natural gas. The rationing sparked riots. And like most market interference, it failed to cut back on consumption. But it's Iran's oil depletion that promises to cause the real problems.

At the current rate of global consumption, and if Iran indeed has less than half the reserves it claims, Iran will run out of oil in ten years rather than thirty. Iraqi oil will therefore become even more critical for Iran's economic survival. And even if Iran took over all of Iraq's oil, this would still only add a few years of longevity. How could Iran not be tempted to take over Saudi Arabia's oil fields, even if they're not as full as Saudi Arabia claims?

Iran has many other reasons to expand at the expense of its neighbors. Like the Soviet economy, Iran's economy suffers from a morbidly inefficient state sector. Unemployment is around 11 percent (according to the government, which means it's a lot higher). Inflation is at 16 percent and possibly as high as 50 percent. And most telling of all, petroleum accounts for 80 to 90 percent of Iran's exports—the perfect storm for a country with a large army and weak neighbors.

With 75 percent of its population under twenty-five, Iran clearly needs a change in course. America's neocons would like us to believe that Iran is in a prerevolutionary state, the Iranians ready to rise and depose the clerics and hard-liners and install a more pragmatic regime. This may or may not be true. But there's no evidence whatsoever that the government that would succeed the mullahs would either wean itself off oil or reconsider Iran's ambition of dominating the Persian Gulf and its oil. Iran knows it is running out of oil and must do something—and quickly. It has no intention of letting itself become the Bangladesh of the Gulf.

In the meantime, there's an easy way to help Iran's economy—alleviating its need to gobble up more territory—and smooth relations with Iran. The West should lift sanctions to help it extract its oil more efficiently. Iran's current recovery rate is 24–27 percent. The rest of the world's producers are closer to 35 percent. By giving Iran access to the modern equipment needed to boost its recovery rate, as well as develop South Pars, the United States can ensure Iran doesn't slip into early penury, forcing it to sail across the Gulf and take Saudi Arabia's oil.

At any rate, one thing is clear: The worst thing America could do would be to leave the status quo as it is.

A complaint you often hear in the Middle East is how Americans don't appreciate this or that country. A Saudi will tell you it's dangerously shortsighted for the United States to ignore Saudi Arabia, with its 24 percent of the world's oil reserves. How can the Americans ignore a country that's a keystone of the world's economy? There is no one in the Middle East who's not enraged that the United States defers to Israel, a country with no oil and of little strategic importance. Arabs and Iranians alike feel slighted by America—humiliated and bent on revenge.

I heard this same grievance from Ayatollah Khomeini's former aide, Amin, the one who now owns a bookstore in Paris. Amin gave me a quick primer on why he thought America has historically allied with the wrong players in the Middle East.

"The United States in the Middle East has always stood on four very wobbly legs," Amin told me. "Pakistan, the Shah of Iran, Saudi Arabia, and Israel."

Each of the four, Amin is convinced, has failed the United States or will do so. He offered a quick *tour d'horizon* to make his point.

"Pakistan is not a country, it's an army," he said—not unlike Saddam's Iraq.

Amin reduced Pakistan to five provinces ripped out of the British Raj, its borders drawn for British convenience rather than that of the Pakistanis. "The country cannot hold together," he said.

My conversation with Amin took place three months before Benazir Bhutto's assassination, but there were already signs Pakistan was coming off its hinges. President Musharraf was unable to control the tribal areas along the border of Afghanistan, let alone capture bin Laden for the Americans.

"As the Pakistani army goes, so goes Pakistan," Amin told me. "In twenty-four hours a coup could change American fortunes in that country. Wasn't it clear enough in Pakistan's failed hunt for Osama bin Laden? It couldn't or wouldn't help."

It was hard to argue against the point that Pakistan has been a waste of money. In 2007, the United States gave $52.6 million to Pakistan's Frontier Corps—a tribal force meant to keep peace along the wild and historically ungovernable Afghan-Pakistan border—to do something about al Qaeda and the Taliban's taking refuge there. Another $97 million was to be spent in 2008. But the money got us nothing, neither bin Laden nor the Taliban leader, Mullah Omar. And it certainly didn't buy stability.

"As for Saudi Arabia," Amin went on, "it's an archaic political structure—Bedouin tribes incapable of coping with the twenty-first century. Do you think it's an accident that there were fifteen Saudis on those planes on September 11? And lest you forget, they were the most Americanized Saudis, the crème de la crème of Saudi Arabia."

I had made up my mind long ago that Saudi Arabia was yet

another virtual country. Its borders are artificial, and it's ruled by fragile tribal coalitions that will crack under pressure. Yet all along the United States has treated Saudi Arabia not only as a friend but as if it were a force capable of defending our interests in the Gulf.

Amin's views of the second wobbly leg, the Shah of Iran, were predictable.

"You anchored your national security on a diseased liver," he said, referring to the United States' decision to support the terminally ill Shah, rather than Iran itself. "In your Cold War myopia, all you could see was that the Shah banned Iran's Communist Party."

"And then there's Israel," Amin said, laughing without humor.

It didn't surprise me that Amin reserved the worst for Israel. In the two decades I've spent in the Middle East, I've seen how truly mysterious the region's Muslims find America's attachment to Israel. Aside from possessing no oil, Israel is demographically insignificant. Muslims look at Israel as an American colonial fort, one not worth the upkeep. "Why the Israelis and not us?" they'd ask me. They're stung by the apparent unfairness and injustice of it, and see it as simple racism: America picked one Semitic tribe, the Jews, over another, the Arabs.

"Israel's greatest conquest wasn't the West Bank and Gaza," Amin told me. "It was the American imagination." Where once the United States looked at the Middle East through the prism of Moscow and the Cold War, he said, "it now sees everything through the prism of Tel Aviv."

"The United States is prisoner to a narrow collective memory," he added. "A country that was manufactured in Hollywood."

And Iranians are doubly aggrieved, he said, because it's not just Israel we favor. They see the same racial and political prejudice in our bias toward Sunni countries. Why does the United States shower attention on corrupt Pakistani generals and grotesquely corrupt Saudi princes when neither can field a real army? Can't we see the disparity in the raw numbers? The numbers alone should be enough for us to take Iran more seriously. But the United States is unable to comprehend the durable and the permanent.

"Don't you Americans remember history?" Amin asked in genuine frustration. "Wasn't the first post–World War II nuclear crisis over Iran? Over Stalin's attempt to seize Iranian oil fields? Still today the United States ignores Iran's real status as the preeminent Gulf power. It treats Iran like a pariah. Even under the Shah, you looked at Iran as a heavily fortified castle, a far outpost of the American empire, manned by *your* friendly if primitive natives."

Although Amin didn't claim to have information that isn't public, he's convinced that the Iranian "nuclear threat" is fabricated, by both sides. The Iranians want the world to believe they're building a nuclear bomb mainly to get attention, to have a chip to play at the global poker table. Indeed, one day they will make a bomb, Amin said, but right now they're only interested in being treated as a serious player. They want to be given their due, if for no other reason than as a deterrent to an American or Israeli attack, as Saddam attempted to do when he made the world believe he still possessed weapons of mass destruction.

What about the view that the Iranian leaders are apocalyptic Shia ready to attack Israel with a nuclear bomb? I asked.

Amin replied with what seemed like a digression. "Did you know that when Arafat went to see Khomeini after the revolution, Khomeini couldn't understand a word of Arafat's Arabic?"

Amin's point was that Arafat's inability to talk to Khomeini in the prophet's language is a metaphor for how far apart the Iranians are from the Palestinians. Iran sees the Arabs, and particularly the Palestinians, as very much subordinate to their core national interests. They're not about to go to war with Israel over the Palestinians, especially at the risk of a nuclear confrontation.

I knew the Iranians had told us over and over through diplomatic back channels that they're not particularly concerned about the fate of the Palestinians or the existence of Israel. Iran will accept whatever settlement the Palestinians accept, they assured us, whether it includes returning Jerusalem or not. I heard the same thing as recently as March 2008, when a politburo member from Lebanon's Hezbollah told me that Hezbollah would be "no more Palestinian than the Palestinians." In other words, if the Palestinians agreed to settle with Israel, so would Hezbollah. Only a serious engagement with both Iran and Hezbollah can test this claim.

Amin thought it was a critical, even fatal, error for the United States not to have any idea what Iran really wants. Why do we take seriously Ahmadinejad's mad ranting about destroying Israel? Haven't the Arabs been making the same threat since 1948, and we've ignored them?

Finally, Amin was convinced time is on Iran's side.

"Do you know what the consequence of your not understanding Iran is?" he asked me. "Iran today is a superpower, if only by default."

Amin was certain this was thanks to America's never giving Iran its due, to ignoring the most populous, stable, powerful country in the Persian Gulf—a state that has existed for thousands of years within the same borders. Instead, the United States made a shortsighted bet on failing Sunni states lurching toward collapse.

The consensus in the Persian Gulf is that the first Arab sheikhdom to fall will be Bahrain, with a tap by Iran.

A small island nation at the top of the Persian Gulf, Bahrain has only a ceremonial army. Whenever there's a problem, the Saudis send a reinforced battalion across the causeway linking the two countries to put it down. Iran could occupy Bahrain in an hour.

And as with the UAE, the Iranians don't even need to invade. Bahrain has a population of just over 700,000, and 70 percent are Shia Muslims. Iran funds Bahraini Shia clerics, charities, and schools. Many senior Bahraini clerics are in exile in Qum, Iran. Not only are Bahraini Shia sympathetic to Iran, they are even more so today now that the Bahraini Shia's historical center of learning and spiritual guidance, Najaf, is in Iranian hands. And it's not as if the Iranians keep to themselves their ability to meddle in Bahraini politics.

An adviser to the Bahraini king told me that Iran was responsible for civil disturbances that broke out there in late 2007.

"The Iranians like to give us a taste of what they're capable of," he told me. "Little reminders now and then."

Bahrain was part of Iran for centuries—until 1782, when the Al Khalifa family, a band of pearl divers and pirates, seized the island from Iran's declining Qajar Dynasty. In order to hold on to it, the Al Khalifa quickly signed a series of treaties with Britain, turning the island into a British protectorate by the nineteenth century. When Britain left the Persian Gulf and gave Bahrain its independence in 1971, Bahrain immediately offered naval basing rights to the United States—with the express purpose of dissuading the Shah from seizing it, as he had the three islands he seized from the UAE.

For Iranians, then, Bahrain represents the worst kind of colonialism. It's as if during the Civil War, Canada had seized the state of Maine. Would America simply shrug its shoulders and let Canada keep it? Bahrain may be an independent, sovereign country in the West's view, but the Iranians consider it stolen property that one day they'll reclaim.

In July 2007, a close adviser to Iranian Supreme Leader Ali Khamenei made that very point in an interview.

"The public demand in Bahrain," he said, "is the reunification of this province with the motherland, Islamic Iran." Although the adviser claimed he was speaking privately, no official in Iran repudiated the interview. The Bahrainis were left to interpret it as official policy.

The king of Bahrain, Sheikh Hamad, came to power only in 1999. He understands just how vulnerable he is. In fact, ever since I first met him, at the Dorchester Hotel in London a couple of years ago, it has been all he could talk about.

As far as I could tell, Hamad had traveled to London with a modest entourage of twenty or thirty people. Dressed in a canary yellow shirt and black slacks, he looked like any other rich Bahraini on vacation. He had no interest in trying to keep up with fellow Arab royalty, who flew to London in their Boeing 777s with hundreds of retainers. But he also traveled light partly out of necessity. With no oil to speak of, the Bahrainis have to live within their means.

We first met in the Dorchester's oblong lobby, which was getting a face-lift at the time. Sheets of plywood covered one wall, with jack-hammers drilling behind it, causing the furniture to bounce on the floor. British aplomb ruled, though, and afternoon tea continued. Taking his cue from his former occupiers, Hamad pretended to ignore the deafening racket.

Since Hamad and I couldn't hear each other over the din, we agreed to meet again when we were next in London. Before shaking hands goodbye, he invited me to the Formula 1 car race in Manama, Bahrain's capital city. (I never managed to run in those circles, and missed it.)

Two months later, Hamad and I met again at the Dorchester. The renovations now complete, we talked in a small conference room off the lobby. Hamad's son, Crown Prince Salman, joined us. In January 2007, Hamad would appoint Salman deputy commander in chief of the military, a move many interpreted as a means for Hamad to exert tighter control over his kingdom.

For the first fifteen minutes we talked about Iran's newly elected president, Mahmoud Ahmadinejad. Hamad listened closely as I told him about the rumor going around that Ahmadinejad had participated in the assassination of an Iranian Kurd in Vienna in 1989. No one knew for sure whether the Ahmadinejad in Vienna was the same Ahmadinejad who was now the president of Iran. But it was not an unimportant question. If indeed President Ahmadinejad was a cold-blooded assassin, we'd have a bigger problem on our hands than we feared.

When I finished, Hamad threw up his hands. "What difference does it make? They're all terrorists."

I was pretty sure Hamad didn't mean the Iranians. He was too polite to spell it out to an American, but what I took it to mean was that the Bush administration terrified him. As far as Hamad was concerned, the United States created the Iranian Frankenstein in the Gulf by invading Iraq. But at the same time, it was absolutely clear in his mind that if it weren't for the U.S. fleet floating between him and Iran, he would lose his crown. But how long would the fleet be there?

Losing an island of 700,000—a Persian Gulf country without oil—may not seem like much of a loss in the global scheme of catastrophes. But it very well could prove to be the first domino in Iran's seizing the Arab side of the Gulf. The "domino theory" deservedly earned a bad reputation during the Vietnam War. But the Persian Gulf isn't Southeast Asia: Iran's successful inroads into the Arab world—Syria, Lebanon, Gaza—suggest there really is a possibility that one country tipping over would knock over the next. An Iranian takeover of Bahrain would be a lesson the Arabs would never forget. "If you want to scare the monkeys," as the Chinese saying goes, "kill the chicken."

There is also the important question of the U.S. Navy's 5th Fleet, based in Bahrain. If Sheikh Hamad is deposed and replaced by a government friendly to Iran, the United States will have no place to dock or gas up its carriers in the Gulf. The island of Diego Garcia, which is in the middle of the Indian Ocean, is the next closest naval base—much too far away to allow us to efficiently patrol the Gulf.

There used to be a saying, "As goes Egypt, so goes the Middle East." It might be more apt to say, "As goes Bahrain, so goes the Persian Gulf."

For fifty years, the Communists were the face of the world's liberation movements, the champion of the poor, dispossessed, and oppressed. In Iranian eyes, that torch has passed to Iran.

Iran's revolution in the Middle East has less to do with religion than with politics and economics. Iran has exploited Shia discontent, but it also has promised to redress global economic inequality, Third World political impotence, colonialism, and injustice. Iran has taken over from the Communists in the war of conviction, and with the bond of belief, salvation, and the hereafter, it's the greatest threat to the Middle East since the Ottomans.

The reason President Ahmadinejad solicits the support of Venezuela's populist president Hugo Chavez, and even the descendants of Che Guevara, is to tap the legacy of world revolution—the have-nots against the haves. It certainly helps that Tehran looks like a socialist country. Walk around Tehran and you'll notice there are no palaces—none of the grand, sprawling compounds like those Saddam Hussein or the Saudis built for themselves. Although Iran's mullahs possess great fortunes, they're not on display. Iran successfully portrays itself as a populist country, one committed to helping the downtrodden.

Iran is using that same revolutionary appeal to succeed in Iraq. As it becomes more apparent that the allies will not be able to reconstruct Iraq, Iran's populist, almost socialist image will become an irresistible beacon for Iraqis. Iran has stated over and over that it will not allow Iraq's oil wealth to be stolen by a minority, as they accuse the Sunnis under Saddam of having done. The Iranians are offering Lebanon as the new paradigm: didn't Iran quickly and with little corruption rebuild the Shia areas of Lebanon that were bombed in the 2006 war?

None of this means Iran will force a Shia republic on Iraq or Bahrain. That's too blunt an instrument for Iran's imperialist strategy. And anyhow, the Iranians understand that identities in the Middle East change. The Maghreb, a swath of northern Africa, was Shia for longer than it was Sunni. Egypt was a Shia country during the Fatimid era of the tenth to twelfth centuries. And in Syria today, there's anecdotal evidence that Sunni and minority Alawites are converting to Shia Islam in solidarity with Hezbollah.

Iran is prepared to adjust its goals, to bend to Iraqi nationalism, sectarian divisions, the peculiarities of the Bahraini Shia, or whatever else is necessary to extend its influence.

Iran will continue to hold itself out as an incorruptible power, unlike the United States, which has been dirtied in one corruption scandal after another in Iraq. The United States still isn't able to get the electricity back on in Baghdad, while one of America's and Britain's largest exports to Iraq and Afghanistan is private security companies, mercenaries.

Today in Kabul, you can't miss the contrast. The American and British embassies are surrounded by blast walls, standoff cement barriers, and razor wire. The Iranian embassy, by comparison, is enclosed by a simple wall, with families picnicking on the trim lawn in front. If there are Iranian security guards, you can't see them.

As much as the Americans like to see themselves as the defenders of democracy, Iran's anticolonialist message is the one people in the Persian Gulf are listening to.

8

White Knights: How Iran's Shia Are Winning the Hearts of the Sunni Palestinians

Large swaths of the Middle East are coming under Iran's sway: Lebanon, Iraq, Kurdistan, Afghanistan, Bahrain, the United Arab Emirates. From Sunni to Shia, Arabs to Turks, Iran's influence is spreading—particularly to the most volatile parts, like Gaza. Iran thrives on poverty, misery, and anger, making hellholes like Gaza easy prey. It's not yet a contagion there, but it's fast becoming one.

Over the past twenty years, since the end of the Iran-Iraq War in 1988, Iran has quietly but steadily hijacked the Palestinian cause. It started with Palestinian exile groups in Lebanon, but within a few years expanded to the Palestinian territories. This was an unpredicted turn of events, as Palestinians historically have been the wards of the Sunnis, particularly Egypt, Jordan, and the Arab Gulf states.

Iran's growing influence over the Palestinians is indisputable. According to a 2007 Pew Research poll, 55 percent of Palestinians have a favorable opinion of Iran. Forty-seven percent have a favorable opinion of President Ahmadinejad, versus 40 percent who don't. (Keep in mind the poll was taken at a time when Ahmadinejad's public statements were alarming almost everyone in the Middle East, including Iranians.) Fifty-eight percent of Palestinians support Iran's development of a nuclear bomb, making the Palestinians the only Arabs who do.

Iran overcame sectarian and ethnic differences by offering the Palestinians a real plan for fighting Israel, and providing cash and arms to any faction ready to do so. The Iranians are trying to convince the Palestinians to abandon pointless suicide attacks against civilians for a more traditional military struggle. Palestinian suicide bombings have dropped off steeply, replaced by rocket attacks. It's more than likely because of Iran, which has been urging the Palestinians to adopt more conventional military tactics.

The one thing that's certain is that the Palestinians have made a definite shift away from their discredited, tired secular leaders, Yasser Arafat's successors. This didn't come as a surprise. But again, the turn to Iran did. The Palestinians' natural course should have been to drift toward Osama bin Laden and *takfiri* Sunnis, if only because they share the same religious tenets and Islamic philosophical influences. (Bin Laden's early mentor was a Palestinian.) The Palestinians' embrace of Shia Iran was as if Ireland woke up one morning and abandoned the pope for the Anglican Church.

And it isn't just in the West Bank and Gaza that Iran has been chipping away at Sunni Islam. As we've seen, Iran has made inroads into Iraq's Sunni Kurdistan. Also, during the 1982–2000 war in Lebanon, Hezbollah picked up increasing support among Lebanese Sunnis, which in itself was remarkable because Lebanon suffers some of the worst sectarian divides in the Middle East.

In a July 26, 2006 poll, 87 percent of Lebanese supported Hezbollah and Iran's war with Israel, while the war was still going on. Broken down by sects, 80 percent of Christians supported Hezbollah during the conflict, and 89 percent of Sunni Muslims. Sunni and Christian support for Hezbollah fell off during Lebanon's recent constitutional crisis over the election of a new president, but that only served to remind Hezbollah that war against Israel, rather than against other Lebanese, is what will further Hezbollah's plan to turn itself into a broad-based, multisectarian liberation front.

How far does Hezbollah's writ extend among other Sunni countries? In a 2006 poll taken in overwhelmingly Sunni Jordan, more than 60 percent of respondents considered Hezbollah a legitimate resistance organization, the successor to the PLO. As for Iran, in a 2007 Pew Research poll, 46 percent of Jordanians said they looked at the country positively, versus 53 percent negatively. Jordanians were among the Arabs who voted Hassan Nasrallah the most popular leader in the Middle East.

What's remarkable, again, is the context. The poll was conducted as Iraq was going through its worst sectarian violence. Jordanians, who have strong family and tribal ties to Iraq's Arab Sunnis, should normally have rejected anything associated with Iran and the Shia. Even factoring in that more than half of Jordan's population is Palestinian, it is remarkable that Iran enjoys this kind of support.

Iran has also started to pick up support in Sunni Egypt, a country that was a birthplace of Arab nationalism as well as many of the major nineteenth- and twentieth-century Sunni Islamic revival movements, all of which are deeply hostile to the Shia. Forty percent of Egyptians look at Iran favorably, while 50 percent don't. And then there's Sunni Morocco, where 42 percent of poll respondents back Iran, and 16 percent don't.

So how did Iran and Hezbollah manage to win over the Sunni? Understanding who Hezbollah secretary-general Hassan Nasrallah is, his appeal, and what he means for all Arabs, goes a long way in answering the question. By rewriting Hezbollah's script, tapping a vein of anger and defiance, and turning Hezbollah into a virtual state and its militia into a modern guerrilla force, Nasrallah has put Palestine, Jordan, and Egypt under Iran's shadow. Iran still has a long way to go. But Israel's encirclement is closer than it has been since the 1967 and 1973 wars. If Iran succeeds, and Israel's back really is put to the sea, the rules change once more.

• • •

Nablus is perhaps the most militant town on the Palestinian West Bank. The Israeli army enters it only in force, preferably in armored jeeps and tanks. I was there nearly a year after Israel's 2006 war with Hezbollah, trying to find out how the Israelis had managed to so sharply curtail suicide bombings. As it turned out, I learned something else entirely.

Nablus's main square was a circus, with bumper-to-bumper traffic, old Mercedes and Nissans belching black, oily smoke, and boys pushing carts and weaving through them. Donkeys loaded down with fresh vegetables occupied the sidewalks.

A man in a four-wheel-drive all-terrain vehicle jumped the curb onto the sidewalk in front of me. He swerved at the last moment to avoid a vendor's cart and screeched to a stop, waiting for traffic to give him an opening.

"We need Hassan Nasrallah here to impose a little order!" he shouted to no one in particular.

I had one of the little epiphanies you get visiting the Middle East: There was a craving here for order, the kind of order Hezbollah had imposed in Lebanon. The kind I'd seen at the Hezbollah martyrs' school in Nabatiyah.

Hassan Nasrallah isn't a name you'd expect to hear evoked in Nablus, which is known for its hard-line Sunni clerics—the ones who historically looked to Cairo or Mecca for spiritual guidance rather than to a Shia imam.

Onlookers laughed at the man in the ATV, who drove off the wrong way through a knot of taxis. They leaned on their horns as he cursed them. This gave me an idea.

I walked into Nablus's old covered bazaar, a dark warren of shops where you can buy anything from pomegranates to Chinese electric fans. It was cool there, with only the thinnest slices of sunlight making it through the rusted metal roof. Here was where I would conduct my impromptu poll.

Shu rayak 'an Hassan Nasrallah? I asked the shopkeepers. What's your opinion of Hassan Nasrallah?

At first I got only shrugs. It seemed no one was willing to speak his mind to this odd American wandering around asking politically sensitive questions. Then a man with a dappled gray mustache who stood in front of a glass refrigerator filled with milk and *labneh,* cultured milk, decided he couldn't hold back.

"He is a great man," he told me. "A hero. A warrior."

The man pointed at a picture behind a refrigerator. It was Hassan Nasrallah.

"Where's Arafat's picture?" I asked.

He shrugged his shoulders.

Arafat was obviously a man of the past. Not only was he dead, he was forgotten. And the organization he founded in the fifties, Fatah, was also a spent force. Fatah wasn't going to liberate Nablus. In fact, Fatah had been politically bankrupt for the last two decades, causing only more misery for the Palestinians. Nasrallah was the general on the white horse now, not Arafat. Who cared if Nasrallah was a Shia imam? He knew how to fight.

Others opened up, and it was soon clear that everyone in the market knew who Nasrallah was. After all, only a year had passed since the 2006 war in Lebanon. But what surprised me was how uniformly passionate they were about Nasrallah. Ten years earlier, Nablus was a city that stood behind Saddam Hussein. And after that, Osama bin Laden.

At my next stop, I met the leader of a cell of the Al-Aqsa Martyrs' Brigades, a Palestinian militant group linked to Fatah. Wanted by the Israelis, he was holed up in Nablus's sprawling Balata refugee camp, moving constantly from house to house to avoid Israeli assassination squads. I asked him about Nasrallah.

"I love that man," he said.

He too couldn't have cared less that Hassan Nasrallah and Hezbollah were the creations of Shia Iran. Or that Nasrallah didn't bother to hide the fact that he answered to Tehran. All that mattered

to him was that Nasrallah had taken up arms against Israel. He'd
have followed a Christian general into battle as long as there was a
chance of defeating Israel.

The foundation of Nasrallah's popularity in Lebanon, Egypt, and
Jordan goes back to the same event: Nasrallah beat the Israelis on
the field of battle, David slaying the Israeli Goliath. In Iran, Nasrallah's success on the battlefield vaulted him into a position of near
reverence.

Ahmadinejad sent a "greeting card" to Nasrallah to mark the first
anniversary of the 2006 war. "The wonderful victory of the Lebanese
people over the Zionist occupiers," he wrote, "is a result of faith,
unity, and resistance."

Arabs today look at Nasrallah as a sovereign leader, with the
stature of a Bismarck or a de Gaulle.

Born in 1960 in Christian East Beirut, Hassan Nasrallah, like Imad
Mughniyah, was the son of a poor vegetable vendor. The Nasrallahs
were from Bazuriyah, a small village in the Shia south. Nasrallah
grew up in Christian East Beirut, learning early on what it was like to
be a second-class citizen to the Christian Maronites there. A
Lebanese military officer told me that Nasrallah worked for a while
in a barbershop that catered to Christian Maronite army officers,
which only deepened his resentment. Nasrallah was another internal
exile, like Mughniyah, cut off from Lebanon's larger society.

When the Lebanese civil war broke out in 1975, the Nasrallah
family was forced to flee south back to Bazuriyah. Nasrallah, a stu-
dious and pious boy, went to the Iraqi city of Najaf for religious studies. Along with many Shia Lebanese students, he was expelled from
Iraq in 1978. He returned to Lebanon and joined Amal, the Shia umbrella party.

Like many Lebanese Shia from the south, Nasrallah at first did
nothing to resist the Israelis. An Israeli general who was in Lebanon
at the time told me he remembers Nasrallah hosting Israeli officers

for tea at the family house in Bazuriyah. But something turned him. In late 1982 or early 1983, the twenty-two-year-old Nasrallah, like Mughniyah, put himself under the flag of the Revolutionary Guards in Balabakk, turning in his Koran for a Kalashnikov.

This wasn't a difficult choice for Nasrallah. He knew Amal was incapable of organizing a resistance to the Israelis. And anyhow, Nasrallah didn't think Amal had done enough for Lebanon's Shia. Like the PLO, Amal was corrupt and ineffective; and just as the Gulf Arabs would never lift a finger for Lebanon, neither would Amal. If nothing else, the Revolutionary Guards were a fresh face. Nasrallah would give them their chance.

Nasrallah's contact in the Revolutionary Guards was the same man Mughniyah had gone to see in Balabakk in 1982, Sheikh Hossein. And Nasrallah agreed to the same draconian rules: Keep Iran's hand hidden at all costs. Never discuss anything important on the phone. Deal in cash. Use the name Islamic Jihad Organization for attacks against the West. In other words, Nasrallah, like Mughniyah, signed up to become a clandestine operative—a terrorist. The only difference between the two was that Nasrallah had had religious training.

Sheikh Hossein didn't care that Nasrallah wasn't a disciple of Ayatollah Khomeini, or that in Najaf, Nasrallah had fallen under the influence of Khomeini's theological rival, the Da'wa Party. Sheikh Hossein cared only that this passionate young man agreed to take Iranian orders.

At some point Nasrallah became Mughniyah's boss, his go-between with Tehran. The Iranians named Nasrallah "Iran's representative" to the Islamic Jihad Organization. While Mughniyah would become a celebrity of sorts as the public face of Hezbollah terrorism, it was really Nasrallah who was the mastermind. It's a history that even today Nasrallah would like us to forget.

Nasrallah's name surfaced in connection with the April 18, 1983, bombing of the U.S. embassy in Beirut, which killed sixty people.

(Mughniyah would be tied to the embassy attack only after he became the subject of press speculation. Otherwise, there's no good evidence he was involved in it.) Nasrallah was also directly involved in the mid-1980s kidnapping of Western hostages in Lebanon. It was Nasrallah who gave the final orders to release them in 1991. And in 1996, when Nasrallah started raising objections about international terrorism, he put them aside at Tehran's insistence, dutifully training the attackers for the Khobar barracks truck bombing in Saudi Arabia—Iran's final terrorist act as of this writing.

The Iranians had complete trust in Nasrallah, both to follow orders and to make the right decisions when he acted on his own. Unlike Mughniyah, Nasrallah never freelanced. He never pushed the Iranians to carry out attacks they hadn't already decided on. When Nasrallah's son was killed fighting the Israelis in 1997, Nasrallah took the news calmly: it was a necessary death to drive out the Israelis. Nasrallah never asked the Iranians to take revenge. He was a loyal and obedient lieutenant, reassuring his Iranian handlers that Hezbollah kept no secrets from Iran.

Still, while Nasrallah was Iran's trusted caretaker of its interests in Lebanon, he was never its water boy. The Iranians treated him as a respected equal, as if he were a general in the Revolutionary Guards. And as Nasrallah's star rose, they were obliged to defer to him, treating him now as a victorious general. Nasrallah wasn't a soft cleric, cloistered in a mosque reading the Koran. He was a charismatic field commander—the only path to earning respect in today's Middle East.

It was February of 1986 when the United States first caught sight of Nasrallah in the south of Lebanon, fighting with the Islamic resistance. He and Imad Mughniyah crossed into the Israeli security zone to set up an ambush of an Israeli patrol, capturing two soldiers on February 17. It's unclear whether the Israeli soldiers died during the ambush or were executed. It made no difference to Nasrallah, because he had succeeded in infuriating the Israelis and flushing them out into the open, making them better targets.

The more frustrated the Israelis became, the more force they brought to bear in southern Lebanon, which is exactly what Nasrallah wanted when he'd kidnapped the two soldiers. Nasrallah needed the Israelis to overreact—to shed Lebanese blood, infuriate the south's Shia, help Hezbollah win more recruits. Ten years later, when Nasrallah was secretary-general of Hezbollah, he applied the same lessons he had learned in the south.

By March 1996, the cease-fire between Israel and Hezbollah had broken down, and Hezbollah was shelling northern Israel. Between March 4 and April 10, Hezbollah killed seven Israeli soldiers, pushing Israel to the brink once again. On April 9, Israeli general Amiram Levine gave Hezbollah and the Lebanese fair warning. "The residents in south Lebanon who are under the responsibility of Hezbollah will be hit harder," he declared, "and Hezbollah will be hit harder. We will find the way to act correctly and quickly."

Over the next four days, Israel shelled Hezbollah positions across the south and around Beirut, blockading Beirut, Sidon, and Tyre from the sea. The Israelis played the part Hezbollah had scripted for them perfectly. The Israelis' crashing around the south convinced the Lebanese that the Israelis intended to reoccupy Lebanon. Hezbollah would get the war it wanted—but just to make sure, Hezbollah fired more rockets into Israel.

What happened next permanently altered world opinion about the war, about Hezbollah, and about the Israeli occupation of Lebanon.

Qana is believed by some to be the biblical city of Cana, where Jesus is said to have turned water to wine. Though Qana wasn't known to be pro-Hezbollah, it had the misfortune of being in the middle of Israel's onslaught, Operation Grapes of Wrath. As the fighting closed in on Qana, about 800 villagers took refuge in a United Nations Interim Force in Lebanon (UNIFIL) compound.

On April 18, 1996, on a clear blue morning, a Hezbollah position just outside Qana, according to Israel, fired two Katyusha rockets and eight mortars at an Israeli position on the Red Line, the northern limit of Israel's "security zone." Fifteen minutes later, the Israel Defense Forces (IDF) returned fire, shelling the area with heavy artillery— 155mm guns. Most of the shells were detonated by proximity fuses, meaning they exploded in the air to cause maximum casualties.

According to the IDF, it fired 38 shells. At least 13 exploded in or above the UNIFIL compound; 106 people were killed, and 116 injured. Tehran didn't rejoice about the dead, but it was a political bull's-eye. You could almost hear the champagne corks, at least symbolic ones, going off in Tehran.

The "Qana Massacre" triggered an immediate outcry in Lebanon and the rest of the Muslim world. The Israelis shouldn't have been surprised, and probably weren't, but still they felt a sense of bafflement about the furious reaction.

"I don't see any mistake in judgment," Israeli lieutenant general Amnon Shahak said. "We fought Hezbollah there [in Qana], and when they fire on us, we will fire at them to defend ourselves. . . . I don't know of any other rules of the game, either for the army or civilians." The United States came to Israel's defense, accusing Hezbollah of hiding in built-up civilian areas, which did nothing to endear the Americans to the Lebanese.

The world saw Israel and the United States as condoning the murder of women and children. It was seen as evidence of Israel's impotence: the Israelis couldn't stop Hezbollah, so they slaughtered refugees, punishing the innocent. The "Qana Massacre" and its fallout also seriously undermined Israel's deterrence credibility—a vicious retaliation had done nothing to stop Hezbollah attacks. Instead, it undercut whatever moral high ground Israel still had left in Lebanon. It didn't matter whether the IDF had hit Qana on purpose or not; the perception was that the IDF didn't make mistakes.

The "Qana Massacre" turned Hezbollah into the moral victor.

Qana's dead evoked the seventh-century martyrdom of Imam Husayn at Karbala, galvanizing Hezbollah's rank and file. Nasrallah now had proved himself a brilliant strategist as well as a general and a soldier.

These were Nasrallah's earliest victories, establishing his reputation as a warrior priest. Although he started out on the same footing as Imad Mughniyah, one crucial difference separated them—a difference that turned Nasrallah into a leader, the head of a sovereign state in all but name, while Mughniyah remained a foot soldier who only knew how to throw grenades.

Mughniyah lost Tehran's confidence because he could never completely turn the corner from terrorist to guerrilla commander, as we saw during the hijacking of Kuwait Airways flight 422 in 1988. But the 1990s were a time when Nasrallah and Mughniyah's old mentors, the Revolutionary Guards, were incorporated into the regular military and the revolutionary commanders retired. Sheikh Hossein was recalled to Tehran and put on ice. Unable to understand that Iran was maturing into a classic statist power, Mughniyah couldn't adapt.

Nasrallah, on the other hand, sensed the shift of winds in Tehran. Though he was at the center of Hezbollah's notorious terrorist campaign of the 1980s, he easily made the shift away from terrorism along with Tehran. Conclusive evidence of the transformation would come during the 2006 war in Lebanon, when the Nasrallah-led Hezbollah didn't so much as touch a hair on the head of any American in Lebanon—a restraint Mughniyah, on his own, would have been unable to show. Nasrallah was now a victorious de facto head of state, taking and holding ground and commanding a military to match.

Since his assassination in February 2008, Imad Mughniyah has become an iconic legend among many Shia. But it's Hassan Nasrallah who is seen as the man who'll liberate the Middle East—the modern-day incarnation of Saladin, the twelfth-century Kurd who drove out the Crusaders and recaptured Jerusalem. The Palestinians are convinced it will be Nasrallah who frees them, liberates Jerusalem, and drives out the modern-day Crusaders, the United States and Israel.

Shortly before the invasion of Iraq in 2003, I got an idea of just how far one Sunni-Shia barrier had come down when a British journalist and I made a trip to Lebanon's most notorious Palestinian refugee camp, 'Ayn al-Hilwah.

Sitting on high ground just outside the ancient city of Sidon, 'Ayn al-Hilwah is the largest Palestinian refugee camp in Lebanon. It's also one of the poorest, most densely populated, and most lawless parts of the Middle East. Within the camp's confines, there's every kind of terrorist and criminal. One of the bombers in the 1993 World Trade Center attack lives there, as do groups affiliated with Osama bin Laden, Usbat al-Islam and Jund al-Sham. There's a Lebanese army checkpoint outside the entrance, but the army would never dare set foot inside the place. It would have to raze it first.

A single dirt road runs through the middle of 'Ayn al-Hilwah, but it quickly dissolves into alleyways so narrow you can touch the houses on either side just by raising your arms. Open sewers run through the alleyways, and the electricity is usually off. The shouts of children ring through the camp. Every once in a while you catch a glimpse of the cobalt Mediterranean, fishing boats riding anchor. Amid all the misery, it's a reminder you're still in Lebanon.

If I went back on my own, I could never find Munir Al-Maqdah's office—just as Maqdah, a Fatah military commander, wants it. As instructed, the British journalist and I waited in a trash-strewn lot. Three fedayeen, Palestinian freedom fighters, drove up in an open jeep. One got out, motioning us to follow. We walked in silence, through an even narrower maze of alleys, and at one point we had to cut through someone's house. Our escort shouted through the open door. A woman with a little girl in her arms ran into a back room. We followed our escort up a narrow stairway to a door with a curtain hanging over it, and he left us there to wait for Maqdah.

We'd asked to see Maqdah to hear what the Palestinians thought about the invasion of Iraq. In the first Gulf War, they almost all had stood behind Saddam Hussein. Saddam had supported them over the years, at least in name. After the second intifada started in September 2000, Saddam would give money to families of Palestinian suicide bombers. Now how did they feel about his approaching end?

Maqdah walked in, gave us a nod, and sat down on the couch next to me. This wasn't the first time he had talked to foreigners. Though he was more comfortable fighting than chatting, he was prepared to give yet another Sisyphean sermon about how wronged the Palestinians were. Then again, why wouldn't he talk to us? With a Lebanese arrest warrant hanging over his head, he had nothing to lose.

"What do you think about the invasion?" I asked.

"The United States has gone to war against Islam," Maqdah said. He meant that the United States had gone to war against all Muslims, not just Iraqi Muslims.

But what about the fact that the invasion was getting rid of a tyrant no one liked anymore? I was about to ask Maqdah this question, but at that moment an old fax machine in a bookcase began to clatter. Maqdah rose and stood over the machine as it came out. He read it, then handed it to me.

Dated March 22, it was from the Al-Aqsa Martyr Brigades: a call to all Muslims to go to Iraq to defend the *umma*, or Muslim nation, and combat the American, British, and Zionist invaders who want to divide the Muslim world, Shia from Sunni.

There wasn't a single word about democracy, modern education, women's empowerment, weapons of mass destruction, or even Saddam's dictatorship—nothing about the reasons Americans thought they were going to war. I read to the end of the fax. The name Saddam Hussein, the Palestinians' onetime ally, wasn't there.

Maqdah didn't care about Saddam either. For Maqdah, the old world—Saddam's world—had only divided Muslims, as it had failed the Palestinians. Only Islam could take back what the Palestinians had lost, the land they had lived on for thousands of years. The allies wouldn't be fighting Saddam Hussein, then, but the faithful. It doesn't matter what you call it—jihad, nationalism, or simply an anticolonial struggle. The point was that Saddam no longer counted; only Muslims did, Sunni and Shia fighting side by side. It was more evidence of how quickly the Middle East was embracing Islam, shedding whatever secularism was left.

The Al-Aqsa fax turned out to be right about the invasion's dividing Muslims, but not in the way Al-Aqsa had expected. Within a year, the Iraqis themselves would start a civil war, Shia against Sunni. I would see Maqdah again, but never got the chance to ask for an explanation. But I think I know the reason for his misplaced confidence that there would be an ecumenical jihad in Iraq.

In the mid-eighties, Maqdah had thrown his lot in with Iran, fighting with the Islamic resistance. Although he was still taking Arafat's money, he now took his orders from Tehran. In 1994, after the Oslo Accords were signed and money from the PLO stopped coming, Maqdah broke with Arafat. He signed up with the Revolutionary Guards and integrated his forces into Hezbollah's.

One of Maqdah's lieutenants told me that Mughniyah had often operated out of 'Ayn al-Hilwah, coordinating with Maqdah. He said that Mughniyah had been in the camp as recently as July 2007, a little more than six months before he was assassinated. Predictably, neither Mughniyah nor Iran cared that Maqdah was a Sunni Muslim. If Maqdah was willing to join the Iranians' cause, they were more than willing to have him—one more Sunni crossing sectarian lines.

And Maqdah certainly was ready to serve under a new flag, as his confidence in Arafat had steadily eroded over the years. In 1993, when Arafat signed the Oslo Accords, he lost the loyalty of many Palestinians. Arafat ceded 78 percent of Palestine to Israel, and got nothing in return other than a vague promise to grant the Palestinians statehood at some undetermined future time—which for them meant never. After Oslo, Maqdah saw Arafat as an Israeli collaborator rather than a liberator. Oslo was an agreement to look after Israel's security rather than that of the Palestinians. The Israelis have their own views about what went wrong with Oslo, but it's Maqdah's that interest us here.

Arafat was just another ineffective exile, as were his lieutenants. Almost all of them were born in refugee camps in Jordan, Syria, Egypt, and Lebanon and had long ago lost touch with the real Palestine. Arafat's war on Israel, which started in 1965, was fought by exiles, Palestinians who wanted to go home. Their attacks reeked of desperation and futility, gaining the Palestinians nothing but a reputation for being terrorists. Maqdah, himself an exile, finally came to understand that the hijacking of a Western passenger airliner only served to strengthen Israel. It did nothing to get him out of this miserable refugee camp.

With Arafat's decline, luring a fighter like Maqdah was easy for the Iranians. Iran's message was simple: Fight Israel on the field of battle, take ground, take back all of Palestine—no more compromises like Oslo. Just as important, the Iranians were ready to step in with money when Arafat wouldn't. And unlike the Saudis and their Palestinian beneficiaries with their hypocritical moral codes, the Iranians didn't waste their money on Beirut nightclubs and whores.

Though the Saudis shared the same religious beliefs with Maqdah—Sunni Islam—they could never win his respect. Hiding behind the walls of their multibillion-dollar palaces, the Saudi royal family never sent their spoiled princes to Lebanon to fight the Israelis. In fact, when has any Saudi ever died fighting the Israelis? Never.

Maqdah saw the Saudis as a spent race. At 35 percent, Saudis take the prize for having the highest percentage of obese people in the world—more than the United States, at 33 percent. When a Palestinian like Maqdah sees a Saudi prince, he sees not a resistance fighter but a soft billionaire like Prince Al-Walid bin Talal, who bought the world's most expensive and luxurious private jet, the Airbus A380, to convert into a "flying palace." No, the Saudis weren't an option.

Maqdah didn't share much with the Iranians in terms of beliefs.

He didn't particularly like them, or Hezbollah for that matter. But the Iranians had a strategy—one they'd never give up on, even at the risk of massive Israeli retaliation. A plan that Maqdah and other Palestinians wanted to be part of, to pull them out of their sea of despair. As it did with the angry, poor, young Shia men living in Lebanon, Iran knew how to tap the vein of Palestinian defiance.

And it wasn't only individual fighters like Maqdah the Iranians were winning over. They also undertook a patient, systematic effort to win the most influential religious and political Sunni organization in the world: the Society of the Muslim Brothers, or the Muslim Brotherhood, an organization the Palestinians gravitated to in the seventies and eighties. And incredibly, considering the inborn hate of the Muslim Brotherhood for Shia Iran, Iran made inroads.

The mission of the Muslim Brotherhood, founded in 1928 by an Egyptian schoolteacher named Hassan al-Banna, was to purify Islam. Relying on a strict interpretation of the Koran and the sayings of the prophet, the Muslim Brotherhood, like the *takfiris,* wants the return of the Caliphate. Today, with branches in every Muslim country in the world (often going by other names), the Muslim Brotherhood is the largest, most broad-based populist movement in the Arab peninsula. The Muslim Brotherhood is another of the cauldrons from which al Qaeda emerged.

Following the 1979 Iranian revolution, Saudi Arabia poured money into the Muslim Brotherhood, into its madrassas, charities, and fighters in the Afghan war against the Soviet army. This was part of the same Saudi effort to counter Khomeini's revolution, which the Saudi royal family saw as a threat to its legitimacy. The fact that three decades later Iran had started to co-opt Palestinian members of the Muslim Brotherhood, in spite of all of the Saudi money, was a marked defeat for Saudi Arabia.

Iran's campaign continues today. It's making a run at the Egyptian and the Jordanian Muslim Brotherhoods with persistent calls for uniting in the struggle against Israel. If Iran succeeds in truly turning a Sunni fundamentalist organization like this, it will have changed identities in the Middle East in ways we've never seen.

In approaching the Palestinians, the Iranians started cautiously. In the eighties, Iran had done well winning over small Palestinian factions based in Damascus and Beirut—the ones cut loose from the PLO by the 1982 Israeli invasion. But now Iran's sights were on the PLO itself.

Iran knew it didn't stand a chance of seizing the PLO by force, or by voting out Arafat democratically. On paper, the PLO's legislative authority is the Palestine National Council, which is nominally democratic but in fact was in Arafat's pocket. He was too wily to let an election slip away from him; the Iranians would have to break up the PLO piece by piece, right under Arafat's feet.

They started by trying to win over the Palestinian Islamic Jihad, or PIJ, which would give them a foothold in the West Bank and Gaza. It didn't take long to enlist the PIJ's spiritual leader, Abd al Aziz Awda, who assured the Iranian emissary that PIJ cells in Gaza were ready to die for Palestine if they only had money and weapons. The Iranians were encouraged and gave him money, but the Revolutionary Guards needed to carefully vet Awdah and the other PIJ leaders, as it did its other proxies. The Guards were forced to move slowly—too slowly, as it turned out, for Tehran's liking.

By early 1990, Ayatollah Khamenei, the successor to Ayatollah Khomeini, was frustrated Iran wasn't making faster progress in the occupied Palestinian territories. Enlisting the exiled PIJ leadership in Damascus was fine, but that wasn't getting Iran any closer to unseating Arafat, or taking Jerusalem.

In a meeting of Iran's Supreme National Security Council, Khamenei ordered an "increased commitment" to winning over the Palestinians. He turned to the Revolutionary Guards' representative and instructed him to form a Palestine Committee to coordinate a new Palestinian campaign. The Revolutionary Guards were to force the groups Iran was in touch with to work together: the PIJ; the Palestinian Struggle Front; the Popular Front for the Liberation of Palestine; the Popular Front for the Liberation of Palestine–the General Command; the Abu Nidal Organization.

Khamenei didn't care that many of these Palestinian factions were avowedly secular, or even communist. Or that Abu Nidal's organization was a bizarre cult led by an insane recluse. What he cared about was recruits—putting Iran's hand on membership lists, the names of alienated young men ready to fight in a military struggle.

What Khamenei really wanted, though, was for the Revolutionary Guards to win over Hamas, with its 300,000 members. Hamas alone would give Iran the voice it wanted in Gaza.

But getting to Hamas wouldn't be easy. Revolutionary Guard officers couldn't travel to Gaza, where the Hamas leadership lived. Even getting to their members living outside the territories, in camps in Jordan, was difficult, because Iranian officials couldn't easily travel to them without coming to the attention of the Jordanians.

Hamas was founded in 1987, its leadership coming almost exclusively from Gaza, from the same overcrowded refugee camps that spawned the PIJ. Like the PIJ, Hamas was an offshoot of the Egyptian Muslim Brotherhood. Its early funding came from Saudi Arabia and the Gulf. By the mid-1990s, Hamas had emerged as a unified, populist movement that could speak for the vast majority of Palestinians in Gaza.

Iran knew that winning over Hamas would be tantamount to winning Gaza. But again, the problem was getting to Hamas's leadership. Then, thanks to an epic blunder, the Israelis gave the Iranians the break they needed to turn Gaza into an Iranian base.

During the first intifada, in 1992, Israel decided it could put a quick end to it by expelling 415 members of Hamas's leadership, shoving them across the border into Lebanon. Israel hoped that exiled in Lebanon the Hamas leaders would fade away. But what Israel didn't anticipate was that Hezbollah would be at the border the same day the Hamas leaders crossed it, waiting with tents, clothes, and food. Or that within days a Revolutionary Guard officer would travel to the south to make sure the Hamas leaders didn't lack for anything. Iran's plan was clear from the start: Teach Hamas discipline, convince it to give up throwing stones, and turn it into a military and political force that would take Gaza.

It wasn't long before the expelled Hamas leaders drifted north, to Beirut, where Hezbollah provided them apartments and small stipends. Some made it to the Biqa' Valley for military training. In 2005, when I met one of the Hamas leaders expelled in 1992, he was still in the southern suburbs, living in a Hezbollah apartment and protected by Hezbollah guards.

For Iran, it was as if Hamas had dropped out of the sky into its lap, an act of divine intervention. Israel's error was the only way the Iranians could ever have gotten to Palestinian internal exiles like Hamas—proving once again that forging an empire isn't simply an act of will; it has as much to do with luck and the stupidity of the enemy.

The whole of the Arab world saw how Iran had come to Hamas's rescue. Where was Saudi Arabia, the rich Arabs—America's allies? No Saudi charity was in Lebanon to take care of the Palestinians. No Saudi diplomat went south to check on their welfare. In all fairness, southern Lebanon was Iran's preserve. But that's not the way the Muslim world saw it. With the Hamas blunder, Israel unwittingly had boosted Iran's standing in the Middle East.

Today it's still not clear whether Iran will manage to fully co-opt Hamas. Still, what's certain is that the ties forged in the early 1990s exist and are becoming stronger. Hamas is allied with Iran, taking Iranian money and guidance. In itself that's an unprecedented shift in modern Middle Eastern history, almost as if the United States were to suddenly co-opt North Korea in an Asian security pact. It was definitely a turn in history no one was prepared for.

Hamas today threatens to be the third Iranian domino to fall, after Lebanon and southern Iraq. And the next ones after Hamas, the Iranians tell the faithful, will be Jordan and Egypt, two countries that currently recognize Israel. If Iran succeeds, Israel will find itself completely besieged—Israel's second-worst fear after a nuclear attack.

One man who's afraid that day is closer than we think is Avi Dichter, Israel's minister of public security.

"Hamas has become the subcontractor of Iran," Dichter told me during an interview in his unofficial office, in a place he asked me not to identify.

I had come to talk to Dichter about Israel's success in stopping suicide bombing. But I also wanted to ask him about Iran. As head of Israel's internal security service, the Israeli FBI, from 2000 to 2005, he knew more than any other Israeli about Iran's influence on the Palestinians.

I watched as he knotted his tie, peering into a small mirror propped up on his desk. With his chiseled face and self-deprecating way of speaking, Dichter couldn't be taken for anything other than a battle-hardened counterterrorism expert—not the self-appointed kind you find on American TV. He was a soldier's soldier, and had a record to back that up: on his watch, Israel had beaten Palestinian terrorism, more or less putting an end to suicide bombings. It matters little whether it was thanks to Palestinian second thoughts, good police work, targeted killings, the controversial West Bank wall, or just plain intimidation. Dichter's knowledge was hard-won.

And indeed, Israeli intelligence knows the Palestinians—their families, clans, factions, squabbles, the way they think. Israeli security listens in to all cellphones in the West Bank and Gaza, and the borders demarcating Palestinian areas are tightly monitored. The Israelis keep vast databases on the Palestinians, including the refugees living in camps all over the Middle East.

The Israelis' job is made much easier by the Palestinians' relative transparency. Unlike the Shia, whose telephone conversations are impenetrable to outsiders—remember *taqqiyah,* the Shia code of silence?—the Sunni Palestinians talk, gossip, and plead their case openly. They complain about injustice, their plight, how the world ignores them, how the Arabs have abandoned them. And they do it on the phone, on lines the Israelis are listening to. In the same conversations they give away details they shouldn't, which is one of the key reasons Israel has been so effective against Palestinian terrorism.

But Iran, as Dichter knew better than anyone, is a different story. Thanks to Palestinian indiscretion, Israeli security was able to easily monitor Iran's contact with Hamas, and when the Israelis found out that Iran and Hamas had made contact, they became alarmed. This was a problem they knew wouldn't be easily containable, especially if the Hamas members expelled in 1992 found their way back into Gaza.

"It's interesting," Dichter told me, "because when Hamas first went to Iran, Iran refused. The Iranians wanted their relations to be similar to those they had with the PIJ—through Hezbollah. But Hamas refused; they didn't want to be beneath Hezbollah."

Dichter's point was that Hamas didn't want to be brought down to the same level as the PIJ, terms Iran agreed to. Enlisting Hamas was a huge catch for the Iranians, Dichter admitted, the foothold in the territories they had so long sought.

"Since 2001, we've seen an increase in the level of coordination and training by Iran," Dichter went on. "We now have Hezbollah in Lebanon, which is a battalion of the Iranian army." More important, he said, "Hamas has started to be built as another arm of Iran." Just like Hezbollah.

Dichter was certain things were going to get worse. "The strategic aim of Hamas [and Iran] today is to take all capability that they have in the Gaza strip and transfer it to the West Bank," he told me.

Dichter had no doubt about the damage the Palestinians, funded and organized by Iran, could do to Israel. Referring to Israeli losses during the second intifada expressed as a proportion of population, he said, "What we've lost is the equivalent of 45,000 Americans."

And Israel holds Iran responsible? I asked.

"Yes."

Dichter is a self-acknowledged hawk on Iran, but because he is the minister of public security, his word carries a lot of weight in both Tel Aviv and Washington. He's convinced Iran is Israel's main enemy, having turned the Palestinian question into an intractable problem.

There's little chance Iran will give up the Palestinian cause easily, and it certainly won't under Israeli threats. For one thing, the Iranians still are convinced they have to champion the Palestinians as an essential vehicle for dominion over the Arabs, to steal the fire of Sunni Arabs. It's hardwired into the Iranian regime's mind that every revolution or empire needs a cause bigger than itself. Rome, Napoleon, the Soviet Union each had one. Without the Palestinians, Iran is just another country with raw territorial ambition.

Westerners tend to think of the Middle East as a place where religions are set in blood and stone. Palestinians are Sunni, Persians are Shia, Iraqis are a mix of Sunni and Shia, and so on. The Iraq civil war seared into our consciousness the idea that there's an unbridgeable divide between Sunni and Shia.

But sectarian divides do break down under the right circumstances, usually when there's a common enemy like Israel or the United States. The spectacular rise of Nasrallah's popularity in Nablus, for example, is due solely to Israel.

The fact that Saddam Hussein, a secular leader, was forgotten—his name nowhere to be heard in Nablus even just six months after his execution—is more evidence we're living through the twilight of a secular Middle East. Thirty years ago, the Middle East was far more secular than it is now. As late as the 1993 Oslo Accords, Yasser Arafat could count on overwhelming support in Nablus, even among the religiously conservative. Today the most powerful force there is Hezbollah, led by the warrior priest Hassan Nasrallah. After Arafat was buried, the Palestinians thought they were left with two choices: surrender unconditionally or ally with Nasrallah in battle.

Most Americans looked at Saddam's execution as a fitting end; he was the Arabs' Hitler. The United States saw Iraq as another battle won in our long struggle against totalitarianism and fascism. But our fixation on dictators caused us to miss the rise of Nasrallah; the culture of resistance he represents, one born of humiliation and defeat; and the conviction that Islam and war alone will deliver the Middle East from occupation. Like the Israelis, the Americans are still fighting World War II, even in the teeth of a completely new set of facts.

Again, it was the 34-day war in 2006 that changed everything. Across the Middle East, a wave of sympathy followed Nasrallah's victory in Lebanon—a wave in which Shia and Sunni joined together. Every time I go back to Damascus, Cairo, or Jordan, there are fewer bars and restaurants serving liquor, in deference to Islamic law. Muslim beliefs are taking tighter hold of the Middle East. The state is withering away, giving ground to a stateless, powerful, and cross-sectarian movement inspired by Nasrallah.

All this points to another Iranian learning curve. The first was their transition from radicals to pragmatists, learned from lessons on the ground in Lebanon. Iran abandoned terrorism for a more classic military struggle; the anarchists turned Machiavellian statesmen.

But there's another arc Iran traveled: It coalesced its sympathizers from rigid, exclusionary sectarian factions into a united Islamic front, unlike anything that has been achieved in Islam's history since the Crusades. By co-opting two radical Sunni organizations, PIJ and Hamas, Iran has taken a big step in unifying Muslims. An out-and-out civil war in Iraq, Shia against Sunni, or even one in the Gulf or Lebanon could undo Iran's progress. But until then we should count on the Iranians holding on tight to the Palestinian cause.

The Palestinian domino hasn't tipped over just yet, in the sense that Lebanon and Iraq have. But it's on its way. And once Iran has successfully co-opted Palestinians, what's to keep them from doing the same in Jordan and Egypt, overcoming sectarian differences? If there's a full-on war between the Palestinians and Israel, Jordan and Egypt will find it almost impossible not to fight under Iran's banner. In fact, they've already started.

Jordan, for example, has a majority Palestinian population, many of whom live in refugee camps. Historically, most Palestinians living in Jordan were loyal to Yasser Arafat. But after Arafat's death in 2004, and with Hamas's electoral victory in 2006 and the violent takeover of Gaza in June 2007, Hamas has recruited more and more of Arafat's onetime followers among the Palestinians in Jordan. They're more radicalized than ever, more susceptible to Iran's influence.

Much of Iran's influence passes through Jordan's Muslim Brotherhood, which goes by the name the Islamic Action Front, and whose platform is very much like Iran's: free the West Bank, lift the Israeli embargo on Gaza, create an Islamic state in Palestine. The largest opposition party, the Islamic Action Front was at one point so powerful in Jordan, it threatened to win a plurality of the vote in free and fair elections—a nightmare that frightened the Jordanian government into restricting its election laws for the November 20, 2007, parliamentary vote. The Islamic Action Front's vote count was set back, but the Iranians see that as temporary.

And this wasn't the Iranians' only entrée into Jordan. Another came clandestinely through the Popular Front for the Liberation of Palestine–the General Command. The PFLP–GC was nominally under the thumb of Syria, but Damascus never had enough money to keep it going, and after 1982 a large part of it went to work for Iran.

The PFLP–GC helped the Iranians carry out terrorist attacks in the mid-eighties. Some still believe Iran carried out the mid-flight bombing of Pan Am 103 in December 1988 with its help. But by 1996, Iran had abandoned terrorism, and it needed the PFLP–GC to expand Iranian political influence.

Iran used the PFLP–GC to recruit from other Palestinian factions in Jordan's refugee camps. Those recruits came to Lebanon for training, and returned to Jordan to set up the core of a new military force. The PFLP–GC also helped Iran establish Jordanian Hezbollah, a clandestine organization. Jordanian Hezbollah didn't have a visible effect, but just getting a toehold in Jordan was enough to convince the Iranian Ministry of Intelligence to keep funding it.

As its pool of Palestinian recruits increases, Iran comes ever closer to provoking a Palestinian uprising, overthrowing the Hashemite Kingdom of Jordan—America's most steadfast Arab ally in the war on terrorism—and encircling and showering Israel with rockets. It will be poised to shell Israel into extinction.

But will it?

In uniting Sunni and Shia, Iran achieves the universality required by all successful revolutions. As more and more Muslims accept Iran as a protective power, Iran will become a truly serious threat to Israel, even without a nuclear bomb. The question then becomes whether Iran truly intends to destroy Israel.

This is doubtful. President Ahmadinejad's threats aside, Iran has shown a history of acting pragmatically. In its relentless push toward winning Lebanon, the Gulf States, and the Palestinians, the Iranians have acted more rationally and consistently than the United States has. The Iranians have pulled back from confrontation with the United States in Iraq. They have avoided confrontation with the U.S. Navy in the Gulf. And they have restrained Hezbollah from being dragged into a civil war in Lebanon.

It's a small detail, but the Iranians are also careful with their money. They haven't sprayed money all across the Middle East, providing arms and cash to shadowy fighters who would ultimately turn on them and wreak havoc worldwide, as the Saudis and Americans did during the Afghan War against the Soviets. And the Revolutionary Guards have established a reputation for being incorruptible. In 1988, when they caught the head of an obscure Palestinian organization stealing money from a student aid program, they very publicly cut off the organization's funding.

For the last fifteen years, Iran has demonstrated a consistent, coherent strategy: It tests its strategy, vets its proxies, judges who is serious and who isn't, and makes plans accordingly. Whereas the United States, especially under George W. Bush, threw money at untested and unreliable exiles, governments, and contractors in Iraq and Afghanistan, who mostly pocketed it. The money is beyond auditing, and no one knows how much ended up in the hands of America's enemies.

Iran knows it is winning. It knows one day the United States must come to terms with that reality. Instead of falling back on the outdated, incorrect notion that Iranians are a riot of mad, scowling, turban-wearing mullahs, the West needs to realize the Iranians are potentially partners in a Palestinian settlement. But this can only be determined through serious engagement.

In any case, Iran definitely knows that a nuclear confrontation with Israel isn't winnable. The Iranians know that Israel would massively retaliate with their own nuclear weapons, and everything Iran has worked so hard to win would be lost.

9

WINNER TAKE ALL:
WHY THE SHIA WILL PREVAIL—
AND THE OPENING IT OFFERS

There's a war going on today for the soul of Islam, and Shia Iran is winning. Over the past four decades, three political currents—all grounded in Sunni Islam—have failed. Failed to catch fire, failed to defeat Israel, failed to drive out Western colonialism. Defeat and failure have left a void. And as we know, Iran loves nothing better than to move in and fill a void—in Iraq, in Afghanistan, in Kurdistan. And now throughout the rest of the Middle East.

The first failed political current was Arab nationalism. Arab nationalism was supposed to be a panacea for everything that was wrong with the Arabs, but it gained them nothing. The Arabs never could come to look at themselves as a single people. With so many different tribes, sects, and political factions, a true Arab identity was a fantasy. And today, with the catastrophe in Iraq, it's dead and buried.

The second was the Sunni Islamic revival, Sunni fundamentalism, the same movement that brought us Osama bin Laden. As early as the seventies, Sunni fundamentalism turned messianic, drifting toward nihilism, a force only for destruction. Sunni fundamentalism knows how to tear down but offers nothing to rebuild on. The Koran is not a true constitution or any sort of political prescription. A Sunni layman can take a verse from the Koran, interpret it as he wishes, and use it to justify an act of violence, no matter how senseless, cruel, or wasted it may be. For these reasons and more, which we'll explore in this chapter, Sunni fundamentalists can never be a constructive political or unifying force in the Middle East.

The third failed political current was secular nationalism. It too was a uniform failure: President Nasser of Egypt lost the 1967 war. Ba'thi Syria lost three wars against Israel, in 1967, 1973, and 1982. Ba'thi Iraq lost three wars: the Iran-Iraq War, the Gulf War (1990–91), and the Iraq War (2003). Communism never took hold in the Middle East. For that matter, monarchy failed as well. The five dysfunctional families who run the Arab side of the Gulf have never fought a war or done much of anything except build luxury mega hotels and gamble their money away in European casinos. In every way, Sunni Islam is tagged with defeat. And defeat equals humiliation, the crucible where hatred of the West is forged.

The failing Sunni order is reflected nowhere better than in Syria. Though technically ruled by a Shia minority, the Alawites, Syria has long been a weather vane for Sunni sentiment; the Alawites stay in power at the sufferance of the Sunni. And Syria is also a second home, after Egypt, of the Muslim Brotherhood.

As Syria goes, so go the Sunni. So it's worth taking a closer look at precisely where Syria gave up, and what that portends for the rest of the Middle East.

It was early 2003, and the Syrian intelligence chief wasn't in a good mood. The U.S. invasion of Iraq was inevitable. Tens of thousands of American troops were already in Kuwait. There soon would be American troops on Syria's borders. The last time that happened, in 1982, Syria and the United States almost went to war.

Muhammad Nassif, who goes by the name Abu Wael, got up from his heavy desk, so clean of paper or any other ornament I wondered whether we were perhaps meeting in a ceremonial office—the kind of place a Syrian official might use to meet the enemy, a former CIA officer. He knew I had left the CIA, but in this part of the world it's assumed you never really leave. At least not until you end up in jail or on the gallows.

Abu Wael, who had to be in his seventies, has been a pillar of the Syrian regime. He'd risen steadily, thanks to being an Alawite and to his loyalty and singular ability to keep his mouth shut. He was old-school. The Internet, openness, the media were not in his lexicon. Like Stalin, he was more comfortable officiating at a firing squad than talking to a reporter.

His bona fides in the Syrian government ran deep. When then-president Hafez's brother made a grab for power in 1984, Abu Wael never wavered: he remained loyal to Hafez. Now, with Syria facing yet another threat to its existence on its borders, the untested new president, Bashar al-Assad—a London-trained ophthalmologist and a pale shadow of his father Hafez—relied more and more heavily on Abu Wael.

Abu Wael sat on the sofa next to mine, opened the humidor on the coffee table, and handed me a fat cigar, a Romeo y Julieta Churchill. He watched as I took my time to light it. I'd learned long ago there's a protocol to lighting a cigar in the Arab world; you slowly light the edge of the tip to make sure it's set ablaze. I had stopped smoking cigars a long time ago. Now that I was out of the CIA, what was the point of pretending I was some sort of player in the Middle East? Still, I hoped sharing a cigar with Abu Wael would somehow help me connect with this Syrian fossil. It didn't help in the least, as it turned out.

I'd asked for a meeting with Abu Wael to find out what Syria would do in reaction to the American invasion of Iraq. For his part, Abu Wael was trying to figure out how the United States could commit a cosmic blunder like trying to occupy the most xenophobic Arab country in the world. He was truly baffled.

I offered my view that if the Iraq invasion went well, there might be an irresistible temptation on the part of the Bush administration to keep going, right on to the Syrian capital of Damascus. Already, rumors circulated in the press that the European Command was dusting off plans to invade Syria. (Bizarrely enough, Syria falls under Europe in the U.S. military's command structure.)

On the other hand, I posited that if the invasion went badly and the United States got bogged down in Iraq, Syria might just get through the invasion unscathed. But then again, when is violence on your border ever a good thing?

"It doesn't make any sense," Abu Wael said, interrupting me. "We're on the same side."

Abu Wael was referring to the fact that Syria had helped the United States after the September 11 attacks, providing details about the Syrian Muslim Brotherhood cells in Germany, in particular Mohamed Atta's Hamburg cell. As it would come out in the press, the Syrians also held and interrogated a Canadian Syrian in the United States who was suspected of working for al Qaeda.

The Syrian help was not inconsequential. The Syrians naturally knew the Syrian Muslim Brotherhood better than anyone else, how al Qaeda had co-opted its European cells. Osama bin Laden's mother was a Syrian, from the ruling Alawite sect—the same sect as Abu Wael. The Syrians truly thought they had been of real help to us, and they couldn't understand how they'd become a target of the White House.

I shrugged. I suspected Washington didn't really value its new relationship with the Syrians, and switched subjects. I asked Abu Wael what Iran would do, faced with the prospect of several hundred thousand soldiers massed on its border with Iraq.

Abu Wael stood up. "Let's get lunch," he said.

It never ceases to amaze me what an odd place the Middle East is.

And Abu Wael wasn't doing his part to clear it up. When I got into the passenger seat of his Oldsmobile 88, I noticed a small machine gun between my feet. I bent over to look. It was an Israeli Uzi—a mini-Uzi, the kind tank crews carry in tight spaces. I looked over at him and said this was wonderful, globalization, a Syrian officer owning an Uzi.

"It's not an Uzi," Abu Wael said, wheeling the Olds through traffic. Damascene drivers are some of the most courageous and reckless in the world, flinching at no challenge. But they gave us a wide berth. They obviously recognized Abu Wael's Olds 88.

"But it says Uzi," I said, confused.

"It's not an Uzi," he repeated. I dropped the subject, realizing that Damascus was no different from Washington: you get through it all by denying inconvenient facts. We denied that Syria helped us with al Qaeda; Abu Wael denied that he owned an Uzi.

Over lunch outside Damascus, I never could get Abu Wael around to talking about how Syria would react to the U.S. invasion of Iraq. Nor would he answer my questions about how Iran would react. The understanding between Iran and Syria was that they'd never discuss in public the details of their strategic relationship. I had to suspect, however, that Abu Wael knew exactly what was in store for us.

And indeed he did. After the invasion, I heard from a friend close to Syrian president Bashar that the president had given the "Iraq portfolio" to Abu Wael. This wasn't surprising. Abu Wael, the old-school hard-liner, an expert in insurgencies, had played a key role in the period after the 1982 Israeli invasion, when the Lebanese resistance drove out the United States and later Israel. Abu Wael was a longtime go-between for Tehran and Damascus.

Abu Wael presided over Syria's funneling of insurgents into Iraq—suicide bombers, Hezbollah cadres, Saudi *takfiris,* or anyone who wanted to fight the American occupiers. As soon as they landed in Damascus, the jihadis were immediately shuttled to the border, where they waited for night to cross into Iraq and set roadside bombs or blow themselves up. I could just see Abu Wael at his window, musing over a cigar, *Better they blow themselves up in Iraq than in my country.*

Abu Wael knew the stakes of America's failed invasion of Iraq, the kind of religious extremism it would spawn. He'd seen firsthand the rise of fundamentalism in his own country—the Muslim Brotherhood takeover of the Syrian city of Hama in February 1982, which the Syrian army had to violently put down, killing thousands in what became known as the "Hama Massacre." He'd also seen the influence Hezbollah had won in Lebanon, ultimately undermining Syria's presence there. But the desecularization of the Middle East, if you can call it that, is a force the Syrians couldn't do anything about. Except stand out of its way.

Through it all, Syria's ruling Alawites kept their mouths closed, never acknowledging they were terrified the dam would break. At the same time, they knew they couldn't completely swim against the current. They would have to take sides, ally with either the nihilist Sunni *takfiris* or Iran. Iran was definitely the better bet. It meant giving the Revolutionary Guards a free hand in Lebanon—but it was better than having your head cut off, which is what the Sunni *takfiris* intended to do with the Alawites.

Syria's surrender to Iran can almost be tagged to a single day, a single meeting in July 1990.

The meeting was between the Syrian commander in Lebanon and an Iranian emissary in charge of Lebanon. It led to a historic capitulation, the consequences of which didn't become known for years. But as it would turn out, for the first time in modern history an Arab state, Syria, agreed to defer to a nonstate actor, Iran's proxy army. It was as if the mayor of Los Angeles ceded police authority to a Latino gang to keep order in a barrio.

The Syrian general was an Alawite, a close confidant of Syria's then-president Hafez al-Assad. He'd served in Lebanon almost a decade and knew the country better than any other Syrian. No

Lebanese political figure, with the occasional exception of Hezbollah, dared cross this general.

In the mid-eighties, Hezbollah had taken a couple of potshots at the Syrian general, but he quickly hit back, moving tanks to the edge of Beirut's Shia southern suburbs, threatening to shell them. Hezbollah knew he was serious. If Syria could destroy one of its own cities, Hama, in order to put down a rebellion, it wouldn't hesitate to destroy the southern suburbs. So Hezbollah backed down and stopped shooting at him.

But by the time the Syrian general sat down with the Iranian emissary, the balance of power in Lebanon was shifting. The Revolutionary Guards and their Islamic resistance were beating the Israelis in the south. An unspoken truth hung over the meeting: The Iranian-backed Lebanese were the ones fighting the Israelis, Syria's enemy, and not the Syrians.

The meeting took place in the Syrian general's office in 'Anjar, which butted up against the notorious Syrian intelligence military prison there—a place every Lebanese had heard rumors about. It was both a gallows and a torture chamber.

The Syrian general set the meeting's tone, reminding the Iranian that it was Syria that had given Iran its role in Lebanon in the first place, in 1982, when the first Revolutionary Guards were allowed to establish a base in Balabakk. The intention, the Syrian said, was not to let Iran divide the Lebanese Shia. Rather, it was to help Syria fight the Israeli occupation.

The Iranian knew exactly what the Syrian general was referring to. Hezbollah had been picking up popular support among the Lebanese Shia—but particularly at the expense of Amal, a Shia party that was more secular than Hezbollah and allied with Syria. Every day, the Syrian general was battered by complaints from Amal about how Hezbollah was encroaching on its power.

The Syrian warned the Iranian that Syria would never allow Amal to lose "the initiative." As long as there were Syrian troops in

Lebanon, the Syrian government would ensure Amal remained Lebanon's most powerful Shia party.

The Iranian understood the general's implied threat, that with one phone call, the Syrian president could close the border, block Iranian supplies for Hezbollah, and bring the resistance in the south to a halt. If that were to happen, Iran would lose its only portal into the Arab world, its link to Hezbollah and its access to Palestinian guerrillas. Tehran had no choice but to take the threat seriously.

And the Syrian general wasn't finished. The Lebanese people, he told the Iranian, were tired of Iran. Iranian-backed terrorist attacks had led the world to brand all Lebanese as terrorists. And Iran had completely bungled the hostage issue in the eighties, capturing foreigners and turning Lebanon into a pariah state. Now Lebanon was a place where even Arabs were afraid to visit.

That chaos was a serious problem for Syria, whose economy depends on a vibrant Lebanon. And it wasn't helping Syria internationally either. Syria was a pariah as far as the Americans were concerned, unavoidably tainted by the hostage-taking. The chaos in Lebanon was bleeding over into Syria's economy and politics, and Lebanese warlords were corrupting Syrian officials.

But still the Syrian wasn't finished.

He told his Iranian visitor that Iran had drawn out the Iran–Iraq War longer than it needed to.

At last the Iranian objected. He reminded his host that it was the Iranians—through proxy Lebanese martyrs—who were beating the Israelis in the south. So despite whatever complaints the Syrian general might have, Iran was fighting a just war in Lebanon.

The Syrian general snapped, irritated now, that Syria, not Iran, had planned the first suicide operation against Israel.

The Iranian dismissed the Syrian's retort with a wave of his hand. The Iran-led Islamic resistance was chewing up the Israeli army, he said. Thanks to the Iranians, the Israeli army was losing, for the first time in history. Would Syria really try to put an end to that, out of some kind of misplaced petulance?

This was the key: military victory—not just soothing words, which was all the Arabs had to offer. The Iranian had made his point, and the Syrian general had no choice but to cede it. But the Syrian couldn't back down completely. He had one last thing to say: Iran had to stop using Lebanon as a base for global terrorism. With that, the meeting ended. The Iranian stood to say goodbye, essentially agreeing to disagree with the Syrian. But he had already made a much more crucial point.

The fact that the Syrian commander for Lebanon and the Iranian emissary met as equals was extraordinary. It was as if the tens of thousands of troops Syria had stationed in Lebanon counted for nothing. It didn't matter to the Iranian now that the Syrians had the capacity to expel him and the rest of the Iranians in minutes, or to close Hezbollah's supply lines with a single phone call. That was an empty threat the Syrians would never dare carry out. Because of the Iranian-backed victories in Lebanon, the Syrians were now essentially powerless to stop the Iranians.

As the Iranian walked backed to his car, he was like the cat who ate the canary, certain that Hezbollah and the Islamic resistance were untouchable.

In the eight short years since the start of the war in Lebanon, the Iranians had transformed themselves from troublemakers who were allowed a base there purely at Syrian sufferance, to owning a de facto state in Lebanon—Hezbollah. And there was nothing Syria could do about it. If it tried to close down Hezbollah, it would undermine the legitimacy of the Alawites who claimed to be at war with Israel. This was a reversal of fortune the Syrians had not seen coming. And now it was too late.

It didn't matter that the Syrians had a point as well: The chaos in Lebanon wasn't helping Syria. The Revolutionary Guards had turned Lebanon into a no-go part of the world, where no Westerner would dare set foot, and Syria's economy had suffered along with Lebanon's in a depression.

During the Cold War, Syria might have turned to the Soviet

Union for economic assistance, but that was no longer an option since the fall of the Berlin Wall. Syria always had the option of throwing a bone to the United States, expelling the Iranians. But what could the United States offer Syria? Syria couldn't dispense with Iran as an ally until the United States was prepared to offer a major concession, which is something Washington clearly wasn't prepared to do. In fact, both the George H.W. Bush and Clinton administrations pointedly decided to ignore signs of an Iran-Syria split.

Syria's hands were tied. Not only was it not possible to expel the Iranians, which would lead to a wave of Islamic rage, Syria didn't know enough about the Iranians to take even selective, punitive measures. The Revolutionary Guards had no clear structure. Their officers traveled under aliases. But there were other ways for the Syrians to make their displeasure with Iran known.

In 1990, tension between Syria and the Iranians had grown to the point that it looked as though it would turn into a public brawl. In April, Amal fighters acting under Syrian orders raked the Iranian embassy with machine-gun fire. In Damascus, the Syrians towed away an armored car belonging to the Revolutionary Guards. The Iranians retaliated against Syrian diplomats in Tehran, but decided it wasn't wise to escalate.

In a meeting of Iran's Lebanon committee, foreign minister Ali Akbar Velayati admitted that Iran could not operate in Lebanon without Syria. He went on to express confidence everything would blow over.

Still, something had to give.

As often happens in the Middle East, everything changed with a quick turn of the kaleidoscope. It started on August 1, 1990, when just a week after the meeting between the Syrian and the Iranian emissary, Saddam Hussein invaded Kuwait.

Syria fought, at least in name, on the same side as the United States—a decision that paid off in late 1990 with the passage of the

Taif Agreement. Taif, which had U.S. backing, put a formal end to Lebanon's civil war and officially gave Syria a free hand in Lebanon. Taif legitimized Syria's presence in Lebanon, a long-sought recognition of its role in that country. With the Israelis now losing in south Lebanon, some ten years after they'd invaded, it looked more and more as if Syria had lost the campaign but won the war.

In September 1991, the Syrians, encouraged by their newfound legitimacy in Lebanon, informed the Revolutionary Guards they would have to give up the Sheikh Abdullah barracks in Balabakk— the same barracks Iranian surrogates had seized in November 1982. Turning the barracks back over to the Lebanese state was a signal that Syria would at least go through the motions of handing Lebanon back its sovereignty. Would the Syrians now ask Iran to give up the Islamic resistance too?

Now that Syria had a stronger stake in the stability of Lebanon, the Iranians asked themselves the same question: How far was Syria willing to go in its search for respectability? Iran's giving up terrorism was one thing—Iran could certainly stand to clean up its own reputation—but the Islamic resistance was something else. Something Iran would hold on to. As a member of Hezbollah's politburo told me in March 2008, it was in 1990 that Hezbollah gave up "the tactics of civil war," by which he meant kidnappings and terror, though he couldn't bring himself to say it. In its place, Hezbollah adopted a two-pronged policy: social development of the Lebanese, including building bridges, hospitals, and schools—and military confrontation against Israel.

It was easier to change course when the Da'wa 17, including Imad Mughniyah's brother-in-law—the man for whom Mughniyah hijacked Kuwait Airways flight 422—managed to escape from prison when the United States invaded Iraq in August 1990. Now that his brother-in-law was free, Mughniyah no longer had an argument for holding the Western hostages he'd kidnapped in the eighties—men such as Terry Anderson and Terry Waite.

Although Iran never acknowledged its role, it ordered Hezbollah's Hassan Nasrallah to release the hostages. As soon as Nasrallah passed down the order on December 4, 1991, tensions between Iran and Syria immediately eased. With order restored in Lebanon, Syria's position in the world, along with its economy, would now improve. And in fact, Iran had given up very little. As a bargaining chip, the hostages were worthless to them.

Following the Iran-Contra scandal in 1987, no U.S. administration would dare talk to, let alone negotiate with, Tehran over hostages. Iran realized the hostages were only a liability to them, especially at a time when it needed fighters in the south and it was trying to turn Hezbollah into a legitimate, sovereign government.

Still, this didn't mean that Iran now had intentions of giving up the Islamic resistance. By 1991, even though the Revolutionary Guards were participating less and less in Hezbollah's political and economic deliberations, they still kept two members on Hezbollah's Military Committee. Revolutionary Guard officers oversaw every important attack on the Israelis.

The new arrangement suited Syria as well. Syria was happy that Iran had narrowed its focus to Israel, still the common enemy. Moreover, the war in southern Lebanon was far from Syria's front lines; there was little chance of Israeli retaliation against Syria or Syrian troops in Lebanon. And there was also the fact that Syria had international law on its side: under UN Resolution 425, adopted in 1978, Israel was obligated to leave Lebanon.

Still, Syria would keep a tight grasp on Lebanon's day-to-day politics. The Syrians believed they needed to dominate Lebanese politics, protect their old allies like Amal, and hold on to the old order. Syria never put it this way, but it was quietly fighting the Islamicization of the Middle East, trying to hold back Hezbollah. But as it would turn out, Syria was like the Dutch boy with his finger in the dike; it had no chance.

Nasrallah complained to the Iranians that Syria was denying

Hezbollah the representation it deserved in the Lebanese parliament, just as it had in the first parliamentary elections it ran in 1992. Syria wanted not only to select who in Hezbollah could and could not run for seats, but to limit the number of seats it could win as well. Syria also forced Hezbollah candidates to run in unsafe districts, relying on parliamentary tactics to slow its seemingly uncontainable popularity. The Syrians reminded Hezbollah over and over of the "red line" protecting Amal.

Iran decided to compromise, choosing not to challenge Syria's political interference as long as it could keep the Islamic resistance. Syria was still capable of cutting off the Iranian and Hezbollah logistics line, blocking shipments to the Islamic resistance. So Iran compromised, giving up Beirut, minus the southern suburbs, and parliament to Amal in return for keeping its war against Israel.

If Washington's attention hadn't been on the Oslo Accords, this would have been the moment to drive a wedge between Iran and Syria. Doing so would have involved three simple steps: force Israel to withdraw from Lebanon as demanded in UN Resolution 425; make an important overture to Syria, such as returning the Golan Heights; and finally, in return, demand that Syria expel the Revolutionary Guards. But few in Washington could grasp the loss Israel was about to face in Lebanon, or the long-term boost it would give to Iran.

As it was, Iran and Syria devised an uneasy truce on their own. But it was one that would work almost exclusively in Iran's favor. First, Syria left Iran and Hezbollah alone to fight Israel in the south, the consequence of which was that Iran cemented its reputation as the only Muslim country in the world fighting Israel. Second, Hezbollah was able to turn itself into a legitimate political party in spite of Syria, building on its 1992 and 1996 parliamentary victories. And by not challenging Syria, Hezbollah began to establish its reputation as a mature, responsible player.

Hezbollah basically got everything it wanted. The onetime

terrorist Hassan Nasrallah became its secretary-general, it kept its war going against Israel, and it won legitimacy in the voting booth. It effectively appropriated large pieces of Lebanese state sovereignty, building schools, policing the south, and appointing judges. The southern suburbs competed as the capital of Lebanon, a place neither Syrians nor the Lebanese army was able to enter. Hezbollah—Iran—had redefined the notion of a state. And Lebanon, the country, had for all intents and purposes truly withered away.

Syria rewarded Hezbollah by letting it bring in increasingly sophisticated weapons: cruise missiles, passive night-vision goggles, antitank missiles, advanced high explosives, and communications intercept equipment to listen in on the Israeli military. Although it lacked tanks and heavy artillery, Hezbollah had developed a form of warfare that could still thwart the Israelis, make them give up ground, if nothing else but by attrition. By the early nineties, Hezbollah was indisputably the strongest military force in Lebanon.

By allowing Iran and Hezbollah to fight the Israelis on their own, Syria might have thought it was getting the better end of the bargain. But though the Syrians pretended they were still in charge in Lebanon, they were losing the hearts and minds of the Middle East. Syria was no longer the "front-line state" against Israel that it had pretended to be for the last fifty years. The Iranian Shia-led tsunami was roaring forth, and now the only question for many in the Middle East was whether they would take sides with Hezbollah or the Sunnis. Increasingly, the answer for most was Hezbollah.

The fact that Syria was forced to bow to Iran, and effectively let the Revolutionary Guards run a large part of Lebanon, was a crucial turning point in the modern Middle East. It was more evidence that the old Sunni order was incapable of stopping Iran and the new order it was bringing to the Middle East.

Iran's co-opting the Alawites would also lead to Syria's tacitly breaking with Saudi Arabia—something that had never happened in Syrian history, as Syria's bonds with Saudi Arabia had always seemed unbreakable. But Syria needed a strong ally, which Saudi Arabia was not. Iran replaced Saudi Arabia if for no other reason than Iran did a better job of protecting Syria from Israel.

With the 2005 assassination of former Lebanese prime minister Rafic Hariri, a dual Lebanese-Saudi citizen who was very close to the Saudis, Lebanon itself slipped out of Saudi hands. Hariri, often called "Mr. Lebanon," was the father of post–civil-war Lebanon. He wore many hats, including personally funding Saudi Arabia's favorite charities, helping to manage the Saudi royal family's money and decorating its palaces. Even when Hariri stopped being the Lebanese prime minister, four months before his assassination, the Saudis still saw him as their guy. But his death was a sign that Saudi Arabia was losing its influence in Lebanon to Hezbollah and the Shia, whom the Saudis despise.

Now that the Saudis had lost Syria and Lebanon, the only question was what other pieces Iran would manage to break away from the Sunni firmament.

If Iran succeeds in keeping a lid on Iraq, the more the Sunni Arabs will look to Tehran for a solution rather than Riyadh or Washington. Iran has responsive, reliable proxies in Lebanon, Iraq, Gaza, and Bahrain. Riyadh and Washington don't.

The shift in the balance of power has been evident in various Arab diplomatic overtures to Tehran. In addition to UAE and Saudi overtures to Iran, the king of Bahrain stated publicly that Bahrain supported Iran's civilian nuclear development program. Around the same time, the Saudi foreign minister was casting around, looking for international support, making an urgent trip to Moscow to try to stop Russia from sending more arms to Iran—something he obviously knew Washington could not accomplish.

The Sunni order is failing. Given the character of Sunni Islam—its lack of a clerical hierarchy and its lack of any real central authority, either religious or political—this was destined to happen. Modern Sunni Islam was never a force that could unify or bring discipline to the Middle East. It's probably just as well that it failed.

The Sunni fundamentalists have no real plan other than purifying Islam and imposing strict adherence to Sharia law. The Koran may have been a relevant source of law in the seventh century, but it is not today. Making the Koran the sole constitution for Muslims is like Christians taking the Old Testament as their sole source of law. With Sunni fundamentalists unable to stray far from the Koran's literal interpretation, they lack a constitutional or pragmatic model to follow.

The Shia, on the other hand, have a unique side to their religion—something called *ijtihad,* the "exercise of independent judgment." In effect, *ijtihad* means that a trained Shia imam may interpret the Koran according to reason and precedent; a strictly literal interpretation of the Koran is rare in Shia Islam. As Hassan Nasrallah himself defined it in an interview with an Arabic newspaper, "Ijtihad makes permissible adaptations to the requirements of time and place, permits one to respond to new demands—be they specific or general—upon the individual and community, state and society."

The practice has allowed the Shia to adapt much better to the twenty-first century. For instance, a Shia leader like Nasrallah has the authority to declare wars licit or illicit, while a Sunni *takfiri* would never be allowed to compromise with a *kafir,* a non-Muslim enemy.

Unlike common Sunnis, a Shia cannot interpret the Koran on his own. He needs an intervening authority, a *mujtahid*—someone trained to exercise independent judgment—to help. Nasrallah became secretary-general of Hezbollah not only because he fought on the front lines but also because he underwent years of formal training, in the Koran as well as subjects such as Aristotelian logic. Although Nasrallah falls just short of being a *mujtahid,* he acts as one, issuing edicts based on independent judgment, the Koran, and the sayings of the prophet. Nasrallah's approach to the world reflected the fact that Shia religious education is rigorous enough, and broad enough, to maintain much greater discipline than the Sunni can.

In Sunni Islam, by contrast, there is no hierarchy, and almost no discipline. A religious education may be limited to what a self-appointed sheikh in the mosque might tell you. Sunni *takfiris,* who so easily anathematize civil society and condone murder, are less grounded in Islam. Osama bin Laden is an engineer by training. His deputy Ayman al-Zawahiri is a medical doctor. The man who assassinated Anwar Sadat in 1981 was an army officer. The Sunnis follow these nonreligious leaders unconsciously, straying into messianic interpretations of the Koran. The Shia, by contrast, would never follow a fatwa, a religious order, issued by someone with bin Laden's thin scholarship.

The question comes down to this: Who would America rather negotiate with as the Middle East spirals deeper into violence—a Shia *mujtahid*? Or a Sunni *takfiri* who would as soon cut your head off?

Compare these two kinds of conduct: It came out in a British court that in 2007 Saudi Arabia's former ambassador to the United States, Bandar bin Sultan, threatened to look the other way to make it easier for *takfiris* to conduct attacks in Britain if Britain persisted in investigating his crooked business deals with a British company. This threat, from the West's supposed Mideast ally, occurred at a time when Iran was talking to American diplomats in Baghdad and re-straining Shia militias from attacking our troops.

Unfortunately, in the United States, there's a persistent, mistaken belief that the Iranians are irrational and dogmatic. They were in the eighties, no doubt. But their more recent record shows they've learned to pursue their interests more coldly and rationally, in a way we can understand as well as bargain over. Unless things drastically change, Iran holds more promise than the Sunni as someone we can talk to.

This argument is strengthened by the fact that Iran's dominance in the Middle East is a fait accompli. Iran has already absorbed more land, influence, and control of trade routes than anyone since the Ottomans. Iran's empire is already half built; we can't stop it now short of starting World War III. Effectively containing Iran would mean a thirty-year cold war. It would take a massive effort, akin to trying to push back East Asia's financial might.

It's time for America to look beyond its historical animosity to the Iranians and sit down with them in wide-ranging negotiations. After an agenda is agreed on, the Americans would have to test Iran, and vice versa. It would require the Americans to forget the past, including Iran's terrorist past in Lebanon. But the Americans have certainly done that before with other countries and organizations—Arafat and the IRA, to name just two.

Just as important, there are no alternatives. America's two traditional allies in the Middle East are failing states. Pakistan is held together by an army that gives every sign of cracking. Saudi Arabia is led by a flamboyantly corrupt, greedy royal family, taken seriously by almost no one save the United States. These are the least well-positioned countries to serve our long-term national security interests.

Saudi Arabia has been the undisputed guardian of Islam's "two holy places"—Medina and Mecca—since the Al Saud captured them in 1924. Now, with this seismic shift of power and the question of whether Saudi Arabia will really hold together, do Americans really care whether Iran assumes responsibility for these holy places? Could that really be worse than the Saudis' showering money on Sunni fundamentalists, which brought us 9/11?

The fact remains that Saudi Arabia has no control over its proxies. During the Soviet invasion of Afghanistan, the Saudis, along with the Americans, handed out billions to Afghan proxies without having any idea who they were or what they ultimately wanted. These are the same proxies who turned around to attack the Pakistani army, America's ally, in the lawless northwestern tribal region. President

Musharraf, a man considered a proxy of both the United States and Saudi Arabia, himself was the target of two assassination attempts. And Pakistan, Saudi Arabia's close ally, is not getting any better: as Pakistan's war on al Qaeda and the *takfiris* ground to a halt in 2007, the Pakistanis acknowledged they had lost control of a large part of their country.

Even if the United States didn't take notice, Iran certainly did. In November 2007, in a remarkable *Washington Post* blog titled "Why Not Dissolve Pakistan Too?", Ali Ettefagh, an Iranian who reflects some thinking in Iran, argued that Pakistan is not a country, and its borders and regime are not worth fighting for. Pakistan is a colonialist confection, five Muslim provinces carved out of British India—provinces with different histories, languages, and cultures. And it has been a mess ever since partition, with coups, ethnic slaughter, a thriving narcotics trade. It's the new rear base of al Qaeda.

Pakistan is a "relic," Ettefagh wrote, like Iraq. Neither should really exist as a supposedly unified "country." In the case of Pakistan, Ettefagh argues the five provinces should be divided into separate states.

It's obvious why Iran is succeeding. If you're a poor baker in Beirut's southern suburbs, furious about the fact your country is being occupied and looted by foreigners, whom are you more likely to throw your weight behind? Fat, self-indulgent Saudis who haven't fought a day for people like you? Or Iran's proxy, Hassan Nasrallah, who obeys Islam's antisumptuary laws, living in a small, shabby apartment like everyone else, eating simply, sitting humbly on the floor when he receives a guest, and working to keep Hezbollah free of corruption? For Lebanon, this kind of leadership has been a seismic shift, especially since Lebanon has historically been one of the most corrupt places on Earth.

The Palestinians, too, have suffered corruption. The head of Palestinian security in the seventies was notorious for having married a Miss Universe and being a fixture on Beirut's all-night party scene, his armed goons hanging out in front of nightclubs provoking fights. And Yasser Arafat died with a fortune in the tens of millions of dollars—money that was supposed to have gone to the Palestinian people.

Hezbollah quickly stamps out any hint of corruption, giving itself an invincible populist patina. What poor baker wouldn't want to drive out the Saudi royalty, balance out the vast economic inequities, drive Israel out, and reestablish Islam as the populist force it once was? If the Iranians are able to carry this off, as they intend to, it will be a social revolution of staggering impact.

Symbols of the Sunni Arab Gulf's decadence are everywhere. During a trip to the United Arab Emirates in January 2008, President Bush made a speech calling for the Arabs to ally with the United States and confront the looming Iranian threat.

"Iran," Bush said, "is the world's leading sponsor of terrorism."

But Bush's words didn't attract nearly as much attention as the venue in which he delivered them: the Emirates Hotel, where an average gold-plated suite runs $2,450 a night. The beachfront hotel, which cost $3 billion to build, sits on a 1.3-kilometer stretch of sparkling white sand, every grain of it imported from Algeria.

And that's not the UAE's only superluxurious folly. The famous Ski Dubai is a giant indoor ski resort in one of the largest malls in the world, the Mall of the Emirates. Complete with Alpine chalets and fir trees, it provides 22,500 square meters of slope sitting on 6,000 tons of artificial snow, kept at freezing year-round to counter the almost continual hundred-plus-degree temperatures outside. The Gulf reminds you of nothing so much as Havana in 1959, with its sumptuous beach hotels, the day before Castro's revolution.

A friend of mine who worked in the embassy in Riyadh told me, "Don't underestimate the capacity of the Saudis to suffer"—to simply put up with the grotesque disparity of wealth in their country. But there's more going on here than just a question of haves and have-nots. There's a moral laxness on the part of the Sunni Arabs, a grasping, philistine bent that doesn't lend itself to fighting off a new Persian empire.

I spent some time in the Gulf after 9/11, trying to figure out if it was capable of pulling itself together to prepare for the Iranian tide sweeping away everything before it. One of my best contacts was a security official working for the Al Nahyan royal family in the Emirates. He had no illusions that his country's vast wealth could guarantee immunity from Iran's growing empire.

"Look," he told me, sitting in the lobby of a beach hotel in Abu Dhabi, "the Nahyan are doing the best they can." To make his case, he told me a story.

For several years, he was in charge of personal security for Sheikh Zaid, the now deceased president of the Emirates. One day the electricity went out—a very rare occurrence in that country. Sheikh Zaid's palace had backup generators, so he wasn't suffering. But the longer the electricity remained off, the angrier he became.

Zaid told my friend to pick up the official in charge of Abu Dhabi's power plant. All of them, including Zaid, then drove together out to the plant. Zaid didn't say a word on the trip out, but it looked as though he was about to blow up.

"Stop here," he told the driver when they arrived at the front of the plant. "Now," he said to the power plant official, "take off your shoes." The man did as he was told.

"Okay," Zaid said, "you can walk back to Abu Dhabi, get a taste of the misery you are causing my subjects."

Zaid was also an environmentalist. He decreed that no trees should be cut down anywhere in the Emirates, under any circumstances. And as everyone in the Emirates learned, Zaid kept close track of the few trees that were there. This meant my security official friend coordinated with construction companies to temporarily unearth trees in the middle of the night and replant them before Zaid woke up.

One night this same security official called me. CNN had aired a report about a new technique, developed in Kazakhstan, for seeding clouds. And an American had just shown up in the Emirates claiming he had a license to export the technology. My friend wanted to know what I thought about the guy, and the technology.

The American turned out to be a fraud, and Zaid passed on investing. But it was more evidence of how desperate the Emirates are to modernize, and how willing they are to spend their vast reserves of money to do so. Yet what good would that do against Iranian rockets on the other side of the Gulf?

During my last trip to the Emirates, as the shadow of Iran cast an ever darker shadow over the Gulf, that was my friend's very worry.

"So we have skiing," he said. "Iran could send Ski Dubai, our hotels, and our oil up in flames in a matter of minutes. We can't do anything about it."

The Gulf Arabs indeed realize that the only thing that stands between them and Iran is the U.S. Navy's 5th Fleet, America's willingness to do their fighting for them. This gives the U.S. an enormous leverage over the Gulf Arabs. But the question is, is it worth it for the Americans to protect the Arabs from the Iranians?

The way decadence progresses, it's unlikely the Gulf Arabs' kingdoms will collapse in a day. If oil stays above $100 a barrel, the Gulf Arabs will be able to pay off their enemies, keep the doubters quiet, and keep their indoor ski resorts and gold-plated hotels full. But it won't change the fact that they are defenseless, or that it will be the Americans spending trillions to keep them from being invaded by Iran.

The Iranians know just how high the ethnic barrier is between them and the Arabs. But once again, fortune came to the Iranians' aid in the shape of Osama bin Laden. Bin Laden was a man who truly believed that 9/11 would be the beginning of the end of the United States. In the end, all he managed to do was prove how bankrupt the Sunnis were and make the Iranians look statesmanlike in comparison.

It's a simple matter of comparing bin Laden in September 2001 to Hassan Nasrallah in April 1996, when he provoked the Israelis into shelling Qana during Israel's Grapes of Wrath campaign. Yes, civilians died in both attacks. But Hezbollah's provocation served a strategic purpose, while bin Laden's was slaughter for slaughter's sake. This is a cold-blooded calculation, but it's one that will determine the future of the Middle East.

The team leader of 9/11, Mohamed Atta, was an Egyptian Sunni who drew a different lesson from the Grapes of Wrath attacks. Atta's reaction was blind rage. On April 11, 1996, a week before the shelling of the Qana refugee camp, Atta wrote a will that offered his life in revenge for the Israeli offensive in southern Lebanon. At the time, the Israelis were killing civilians in their sweeps across the south. After Qana, Atta's decision to make someone pay was now written in stone. But that was the difference between Nasrallah and Atta: Nasrallah turned Grapes of Wrath into the last phase of a military victory over Israel. Atta turned it into a justification for aimless slaughter.

Who are these people who turn to random acts of rage and violence? The Sunni who end up in *takfiri* movements share with the Shia the common wound of dispossession. But it's how the *takfiris* react to it that makes them different. The second-generation Pakistani boy who lives in London is neither Pakistani nor British—he's twice exiled, first from Pakistan and second, internally, from British society. He ends up in the corner mosque, listening to a preacher who is more than likely to be self-taught and self-appointed, with scant knowledge of the Koran. There's no comparison between such men and Nasrallah, a man who makes decisions according to the rules and logic of the *mujtahid,* whose interpretation of Islam is subject to discipline and a hierarchy of learning. Who would you rather deal with, a Hassan Nasrallah or a Mohamed Atta?

The young man of Pakistani origin in East London, a typical *takfiri* recruit, doesn't even know what a purified Islamic state would look like. Nor does he understand that the Koran doesn't provide the rules for governing a modern country. But the *takfiris'* "purification of Islam" is an appealing, simple message. As is the call to kill Crusaders and Muslim apostates who cooperate with the West. This was the same simple message used to justify the assassination of Anwar Sadat and the attempts on Pakistani president Musharraf and Egypt's president Nasser.

The *takfiri* doesn't question the sanctioned discrimination against the Shia, who often in Sunni countries aren't allowed to serve in sensitive government positions or perform Shia religious rituals. Even worse, in Saudi Arabia Shia are subject to punitive property seizure and even gang rape. The *takfiris* consider Shia apostates: their irrational hate for Shia, and the West, makes it easy for *takfiris* to recruit young men and women—but that's where their strategy ends. *Takfiris* say they're "weakening the enemy," but what does that mean? They have no second act, which makes the *takfiris* the Khmer Rouge of Islam: shedding blood is the only message.

Hezbollah's flexible doctrine allowed it in 1985 to withdraw its demand for an Islamic state in Lebanon, implicitly accepting a multisect state, permitting Christians and Jews to live under the same secular rule of law. It also allowed Hezbollah to drop terrorism for a classical military struggle. On the other hand, even after the failure of 9/11, the *takfiris* have been unable to draw any lessons from their failure. With the hundreds of suicide bombings in Iraq and Afghanistan, it looks as though they've learned nothing at all.

Which brings us back to the same question: Who would you rather deal with?

10

ULTIMATE SACRIFICE:

MARTYRS, SUICIDE BOMBERS, AND THE

FIGHT FOR THE SOUL OF ISLAM

There's not a single known instance of an Iranian suicide bomber since the end of the Iran-Iraq War in 1988. There's also no evidence that Iran has ordered any suicide bombing attacks by proxies since the Israelis left Lebanon in 2000. Many would argue that the fact the Iranians had ever sponsored suicide attacks at all makes them irrational and impossible to negotiate with. But that's not the way the Iranians look at it.

A suicide bomber, for them, is the ultimate "smart bomb," little different from the wartime soldier who rushes a machine-gun nest to meet his certain death. For Iran, the suicide bomber is part of its military arsenal, a tool with a tactical military purpose. For Sunnis, on the other hand, suicide bombers are used for the vague objective of "weakening the enemy." While the Sunnis can't define the objectives of martyrdom, the Shia can. And the Shia are capable of stopping the violence when necessary.

The misconception many Americans have about Muslims is that they *all* hate the West. Not just the West's politics, but Western culture and Westerners personally. But that's only partially true. Yes, a small fraction of Muslims is driven by blind hate and wants to destroy the West, but most Muslims just want to be left alone. They don't care about a jihad against the West. The problem is separating one from the other.

In January 2008, a bomber walked into the five-star Serena Hotel in Kabul with two confederates carrying automatic rifles and grenades. He blew himself up, killing eight, including Afghans—believing Muslims. The Taliban, the Sunni *takfiris* of Afghanistan, claimed responsibility and threatened to start attacking restaurants Westerners frequent. It didn't matter to the Taliban that Kabul's restaurants cater to aid workers and not NATO troops. The only thing they cared about was that they're symbols of the West.

The intended target of the Serena Hotel attack, the Norwegian foreign minister, wasn't a military target. Neither were the people who died in the lobby. They were just ordinary people trying to help Afghans. Norway is a neutral country in the conflict between Islam and the West. It sponsored the Oslo Accords to stop the killing of Muslims as well as Jews. So the Serena attack had no practical objective other than slaughter, a misguided attempt to "purify" Afghanistan.

Days before that, an al Qaeda group ransacked the American school in Gaza—another act of blind rage against the West. And 9/11, too, was simply an act of hate against the West, with no military objective or, for that matter, comprehensible goal. The World Trade Center could never seriously be considered a military target. Some Muslim clerics would justify its destruction by claiming the people who died there paid taxes that go to a military that kills Muslims, reasoning that won't stand in any sort of rational discourse. In any case, it doesn't disguise the abiding hate these people have for us—the notion that in a clash of civilizations, everyone is a fair target.

There's a set of people in America who have focused on the radical wing of Muslim Brotherhood, on al Qaeda, and even on Iran, lumping them together, claiming they represent a wider hate that drives the Middle East. Since 9/11, without any evidence, these people have tried to make the case that Muslims intend to infiltrate the United States, bring it down from inside, and convert us to Islam. They search the Dumpsters of the world looking for evidence of this dark conspiracy.

But the truth is something different. When the Egyptian schoolteacher Hassan al-Banna founded the Muslim Brotherhood, his real interest was reforming Egyptian society, borrowing from the Koran as social doctrine rather than a call to war. Yes, the Muslim Brotherhood is an anticolonial movement, but mainly because the purification of Islam, the Muslim Brotherhood believed, would only occur if Muslims governed themselves.

Things went wrong when the Muslim Brotherhood's military wing broke off and resorted to violence. This was a reflection of how the Sunni, unlike the Iranian Shia, lack a hierarchy, a central point of authority. At the risk of gross oversimplification, the Sunnis lack discipline because they lack a pope, an institution like Shia Islam's grand ayatollahs.

Even during its worst periods of terrorism, Iran generally stuck to attacking military and diplomatic targets—the Israeli army, the Marines, U.S. embassies. The Sunni *takfiris,* on the other hand, never attempted to make this distinction. Again, Western concepts don't transfer easily to the Middle East. Yet the Sunnis are anarchists. And this isn't a recent occurrence: extreme Sunni movements like al Qaeda have flared up throughout the history of Islam. But they never end up attracting a broad base, and soon disappear.

Sunni *takfiris* believe they're in an existential fight against the West. Like Cambodia's Khmer Rouge, Peru's Shining Path, or even Mao Tse-tung's Cultural Revolution, they believe the West's influence, its intellectual and physical occupation, can only be reversed by erasing every symbol of the West—including decimating their own Western-educated intelligentsia, blowing up the Bamiyan wall carvings, or throwing away their toothpaste.

There's an undeniable lure for Sunnis in the promise of chaos. Osama bin Laden only began attracting a following when he called for the slaughter of Americans: "The ruling to kill the Americans and their allies—civilian and military—is an individual duty for every Muslim who can do it in any country in which it is possible to do it."

Al Qaeda and the *takfiris* are a threat we will struggle with for years. But when we take that part to represent the whole of the Muslim world, we are unable to separate friends from our enemies.

In her hijab, twenty-nine-year-old Palestinian Hanadi Jaradat looked out of place in Maxim's, a seaside Haifa restaurant. But she wasn't enough out of place for the security guard not to let her in—many Israeli Arabs these days dressed conservatively. Besides, the taxi driver she arrived with was an Israeli Arab. And she spoke fluent English.

Maxim's restaurant, owned by a Jew and an Arab, was the promise of what a secular Israel could be, Muslims and Jews living together. Many of the staff were Arab. Haifa, Israel's principal port, is more cosmopolitan than most Israeli cities.

Hanadi sat across from the driver. He'd picked her up at the crossing from the Palestinian West Bank, the one that serves the town of Janin.

The driver wasn't surprised a single woman was traveling alone. Hanadi was well spoken, educated, from a good family. Palestinian mores had been changing for a long time. He remembered the sixties and seventies, when Palestinian women started wearing miniskirts in the first sign of rebellion and sexual liberation. That rebellion would never reach the level it did in the West. Still, it was a sign that Palestinian women were modernizing in spite of the hijab.

Later, the driver said Hanadi was perfectly lucid and calm, just chatting about her family and Janin. It was Saturday, October 4, 2003, the Jewish Shabbat.

Hanadi watched the surfers catching the swell beyond the breakers. Although she had studied law in Jerash, Jordan, the world outside of Janin was alien to her. She'd been a virtual prisoner most of her life, stuck in the West Bank, in a society that couldn't quite bring itself to accept women as the equals of men. She'd been dragged into the resistance against her more cautious nature: her fiancé and her brother were Palestinian Islamic Jihad activists, and no doubt had Israeli blood on their hands. The Israelis had gunned them down in a "targeted killing" in Janin. She was standing next to her brother when he died.

The driver said she listened to a half-dozen of the kitchen staff, Arab Muslims, taking a break to eat. But more than that, she watched two Israeli Jewish families eating their Shabbat dinner. Three generations sitting together, laughing, savoring their day off. Hanadi commented to the driver on how cute the children were, running around the tables.

The taxi driver, now in prison for illegally transporting a West Bank Palestinian into Israel without a permit, isn't a reliable witness. The story he told later to the police undoubtedly was tailored to exculpate himself. Still, Hanadi couldn't help but have noticed those small children, seen their innocence. They were in no way responsible for the deaths of her fiancé and her brother, or the poverty in Janin.

Her last words to the taxi driver were "I'm fine. You had better go now."

As soon as the driver left, Hanadi stood up, walked between the two families, and pulled the pin on her suicide vest. She killed twenty-one people as well as herself. Two families, three generations.

Later, I found Hanadi Jaradat's father and mother in Janin. She was a wonderful girl, the father told me. Kind, a brilliant student.

She had a future. They'd had no idea what she was planning—it came as a complete shock. Of course. The families always claim they suspected nothing.

What did surprise me was the condition of their apartment. The day after the Maxim's attack, the Israeli military had blown up the Jaradats' house in retaliation. The family moved to a filthy second-story apartment on a narrow street with trash piled in the front. The day I arrived, Hanadi's mother was cooking with one of her sisters in the kitchen. But it was nothing like the elaborate meals Palestinians usually make. Most telling of all, they didn't ask me to stay to eat. This was a family who had given up, though I had no idea whether that had happened before or after the Maxim's attack.

I'd noticed in general that the town of Janin was getting poorer, looking more like Gaza, with Arab culture flaking away and the people coming to the end of their self-respect. Historically, along with Nablus, Janin has been a staging ground for Palestinian attacks against Israel. In turn, it has been the target of numerous Israeli sweeps, including a major offensive to clean out the terrorist cells. Hanadi Jaradat had grown up amid violence. She was taught that it was the way you solved problems.

I also met Sami Jaradat, a relative of Hanadi and one of the organizers of the attack on Maxim's. Sami's brother was Hanadi's fiancé, the one killed in a "targeted attack." Sami, who gave Hanadi the bombing vest and filmed her last testament, which aired on television, is now serving twenty-one life sentences in a high-security prison.

"By the power of Allah," she declared in that last testament, "I have decided to become the sixth female martyrdom-seeker, who will turn her body into shrapnel, which will reach the heart of every Zionist colonialist in my country, and every settler or Zionist who has tried to sow death in my country."

It was a telling statement—and a telling attack—because it was directed at civilians rather than a military target, completely unlike anything Hezbollah carried out in Lebanon in the eighties and nineties. Iran by this time was an ally of the Palestinian Islamic Jihad, but there was no evidence the Iranians assisted in planning Hanadi's attack. The Iranians almost certainly weren't in touch with the Palestinian Islamic Jihad cell in Janin that had planned it.

Sami, small and wiry with intense green eyes, was a man who'd be happy to help a foreigner who got lost in Janin, and invite him for a cup of tea. A man you might keep in touch with after your visit.

He was quite insistent that Hanadi was supposed to attack a military target—a military bus or a group of Israeli soldiers. It was never supposed to be Maxim's. So what did Sami think when he heard she'd blown up a restaurant, killing small children?

"One cannot separate the kids from the adults," Sami told me, his green eyes unblinking. "Israeli society is a military one."

I'd heard this logic before. The children killed in Maxim's were going to grow up to be soldiers. Just as the people in the World Trade Center contributed to killing Muslims through taxes they paid. Still, this logic was so contorted, it surprised me. I couldn't help but challenge Sami.

"The Israelis say the same thing about Palestinian society," I told him. "They're all potential terrorists." Meaning, anyone is a legitimate target.

Sami didn't know what to do with that statement. He could only respond that the Palestinians, unlike the Israelis, don't have tanks or planes to fight back. An eye for an eye was all that mattered to him. Weaken the enemy as they weaken you.

What struck me about the attack on Maxim's was the randomness of the bombing, the aimless slaughter. If Sami was telling me the truth, that Hanadi was supposed to hit a military target, the Palestinian Islamic Jihad was incapable of controlling its people or even mounting an effective military campaign. Killing two Israeli families in an Arab/Israeli business was anything but effective. It didn't help the Palestinians' cause in the least.

The notion of martyrdom is so deeply ingrained in the Middle East that even secular groups have embraced it, young men who don't believe in the keys to heaven or the promise of seventy-two virgins.

In Tehran a couple years ago, I spent several days with former members of the Basij, the reserves of the Revolutionary Guards. They had been volunteers, some of them in their mid-teens when they were first sent to the front lines during the Iran-Iraq War.

I sat with one of the Basij on the roof of my hotel, looking over Tehran. In the distance, the Elburz Mountains were covered with snow. We were a world away from south Tehran, the poor part of the city where many of the Basij came from—as in so many conflicts, it was the poor who fought and died in the Iran-Iraq War. But if there was any bitterness or resentment on the part of this now middle-aged man, he didn't show it. Iran was his country, and he had done his duty.

I asked about the keys to heaven, the plastic keys the Basij were rumored to carry into battle, a promise of passage into heaven if they died. The question annoyed him.

"Getting killed wasn't our purpose," he said. "We went to protect and defend our country against an attack. And also we knew that getting killed is a part of war. I wonder what you call a soldier who's been killed for protecting your country. You wouldn't use 'killed' would you? There should be another respectful term for it, no?"

The more we talked, the more it was clear he equated martyrdom with nationalism—a sacrifice for Iran, nothing more. He claimed never to have seen a pair of plastic keys. He also dismissed the promise of seventy-two virgins for martyrs. Heaven for him was too abstract to talk about, and he looked at the promised virgins as Western lies meant to trivialize the Basij's patriotism.

I'd seen the same thinking in the way Hezbollah looked at suicide bombing. It was a military tactic, rather than a way to get to heaven. In all, Hezbollah produced thirteen acknowledged suicide bombers.

Cheap and lethal, they were supposed to force the Israeli army to give up ground, not to "weaken" them. Unlike Hanadi Jaradat's attack in Haifa, Hezbollah suicide attacks were a precision weapon used against military targets.

On November 11, 1982, the Israeli military headquarters in Tyre, Lebanon, was abuzz with the morning routine, a confident optimism in the air.

The Israeli invasion of Lebanon was succeeding. The Israel Defense Forces had completely crushed the PLO, cornered them in the Biqa' Valley and the far north, from where their rockets could no longer reach northern Israel. Yasser Arafat was finished. The Middle East looked as though it was finally going to be cleaned up, or at least the Palestinians subdued. Once the Lebanese civilian government restored its writ, the Israelis could go home.

The Israeli soldiers, many of them just girls with M-16s strapped across their backs, ducked into the military HQ building to get out of the rain. They would have been struck by the beauty of Lebanon's blue-green, silver-flecked sea and the coastline around Tyre that morning. The craggy limestone cliffs poking a finger into the water, capped with limestone houses like castles, would have made Tyre look medieval to them, so different from Israel, with its modern high-rises and shopping centers.

Alexander the Great captured Tyre in 332 B.C., denying the Persians their only port on the Mediterranean. From Tyre it seemed he would march unopposed across the known world, invade Persia, and keep going. Israel, too, felt it could march as far as its political will would take it. There certainly didn't appear to be anyone who could stop it.

The young Israeli soldiers marveled at how calm Lebanon had been, how friendly everyone had been, waving at the Israeli checkpoints. The Israelis had been welcomed by the Shia. Stories about roses thrown in front of the Israeli tanks weren't true, but the

Lebanese Shia really did seem relieved to finally be rid of the Palestinian militias. The Israelis were so confident, they were even talking to the Shia about turning parts of southern Lebanon over to them. Armed and committed, the Shia would keep out the Palestinians.

There had admittedly been some problems. A tank crossing a farmer's field. Israeli checkpoints that weren't always polite with the Shia. But that was seen on all sides for what it was—unfortunate mistakes, easily forgotten in the wake of an invasion.

At a little after eight in the morning, a boy driving a minivan approached the eight-story Israeli military headquarters. The van looked like any one of the thousands of vans racing around Tyre. There was no reason for anyone to be suspicious. The boy asked an Israeli soldier standing out front if he could make a U-turn. No one suspected anything until the van lurched toward the main entrance, where a group of Israeli soldiers had just walked in. By then, it was too late. Even to run.

The van exploded inside the building, killing seventy-five Israeli soldiers and fourteen Arabs. If this had been a missile fired from a helicopter, it would have been called a surgical strike. But it was a suicide bomber, an attack claimed by the Islamic Jihad Organization. The shock was so profound for the Israelis that to this day, official Israeli websites claim the blast was due to a gas leak.

This attack would mark for many Israelis the beginning of the end for the Israeli occupation of southern Lebanon. The Israelis should have pulled out then, many thought, rather than wait for a popular confrontation, like the one that would come in Nabatiyah a little less than a year later. But then again, who knew that this would be only the first of many suicide bombers?

The driver of the van was Ahmad Qasir, a fifteen-year-old from the village of Dayr Qanun al-Nahar. Years later, I went to see his family, hoping to get clues about the event that ultimately triggered one of the most significant defeats in modern military history.

The Qasirs' home is more of a cave, cut into the side of limestone walls. I followed Ahmad's mother into the dark living room. She turned on the lights, revealing several large portraits on the wall.

I recognized Ahmad from newspaper photos, a pudgy boy with a sad expression. After Hezbollah identified him as the driver of the van in 1985, the Lebanese and Arab press descended on the Qasirs' house, and posters of Ahmad appeared all over Lebanon. From his picture, he looked like an improbable hero.

Another picture was of Musa, a second martyred Qasir son. The third was of Abd-al-Mun'im Qasir, a relative, who had died somewhere fighting the Israelis. And in the middle, the largest picture was of Ayatollah Khamenei. There was no doubt where this family stood.

I started by asking about Abd-al-Mun'im.

"He was martyred, but no one knows where," Ahmad's mother told me.

I had never heard of Abd-al-Mun'im Qasir before; for some reason Hezbollah had never announced where he'd been killed and turned him into an icon, as they did with so many martyrs. This was unusual, and I immediately wondered if he was the driver of the van that in 1983 destroyed the U.S. Marine barracks in Beirut. Or maybe the driver of the GMC pickup that blew up the U.S. embassy there in April 1983. I doubted Ahmad's mother knew. There was no point in pressing her.

But she did claim to know the history of the resistance, how it started. When Ahmad drove his van into the military intelligence headquarters in Tyre, Hezbollah didn't exist, at least under that name. It was an ad hoc organization then, its leadership known only to a few people. It certainly was an unknown entity for the Israelis. If they had known about its capabilities, they would have taken precautions.

Ahmad's mother was resigned to his death. By the time I met her, it had happened more than twenty years ago. I had the feeling this is what life had prepared her for, to lose two sons for some cause she couldn't completely comprehend. Did she really feel the anger that had driven her son to kill himself?

I asked her how many Israelis Ahmad had killed. She thought three hundred.

"It was more like three hundred seventy-five," a voice said from behind me.

It was Ahmad's sister, whom I'd been introduced to when I arrived. Though both she and her mother were inflating the true number, I didn't attempt to correct her.

"They weren't expecting it," the sister said. "And it was in the middle of a rotation."

Ahmad's sister knew the story intimately, how Ahmad approached the Israeli sentry and asked if he could make a U-turn. And how instead, as the sentry watched, he'd rammed the van through the front door.

They were surprised the Israelis hadn't seen it coming. But the Israelis didn't know about martyrdom, she said. They disregarded the lessons of the Iran-Iraq War, then in its second year—how tens of thousands of young men heedlessly charged the Iraqi front lines, giving up their lives. For the Israelis, the waves of Iranian martyrs in Iraq must have seemed as much ritual sacrifice as military tactic.

The sister made it a point to remind me that the Iranians exported the tactic of martyrdom to Lebanon. And that her brother was the first Lebanese martyr.

She also pointed out that Ahmad was the first martyr to drive a car into a target. In Iran, the practice was to charge Iraqi front lines on foot.

There was one delicate question I wanted to ask. In a small family village like this, the idea of agnosticism or apostasy—of abandoning your religious beliefs—was unthinkable. Religion was as much a part of the fabric of life here as anywhere in the world.

"Was Ahmad a strong believer?" I asked.

"Of course. He used to pray and fast."

The sister caught on to what I wanted to ask, whether Ahmad had been programmed or possibly was unaware of what he was doing. For a long time we thought that suicide bombers were picked because they were psychologically flawed. She answered my question before I could ask it.

"There is nothing that makes a person rebel more than oppression, right?" she said. "So oppression gives birth to mutiny. Now when you see Israel invading and killing people, while you are not fighting back as is happening in Palestine—well, you are not fighting and dying. To fight and die is better than just dying."

I wanted to get back to Ahmad—the "prince of martyrs," as he is known today in Hezbollah.

"When he was in Saudi Arabia, he started saying that no one will shake Israel more than him," she told me. "His friends in the village would ask what he could do against Israel. He would reply, 'You will see what I will do to Israel.' "

The morning of the attack, Ahmad said nothing to his family. When he left the house, he asked what was for lunch. Anything he wanted, his mother replied. There was nothing unusual about him that morning.

"He was standing next to me as I was washing the dishes," Ahmad's mother said. But not long after he left, they heard the explosion. They were standing outside, next to the fountain on the veranda—you can almost see Tyre from there.

Ahmad's identity was kept secret until the Israelis pulled out of Tyre, so they couldn't take retribution against the Qasir family. In fact, the Qasirs themselves weren't told for two years that it was their son who had driven the van into the Israeli military headquarters.

"They first told us he had been detained," the mother said. "We would look for him in prison. We searched in the beginning in the hospitals."

I asked what part Iran played in Ahmad Qasir's martyrdom.

"While he was in Saudi Arabia, he became psychologically prepared for it," the mother said, sidestepping my question.

His sister put it in historical context.

"For the Shia, the concept of martyrdom comes from the Imam Husayn"—the seventh-century martyr who died at Karbala and is celebrated on Ashura—"who is the symbol of martyrdom and resistance," she said. "The modern concept of martyrdom started in Iran and spread. But this idea is present in the mind of every person. It isn't because there are martyrs in Iran that there are martyrs in Lebanon. No."

I asked her about the details leading up to Ahmad's attack. Was there a fatwa? Was he recruited by the village imam? How was the attack put together?

"God only knows about these things."

I was particularly interested in the fatwa, because it fit my conceptual framework of discipline among the Shia.

She said a fatwa wasn't needed. You only needed oppression and the example of Imam Husayn, the Koran. I still had my doubts. In the 1988 Kuwait Airways hijacking, Mughniyah specifically asked a cleric for a *khayra,* something like a fatwa, before ordering the two Kuwaiti passengers executed. And there were dozens of other incidents we knew about where Hezbollah sought the blessing of religious authority before making an attack.

I asked her whether it was worth it, sacrificing her brother.

She looked at me with an ironic smile that made me wonder whether she'd known about it from the start. Had she talked it over with Ahmad, pushed him, kept up his resolve?

"Of course it was worth it," she said. "Until that day, Israel had never tasted defeat."

"Where is Ahmad now?" I couldn't resist asking.

"In heaven, with Imam Husayn," the mother answered.

The sister added, "For us, in the holy Koran, it says that heaven's beauty is beyond anything you have seen. And those who go to heaven have done great things. The highest ranks are for martyrs."

A conversation I had with Ayatollah Sanei, a reformist grand ayatollah who lives in Qum, only confirmed my impression that Shia ideas about suicide bombings differ substantially from those of the Sunni *takfiris*. The Shia, at the very least, are able to articulate the purpose of martyrdom.

It was April 2005. I walked through a courtyard and up to the second floor of a nondescript building to the ayatollah's office, where I was offered a seat and a cup of sugared tea as I waited for the man who was revered as a *marja' al-taqlid*, a source of learning and moral rectitude, a living paradigm to be emulated by his followers.

I asked him how martyrdom came to be adopted at the beginning of the Iran-Iraq War.

Sanei told me that the idea of martyrdom was not unique to Islam but found in many societies. It was something a society needed, a simple matter of self-defense. It is within human nature, he said, to defend oneself. "Martyr," then, is only a name for those who died defending the greater good.

"Is martyrdom a personal choice?" I asked.

"It's a personal choice," the Ayatollah replied. "Anyone can decide to go or not to go. But the law of God is you should go and fight."

Was martyrdom an important weapon of Islam?

"Yes. In the same way that defense is a worthy value, so is martyrdom. Martyrdom is the great and worthy child of defense."

Did martyrdom make a difference in the Iran-Iraq War?

Sanei wouldn't answer my question, other than to say, "We had no other options."

I persisted and asked whether Iranian suicide bombers helped demoralize the Iraqi army. Or did he think it was just throwing away lives?

"It did have an effect," Sanei said. "But because foreign powers supported Iraq, it wasn't decisive."

I'll say it for Sanei: Belief alone wasn't enough to win a war.

Sanei was quick to defend Ayatollah Khomeini. He said Khomeini had managed to drive all the Iraqi forces from Iran. His military strategy, the embracing of martyrdom, had been worthwhile.

I asked Sanei what he would say if a young man came to him today and asked to go on a suicide mission.

"I would tell him to look at the politics of the world, think about the enemies' plans, think about the people," he told me. "And if martyrdom serves a higher objective, well, then, he decides for himself."

I pressed him further. In that case, why were there no more Iranian martyrs? How were Iranians able to keep an individual choice like that under such remarkable control? Did they have an ability to turn it off and on?

I was getting at the discipline question. I wanted to ask directly if the Shia were more disciplined than the Sunni. But I sensed that framing the question precisely in those terms would offend him.

"At the war's end," he said, "Iran no longer needed suicide bombers to defend itself."

But I wasn't prepared to let it go at that. A few days before our meeting, Jewish Israelis were caught trying to blow up the Al-Aqsa Mosque in Jerusalem. They were arrested. Could this not be construed as an act of martyrdom? The defense of Judaism—a legitimate act of defense?

Sanei answered with a non sequitur. "Whoever wants to desecrate holy places must be stopped by force. With all your souls," he intoned, "eradicate oppression." This was, he said, the same way Khomeini's guidance had inspired the Lebanese. "He had a great impact and saved Lebanon from captivity."

I pressed further. "What about the Sunni suicide bombers in Iraq and Afghanistan?" I asked. At the time of our meeting, Sunni *takfiri* suicide bombers were blowing themselves up in markets and schools every day. Weren't these people doing the same thing Sanei suggested? Looking around, seeing what they perceived as an intolerable injustice, and making the decision to defend themselves?

Sanei started softly, almost whispering. He said he didn't think the chaos in Iraq would lead to a general war among Muslims. Ayatollah Sistani and Iraq's other learned *mujtahids* would prevent it, he said.

"But who are these people?" I pressed. "These suicide bombers?"

"They are criminals," Sanei said, his voice rising. "They are against humanity. Not only are they not human beings, they're not even feral animals. They are worse than desert wolves."

Sanei was angry. And his anger was clearly not summoned for my benefit.

What if these suicide bombers didn't stop?

"They will be stopped by force," he said.

Sanei's point was clear enough now: Suicide bombing wasn't meant to be a free-for-all, a decision made independently by anyone with a grievance, to be carried out when and where he felt like it. It had to be controlled by someone, carefully aimed at a military target, by a leader, a military, or even a state. Otherwise, it was an act of aimless slaughter.

"Why is it that the followers of Ayatollah Sistani have such good behavior?" I asked. "They're not committing suicide operations now."

Sanei paused and looked at me. "It is obvious," he said. "They are rooted in the religion. Their belief in a religious leader brings order."

Sanei didn't say it outright but he might as well have: The Shia are disciplined, unlike the Sunnis, the savage wolves.

In contrast to Iranian Shia, Sunni *takfiri* suicide bombers are less educated, less well vetted, less clear about their objectives. They're more likely to drift off into undisciplined, aimless violence. The difference in quality of recruits was never more apparent to me than when I interviewed a would-be Sunni suicide bomber in April 2007.

I was in Kabul, one of those cities the centuries have passed by. With its stone houses burrowed into the stone hills, it's biblical—and has the worldview to go along with it. I was escorted into an office deep inside the headquarters of the Afghan intelligence building.

A guard pushed a young man through the door toward me. He was little more than a boy, his adolescent skin pimpled and his hands shaking at the idea of meeting an American. He had never met a foreigner before, the Afghan intelligence official told me. He was terrified.

Dressed in a loose-fitting *salwar kameez,* the boy sat in front of me, his hands on his knees. In a soft voice, he told me he'd grown up in South Waziristan, a mountainous region in Pakistan on the Afghan border. Everyone in his family of poor farmers had been a devout believer in Islam and went to the local mosque every Friday, the men and the women segregated.

It was in the mosque where the boy's problems started; two young men from the Taliban approached him, having noticed his piety. They asked him if he wanted to learn about the real Islam. Over the course of two weeks, they inculcated in him a crude obligation to martyrdom: if the boy sacrificed his life he would go right to heaven, to be received by seventy-two virgins amid lush green grass and rivers. This was a description I'd heard from the Sunni—but not, in contrast, from the Shia Basij, with their more reasoned and disciplined view of martyrdom.

When the handlers showed the boy a suicide vest with detonator button, they told him that when he pushed it, it would send a message to God. God then would decide whether the boy was worthy for martyrdom. If he was, God would detonate the vest. I understood now why they'd picked him.

The boy's mission had been to put on a suicide vest, approach the governor of Jalalabad, and blow him up—and anyone else who happened to be standing around. Not only was the governor not a military target, but the bomb would also have killed dozens of civilians, innocent bystanders. But the boy didn't care, and neither did his handlers, the logic being that if you're anywhere near a potential target you're somehow guilty too. (Fortunately for the governor of Jalalabad, the Afghan police discovered the plot, and the boy never got close to him.)

Trying to fathom the depth of his naïveté, I asked the kid whether he'd heard about the Iraq War. Yes, vaguely, he said. But he couldn't fix the year it started or tell me where Iraq was. He also knew nothing about the Palestinian-Israeli conflict. Finally, I asked him about General Pervez Musharraf, the president of Pakistan.

"Well, he's a Jew, of course," the boy said. "An unbeliever who should be killed."

I was stunned. This was an elite recruit for the Sunnis, their ultimate smart bomb? A boy so naïve and uneducated he actually thought the president of Pakistan was Jewish? Once again, I was confronted head-on with the realization that the Sunnis in which we've put so much trust over the years were deranged. In comparison—can the morality of suicide bombing be put on a scale and weighed?—the Iranians and the Shia we fear so much are more reasonable, almost convincing.

Martyrdom was a pillar of Ayatollah Khomeini's revolution. You only need to visit Tehran's Behesht-e Zahra—Zahra's Paradise, or the martyrs' cemetery—to see evidence of a bright, constant readiness for sacrifice. The graves are marked with red tulips, the fountains run with red-colored water—symbols of the blood of martyrs. An endless recitation of the Koran echoes from blown speakers.

Iran encourages foreigners to visit, see for themselves the constant stream of visitors, just how real Iran's piety is. It's a reminder of what happens when Iran is stirred to defend itself, the nation, and

Islam. I've found that relatives in the cemetery are more than happy to talk, indifferent to the camera and tape recorder or to even the most personal questions.

The first couple I found was a man in his fifties dressed in faded shirt and cotton slacks, his wife in a chador pinched together right below her nose. They were seated on the grass next to a flat tombstone with a picture of a clean-shaven boy. The woman sliced a cucumber for me.

The man spoke for his wife. Her brother Nasser had died on the front, during a fight for a place called Masjid Sulayman. He was with the Revolutionary Guards. They'd received a call one morning, a voice on the other end telling them to come collect Nasser's body. When they arrived at the military morgue, they found his corpse shredded by shrapnel.

The man told me Nasser had been a pious boy. He had been wounded several times in the war but hid it from his family and kept volunteering to go back to the front. He was even hospitalized for three months once but never told his family. After his death, one of his commanders paid him the high compliment of comparing his courage to that of Abolfazi, one of Imam Husayn's bravest lieutenants.

"Is martyrdom worth it?" I asked.

"We are Muslims," he replied. "We believe if either our religion or our country is in danger, we have to defend it down to the last drop of blood."

I asked where they thought Nasser was now.

"We believe he is in heaven now. Whoever is martyred for his religious beliefs goes to heaven to be near our imams."

I asked the wife if she dreamed of her brother. Again, I was looking for similarities and differences between the Shia and Sunni.

She said that one time she dreamed she came here to Behesht-e Zahra to dig him out of his grave. But he got angry and told her to stop—he said he did not want to bring the outside world into where he was. He then showed her a key. "I have the key to God's house," he said. She asked him to leave the key there and come back to them. "No!" he said. "What are you talking about? Everyone wants this key." Though the plastic key is a myth for Shia, it is still a strong metaphor.

The couple comes every Thursday to visit Nasser's grave. Whenever his sister is troubled or anxious, she visits his grave to look at his picture. When she does, she told me, her problems go away.

Farther along, I found a woman in her forties, holding up her chador so it wouldn't drag on the ground. She was kneeling over a grave etched with the portrait of a young boy.

"This was your son?" I asked.

She nodded. "Seyed Mostafa."

"How old was he?"

"Fifteen."

"Bache bud," I told her. He was only a child.

"Fifteen and two months."

She told me he had just started high school when he decided to volunteer to go to the front. He was a Basij. His mother argued with him that he should finish his exams before going off to fight. But he said that would be too late.

"He said he was going for the ultimate exam," his mother told me.

She relented and signed a letter of parental approval for him to go to the front. He arrived during a fierce Iraqi assault.

"No one made him go," she told me more than once.

Was she remorseful?

"No. He did it for a good cause," she said. "I'm a mother. I do miss him. But I'm glad he did it for a good reason. For God!" She was convinced Iran's martyrs had won the war with Iraq. And besides, she added, "We will all be gone someday."

Where is he now?

"He is with our imams. He is their guest, with Khomeini." She dreamed of her son sometimes—when she was ill, he would come to her, embrace her. She would ask where he had been. He would laugh, and say I am here now.

Did she regret her son's death? "Not at all. I would have gone myself if I had been asked." She told me her other two sons had fought at the front too, but they came home.

"God didn't want them as martyrs," she said. She insisted I eat a piece of watermelon she'd brought to the cemetery. I was to celebrate in the cult of death too.

I've never seen a reliable poll about the number of Iranians prepared to sacrifice their lives. But the dozens of Iranians I talked to uniformly said they would do so—even the ones who had little confidence in the regime. I'd say offhand that martyrdom in Iran isn't going to pass with the disappearance of the mullahs.

The Iranian families of martyrs I talked to also uniformly justified the act as self-defense, a weapon of war. It served to protect borders rather than Islam. They never talked about "them"—the West—but about specific battles, on the front line, the confrontation of two nations, fighting to take and hold ground. The Iranians also kept looking for references that showed martyrdom was also a part of Western culture. The question kept coming up: Wouldn't you do the same in the same circumstances?

By the time I walked out of Behesht-e Zahra I was convinced that martyrdom for the Iranians was just another weapon, different from their wire-guided antitank rockets, their Silkworm missiles, or the Kalashnikov in that someone had to give up his or her life. It was an articulation of martyrdom I couldn't find among the Sunni.

It seemed to me that Khomeini's real, lasting legacy is martyrdom as a battlefield weapon. He elevated the martyrdom of Imam Husayn into service of the state.

• • •

On July 7, 2005, three suicide bombers blew themselves up in London's Underground. They timed their explosions for 8:50 A.M. to create the bloodiest mayhem possible at rush hour. Shortly afterward, a fourth suicide bomber blew himself up on a bus. In all, fifty-two people were killed, seven hundred wounded. Three of the bombers were British citizens of Pakistani heritage. All were Sunni Muslims.

I was in London not long after the attacks, filming a segment on suicide bombings for Britain's Channel 4. What struck me was that the friends and family of the 7/7 bombers refused to talk, let alone try to explain or apologize. I knocked on doors of people who knew the bombers. Invariably, the doors were slammed in my face. I couldn't help but note the contrast with the families in Behesht-e Zahra, who were more than happy to talk about sacrifice and self-defense, as was Hezbollah.

The attacks shocked Britain. The bombers had grown up in a Western democracy where there were more than enough outlets for dissent and opportunities to change the government from within. None had grown up in the Middle East. None could read the Koran in Arabic. They hadn't been exposed firsthand to the personal grievances that normally provoke people to slaughter civilians in this way. Instead, they picked up whatever justification they needed—not to mention the formulas for their homemade explosives—from the Internet.

The London bombings were similar to Iranian-backed bomb attacks in Paris in the mid-eighties—bombings that also targeted civilian areas, including department stores. There was a difference, though. At the time of the Paris attacks, Iran was at war, the seesaw of battles on the Iraqi front threatening its existence as a nation. The bombings were meant to stop the French from sending more missiles to Iraq. So the attacks—there's no attempt to morally justify them here, only explain the thinking behind them—had a defined military objective, unlike the 7/7 bombings.

There have been just a few other instances when Iran attacked civilians for defined military purposes. In 1992 and 1994, Iranian-backed terrorists attacked the Israeli embassy and a Jewish cultural center in Argentina, killing dozens of civilians. And in 1988, Iran sponsored a plan to bomb five civilian airliners. But as with the Paris bombings, the Iranians undertook these attacks in response to actions they considered provocations—Argentina was in retaliation for Israel's assassination of Hezbollah's secretary-general in 1992, and the airliners attack was a response to the U.S. Navy's shooting down of an Iranian Airbus in the Gulf in 1988.

Questions of moral calculus aside, the Paris bombings strategy worked. The French held secret negotiations with Iran, which resulted in an end to sending arms to Saddam Hussein. The French had a return address for the terrorism in Paris, someone they could bargain with. There was a clear list of demands the French had to meet, and there was nothing on the list that wasn't politically doable. There was a logic to it all—bloody, yes, but still, the point was the French had the option to make it stop.

The British, on the other hand, had no one to talk to to find out what had driven the 7/7 bombers, let alone to negotiate a settlement. The inspiration for the bombing was Osama bin Laden and al Qaeda's war on the West. But there is no traceable al Qaeda command structure. The remnants of al Qaeda are out of touch in the mountains of Pakistan. From the testaments the 7/7 bombers left behind, it was unclear exactly what they wanted. They asked that the "oppression of Muslims" stop, but that included everything from Russians killing Chechens to Indians killing Kashmiris. These were conflicts Britain could do nothing about.

After the 7/7 bombings, Britons were shocked at how closed and hostile the British Pakistani community was, unwilling to grieve or condemn the stupidity of the act. There were exceptions, but it was clear that while the Pakistani community condemned the means, they shared the 7/7 bombers' deep grievance, East versus West.

The 7/7 bombings were a signal of the steep descent into pure hatred these Sunnis feel for the West. Even as Iran-backed Hamas was trading rockets with Israel, they were still ready to talk. The most radical members of Hamas were not slamming the door in the face of journalists—there was still something to talk about, something to negotiate.

These British Pakistanis were different, closer to the Khmer Rouge soldiers I used to meet. They seemed nothing like the Muslims with whom I spent twenty-five years in the Middle East. They were so convinced of the justice of their cause, so convinced that it was an existential clash of civilizations, that they saw no need to explain their murderous tactics. They wanted to bring Britain down from the inside, to purify Islam, start over again, and adopt the Koran as their constitution.

In 2006, Hezbollah crossed the border into Israel. Its goal was to capture Israeli soldiers to exchange for Hezbollah "soldiers" held by Israel. During the course of the war, Hezbollah shelled Israeli cities, but it was in response to Israel's initial shelling of Lebanese cities. And after the assassination of Imad Mughniyah in February 2008, Hezbollah said it would retaliate internationally—possibly at a civilian target—but that was because Israel had struck outside the "agreed" field of battle, Lebanon. Inasmuch as there's order to war, Hezbollah believes it follows one.

Hezbollah's "logic of war" gives us, and Israel, room to talk. There is a way to stop the violence if we are prepared to compromise. But the Sunnis' violence comes from a different well. Or to mix the metaphor, there's no head to the Sunni snake, either to cut off or to reason with. Sunni beliefs, especially when they stray from orthodoxy, are much more sweeping and arbitrary than those of the Shia. You couldn't miss this difference in a conversation I had with a British Muslim *takfiri*.

Muhammad Khan lives in Derby, a small town in the Midlands, where life got worse after the factories closed. Plastic toys were scattered in the backyard of his ground-floor apartment. I walked in through a shabby kitchen, past dirty dishes stacked in the sink.

One of Muhammad Khan's cousins had died following a terrorist attack in Tel Aviv—a suicide bombing at an American-style pub called Mike's Place. The cousin strapped on a suicide vest and went to the bar with another bomber. When the second man blew himself up at the bar's door, either the cousin's vest failed to go off or he lost his nerve and ran. Days later his body was found in the sea, where he had either thrown himself or been thrown.

I talked to Muhammad Khan a year after the 7/7 bombings. He was still trying to justify the act.

"I will say that anyone who sacrifices their life for the sake of Allah," Khan said, "hands up to him."

I asked him if he considered himself British or a Muslim.

"I am a Muslim," he said. "Not a British Muslim."

Muhammad's accent belied the claim. But the way he saw it, being born in Britain was nothing more than an accident. It in no way affected his identity. I felt that creeping anomie again, the one I got when I talked to other Sunni *takfiris*. These were a people who had lost their compass, socially, geographically, ethically. As we talked, Khan kept repeating a particular phrase from the Koran: "striking fear into the hearts of the *kuffar*"—the unbelievers.

For Muhammad, becoming a Muslim involves nothing more than repeating the *shahada*, a witnessing of belief—"There is no god but God, and Muhammad is his messenger." And becoming a suicide bomber is nothing more than witnessing that faith in blood, both the martyr's and the victims'.

And what about the victims who died in the London Underground on 7/7?

"They go to heaven as well," Khan said. "Innocent people go to heaven."

So what did Britain need to do to avoid more attacks like 7/7?

"Accept Allah's law," he said. "End of story. Accept Allah's law and I think you'll have a peaceful life."

In other words, we either convert to Islam or die.

There is no way to argue with these people. I have no doubt the Sunni *takfiris* will go away one day, as other radical Sunni movements have, the day other Muslims turn against them. The question is what happens in the meantime. At this writing Iraq is better than it was during the first years of occupation, but that won't last forever. Chaos is never further than one mosque bombing away. NATO concedes that it's lost a large part of Afghanistan to the Taliban. Which leaves us with the question: What do we do in the meantime, until the violence subsides on its own?

11

MEMORIES THAT DON'T FADE:
WHAT IRAN *REALLY* WANTS

In May 2007, American and Iranian officials sat down together for the first time since the Iran-Contra affair in the mid-eighties. The meetings were held in an Iraqi government office in Baghdad, and the Iranians' demands were straightforward and reasonable.

First, they asked for a U.S. acknowledgment of Iran's role in Iraq—Iran's long-term, vital interest in stabilizing the country, ensuring the chaos doesn't spill over its borders. Second, they wanted assurances about Iran's internal security—an American promise that the United States would not meddle in Iranian politics.

Neither demand came as a surprise. Iran already had a role in Iraq, and had been publicly demanding a larger one for a long time. The unanswered question, though, is what does "acknowledge" mean? That Iran becomes America's new partner in the coalition, replacing the other countries that dropped out? That the West cedes Iraq to Iran? As for meddling, Iran, as we know, has never forgotten that Saddam Hussein tried to stir up the Arabs in Iran's Khuzestan Province during Iraq's 1980 invasion. Since then, the Iranians have been especially sensitive to rumors that the United States has been sending money and arms to Sunni and other Iranian resistance groups within its borders.

On the face of it, Iran's demands were reasonable, ones that the United States could accept if it weren't for domestic politics that constrain the United States from opening up a real dialogue with Iran. The Iranians did not demand that we abandon Israel, let oil go to $300 a barrel, or convert to Islam. The Iranians wanted to project themselves as a responsible power. The question is whether we can trust them.

The Gulf Arabs and the neocons don't. Iran's promises are worthless, they say. They're convinced that in sounding reasonable like this, Iran's only intention is to drive a wedge into any possible anti-Iranian coalition. And that the moment we let our guard down, the Iranians will start a war with Israel.

It's impossible to know exactly what the Iranians have in mind. But if the United States were to go by the standard of what the Iranians *do* rather than what they *say*, there's no evidence they'll start World War III. With all the weapons Iran has brought into Lebanon, it could have done that a long time ago. What America needs to do is ask for a truce with Iran, deal with it as an equal, reach a settlement one issue at a time, and continue along the same course until Iran is ready for détente—and maybe more.

So what do the Iranians really want from the West? And what should the West be willing to give? There's one more essential Iranian characteristic we need to understand if we are to answer that question.

It helps to remind ourselves once more that Iranians don't think like us. Their cognitive framework drives them to empire, and at the same time it informs their sense of justice and fairness. History, which we in the West pay less and less attention to, still plays a defining role for all Iranians.

For the thousand years before Islam, Iran's religion was Zoroastrianism, a monotheistic religion that has left indelible traces on Iran, at times causing other Muslims to wonder if Iran ever fully accepted

Islam. In his insightful book about Iran's Islamic antecedents, *In Search of Zarathustra,* Paul Kriwaczek argues that in many ways, Islam in Iran is nothing more than an accretion on something much older.

"Islam in the Iranian world is like a woman's plain *chador* worn over party finery," he writes, "a cloak that covers, disguises, or incorporates much traditional Iranian, pre-Islamic, Zoroastrian belief." Iran is a country that is at once "cynical, cultured, sophisticated, wise, and deeply religious."

Iranians see Americans not only as a people without a history, but also as a people who have no *sense* of history. An Iranian will tell you about points of history few of us think about—how the major Iron Age nomads spoke early Iranian, and about the Kimmerians, the Scythians, the Sarmatians, and the Alans. How Central Asia's major cities once were all Iranian-speaking.

Iranians will tell you how the sky-worshipping nomads who rode out of the Pontic-Caspian steppe were, with their innovative military tactics, undefeatable. They captured the Danube Valley in the second century A.D. and were conscripted to defend the borders of Roman Britain. They'll remind you that the Iranian nomads made it to France and Spain, and founded a state in North Africa. Even today, there are Iranian speakers living in the central Caucasus: the Ossetes, who number 600,000. They'll also tell you about the ancient kingdom of Samarkand, where people spoke an Iranian dialect called Sogdian. And still today it's important to Iranians that people living in the high Pamirs and Chinese Turkestan speak an early Iranian dialect, Khotanese Saka.

Pure, unadulterated monotheism blew out of the great empty Arab desert—not the Persian plateau, where the equal forces of good and evil battle over divine authority and humanity. The Arabs are dualistic too, but they lack the spiritual and intellectual depth of Iranians. And these are not the musings of some wide-eyed Iranian apologist—I say this despite the fact that the Iranians murdered my CIA colleagues in Beirut in cold blood, and would probably have killed me had they gotten their hands on me in the eighties. They are complex, with a very deep spiritual side.

Balkh, ancient Bactria, is believed to be the birthplace of the prophet Zoroaster. It is the "mother of cities," home to a civilization that goes back to the Bronze Age. It's where Zoroaster made his first convert. Nearby is where Alexander the Great found his Iranian bride, Princess Roxana, who became the mother of his only son.

Alexander the Great, known in Central Asia by the name Iskandar, was for Iranians the first in many waves of colonialist occupiers in the Middle East. Alexander was a barbarian as far as the Iranians are concerned. He burned the Avesta, the Zoroastrian holy book, and undertook a Hellenistic civilizing mission that attempted to destroy indigenous Iranian culture. The Zoroastrians curse him to this day; as the scholar A. V. Williams Jackson put it, in Zoroastrian eyes Alexander the Great was "the predestined tyrant of evil fate."

How does history help us understand the Iran of today? It's the filter through which Iranians look at the world, the deep foundation of their dreams of empire. Call it flawed if you like, but they see the world in stark, Zoroastrian terms, good versus evil. They see it through the prism of colonialism, whether it's Alexander the Great's, the prophet Muhammad's, or American occupation of Iraq. Occupation and colonialism are what drove real Iranian life underground, behind walls, silk curtains, or whatever metaphor we choose to explain the mystery of Iran. The only way Zoroastrianism survived was by going underground.

At all levels, Iran is never what it seems. Just as President Ahmadinejad is not really Iran's leader, his call for the destruction of Israel is something other than it seems. Ahmadinejad is making a rhetorical appeal to Zoroaster's ideal of good and evil—Israel is evil, Islam is unadulterated good. It's classic Zoroastrian dualism, the struggle between Light and Darkness. Zoroaster foretold the end of this battle: the coming of the Mahdi, known as Saoshyant in

Avestan, who would lead Lightness to victory. Ahmadinejad's apocalyptic interpretation of Islam—including money he spent as mayor widening Tehran's streets in anticipation of the return of the Mahdi—reflects a sense of this ancient Iranian religion.

And he is not alone. Christianity, too, sees the world in terms of good versus evil. But the difference is that although Christianity accepts evil in the form of the devil, he was never the equal of good, of God. The devil was a fallen angel, a temptation, but there was never the ongoing struggle, or jihad, between equivalent forces of good and evil.

In one of the best books written on Iran, *The Mantle of the Prophet,* Roy Mottahedeh speculates that Satan, who is barely mentioned in the Old Testament, became important for Jews only after the Babylonian captivity in the sixth century B.C., when they came under the influence of Persian dualistic beliefs about good and evil.

The Iranians reluctantly converted to Islam when it first arrived on the Iranian plateau, though they saw it as an impure, evil force. When Islam began to spread, the poets of Iran likened it to a foreign conquest, describing it with that very term, "evil." The Muslims were invaders. So at the center, always, there remained the Iranians' struggle against evil.

With this complicated worldview, it's little wonder Americans have found it so difficult to understand Iran, how it has so strongly resisted efforts to introduce modernity and accept the nation-state system and the Americans' laws, democracy, and notion of human rights. Americans can't understand how the Iranians can possibly look at the world in mystical terms like this—a battle of good against evil. To many, it sounds like excess cultural baggage better left behind. How can we even begin to base a discussion on Iranian empires dead thousands of years? Combine it all with the Islamic concepts of martyrdom and sacrifice and we have on our hands a country ready to fight to the last drop of blood for what it considers right. If the United States doesn't understand this now, it will in a hundred years, when it's a broken, spent force and Iran is either completely crushed or prevails.

The new Iranian empire is driven by the old one, because Iran's character and interests are enduring. You can overthrow the clerics, replace the government, and change the laws, but Iran will still be Iran, with its entrenched desire to overcome a history of occupation and a determination to come to the aid of oppressed Shia and Sunni alike. Considering the police state they live in, Iranians certainly don't live up to these ideals, but it's still important that this is how they see themselves. It colors every decision they make and everything they do.

On March 17, 2000, during Bill Clinton's final year as president, Secretary of State Madeleine Albright gave a speech at the Omni Shoreham Hotel in Washington, D.C. The people in the audience who knew America and Iran's troubled history were stunned by what she said.

"In 1953, the United States played a significant role in orchestrating the overthrow of Iran's popular prime minister, Mohammed Mosaddeq," Albright said. "The Eisenhower administration believed its actions were justified for strategic reasons, but the coup was clearly a setback for Iran's political development. And it is easy to see now why many Iranians continue to resent this intervention by America in their internal affairs."

She went on. "Moreover, during the next quarter-century, the United States and the West gave sustained backing to the Shah's regime. Although it did much to develop the country economically, the Shah's government also brutally repressed political dissent. As President Clinton has said, the United States must bear its fair share of responsibility for the problems that have arisen in U.S.-Iranian relations."

It was an abject apology, unprecedented in the history of American foreign policy and close to capitulation. But even that wasn't enough. Albright also apologized for American support of Iraq during the Iran-Iraq War.

"Even in more recent years," she said, "aspects of U.S. policy towards Iraq during its conflict with Iran appear now to have been regrettably shortsighted, especially in light of our subsequent experiences with Saddam Hussein."

Albright's speech was meant to be taken as it sounded: an apology, a magnanimous gesture, a breakthrough to Iran. It was a mea culpa for years of misguided policy, an opening no less dramatic than Nixon's trip to China in 1972. It was meant as a détente that would define the Clinton administration's foreign policy.

The trouble was, it landed in Tehran with not so much as a ripple. Albright could have been reading her grocery list for all the Iranians cared. What the Clinton administration had done was reduce America's problem with Iran to the 1953 Mosaddeq coup. As the Clinton administration found out, this was a gross oversimplification, not unlike our belief that Iranians are Islamofascists.

Yes, the United States engineered the overthrow of the Iranian prime minister, Mohammed Mosaddeq. But in fact, all these years the Iranians had looked at that as only one more piece of evidence that the West had colonial designs on Iran, rather than the important turning point in American-Iranian relations we had assumed it had been. As coups go, the Mosaddeq coup was a fairly benign one. Iran was never a true democracy; the Shah could change his prime minister when he wanted to. In not understanding Iran, Washington accepted the easy assumption that we had destroyed Iran's democracy, and that this was the only thing the Iranians have cared about since. The Mosaddeq coup is another prism through which we look at Iran, distorting the country beyond recognition.

At the same time, there's no doubt the Iranians have done their part to mislead us. They'll tell you the Mosaddeq coup is important to them even when they don't give it a second thought. It's part of the same "Iran is never what it seems" complex, which takes us back to the notion of *taqqiyah,* the obligation for a Shia to lie to protect the faith.

I got a taste of this in October 2007, when I arranged to meet Seyed Safavi, the brother of the recently resigned commander of the Islamic Revolutionary Guard Corps, Yahya Safavi. Like his brother, Seyed Safavi is a hard-liner. While a student in Tehran, he was jailed for anti-Shah activities. At the beginning of the Iran-Iraq War he served in the Basij, the reserves of the Revolutionary Guards, and then in the Guards itself. He rose steadily, serving on the front during the war, afterward going back to school to study for a civil engineering degree.

His brother was a key commander in Iran's early terrorism campaign against the West, every once in a while showing up in Lebanon to oversee the hostage-takers in the eighties. The brother was also one of the architects of the Islamic resistance. Yahya rarely gives interviews to the press, so Seyed, who is still supposedly close to his brother, was the best stand-in I could find.

We met in a Holiday Inn around the corner from his office in London. Seyed was wearing a neatly pressed suit and a white shirt with a Nehru collar. His thick beard was graying; it looked as though he pointedly did not want to fit into cosmopolitan London. I asked him about Mosaddeq and the 1953 coup.

"You know it was because of Mosaddeq that I refused to come to London for many years," he told me. He was afraid of Americans, he said, as he was of the British. Even today, he still thinks Britain is the "software" of colonialism and America the "hardware"—the British think up the infernal plots against Iran, and America executes them.

I pressed Seyed on whether Iran had ever moved beyond the Mosaddeq coup, or whether Iran had other aspirations than righting a wrong that occurred more than fifty years ago. Seyed answered that the Mosaddeq coup was a grievous injury to American-Iranian relations, a wound as fresh as it had been four decades earlier.

But is it just Mosaddeq? I pressed.

"The Iranians will never forget what you did to Iranian democracy."

That was all I was going to get. But I was convinced that Seyed knew better. For the last thirty years, his brother had been a general in Iran's growing empire. Seyed's brother hadn't spent all those years nursing a grudge, trying to right the Mosaddeq injustice. He was an Iranian who looked forward, not back. His brother Seyed, I was sure, was only parroting the party line for my benefit.

Iran has stopped thinking about the Mosaddeq coup just as surely as the Chinese have stopped thinking about U.S. support for Chiang Kai-shek, or the Russians about American help for the White Russians at Arkhangelsk in 1918. The United States humiliated Iran in 1953—but they more than paid us back with the 1979 embassy takeover, and by bloodying our nose in Lebanon.

Iran has more important things to think about. It's far more concerned today about preventing a civil war in Lebanon, which would erase the gains it made in the eighteen-year war there; stemming the chaos in Iraq; and not running through its oil faster than it needs to. And that's not to mention the empire it's just starting to build. The United States, on the other hand, has an understanding of Iran that's frozen in time.

The Gulf Arabs understand the currents of history. They know what Iran's rise means, how the balance has shifted against them. It's the reason that Saudi Arabia has started to bend on the issue of Israel, helping the Israelis in Lebanon to defeat Hezbollah. The Saudis are still ready to do much of Washington's bidding, if only to keep the U.S. fleet in the Gulf to protect them from Iran. As part of the same gamble, the Arabs are making a desperate attempt to reconcile with Iran, never excluding the possibility that one day we will withdraw our fleet—the Arabs' Maginot Line. The Arabs have a collective memory of having lived under a Persian empire, and they're terrified.

Iran confused the Clinton administration. After Madeleine Albright's speech was met with indifference by Iran, the Clinton administration never tried another opening, realizing that coming to terms with Iran would cost the United States a lot more than just a very belated apology.

Insights into what the Iranians really want are rare. One came when former Iranian president Akbar Hashemi Rafsanjani discussed that very issue in a private meeting with an Iranian source I can't name. Though he is a former president, Rafsanjani is the second-most powerful man in Iran today: He is chairman of the Expediency Council, an advisory body to Ayatollah Khamenei; a respected *mujtahid;* and a central player in Iran's political and foreign policy spheres. He's a power broker of the highest order.

Speaking for Iran's leadership, he said Iran would fight any war necessary for the security of the clerical regime. Any person, country, or group who attempted to undermine it would become the target of Iranian reprisals. There was no doubt what Rafsanjani meant—assassination, terrorism, war.

In the longer term, Rafsanjani said, Iran is committed to undermining the "unipolar" world—a world with one remaining superpower, the United States. A global American hegemony would suffocate Iran. One alliance to offset it would be with China. Rafsanjani said he personally would like to see an opening up of Iran's oil fields to China and Iran's relying on Chinese arms.

Finally, in extraordinary frankness for a society that lives behind walls, Rafsanjani said Iran's clerical and secular leadership intended to regain "Iran's past greatness." He spoke of the "imperial outlook" that prevailed among Iran's religious leaders, an impulse to promote militant Islam. They wanted to turn Iran into a "citadel of Islam" to help oppressed Muslims worldwide. They wanted to control Mecca and Medina, Islam's two holy cities.

What really struck Rafsanjani's Iranian interlocutor was the phrase "imperial outlook." Here was Iran's most powerful leader after Ayatollah Khamenei, talking openly about a new Iranian imperium. The game had definitely changed since Iranian students overran the U.S. embassy in Tehran.

And there was nothing to suggest Iran's imperial ambition was confined to its clerics. In the spring of 1992, in the first parliamentary elections since the death of Ayatollah Khomeini, the radicals dropped from 42 percent of the seats to just 17 percent. The new Majlis, or parliament, never questioned Iran's aggressive foreign policy, particularly in Lebanon. The Islamic resistance, support for Shia, the security of the clerical regime were all policies that went unquestioned. Iranians, whether they wore clerical robes or not, all wanted an empire.

Iran's aims are rooted not in Khomeini's revolution but rather in what Iranians consider their core national interests. The United States shouldn't count on the emergence of a moderate parliament that will give up Lebanon or oppose Iranian dominion in the Gulf. Iranians are united in their goals. The only thing that separates them is the means of pursuing those goals.

Incidentally, when Rafsanjani talked about Iran's enduring interests, he never mentioned a nuclear bomb or the destruction of Israel. Unlike President Ahmadinejad, Iran's real leaders know that a nuclear bomb is very much a secondary interest. A bomb can come later, when Iran is an acknowledged superpower and no one would dare stop it from acquiring one. Iranian patience has always paid off, and so it will now.

Although none of this became public before now, Rafsanjani's interpretation of what Iran wants can't be ignored. Through all of Iran's postrevolutionary crises, scandals, and mistakes, and into the twenty-first century, Rafsanjani has proven to be the best barometer of Iranian policy and strategy. Even in Iraq he pulls many of the strings—through both the Revolutionary Guards and Iran's Iraqi proxies.

Another clue to what Iran really wants surfaced when Saudi Arabia and Iran began a substantive back-channel conversation in 1995. Immediately, the Saudis understood that although seven years had passed since the end of the Iran-Iraq War, the fact that Saudi Arabia had supported Iraq was still an open wound for Iran. The Iranian envoy told the Saudis that relations would never improve until the two countries came to terms with how badly Saudi Arabia had behaved during that conflict, when it indirectly financed Saddam's invasion of Iran's Khuzestan Province. The Iranian envoy told the Saudis that Tehran would never again tolerate any attempt to divide Iran ethnically between Sunni and Shia.

The Saudis agreed they could live with that condition, and in general found Iran's other demands to be reasonable. The Iranians wanted better accommodation for Shia making their annual pilgrimage to Mecca and Medina. They asked also that Saudi Arabia not host a visit of the Bahai, a sect the Iranians feel is tantamount to apostates.

What the Saudis found remarkable was what the Iranians didn't ask for. They didn't ask for better treatment of Saudi Arabia's Shia, for a cutback on oil production to raise world prices, or that Saudi Arabia sever its relations with the United States.

This was all very reasonable, but the talks went nowhere. One reason was that the Saudis found out that, despite their talk of wanting a truce, Iran was behind the attack on the U.S. military barracks in Khobar, Saudia Arabia, in 1996. Another reason was that Iran was well on its way to stealing Lebanon and the Palestinian struggle from the Arabs.

Now, with Iran's victory in Lebanon, the question for the Saudis is whether the Iranians are any more reliable than they were then.

So what do the Iranians want? Based on their actions and what they've told Western officials, they seem to have six core interests:

Internal security. Iran is 89 percent Shia and 9 percent Sunni. The Sunnis are a small minority, but Iran still looks at them, as well as the Kurds in Iran, as its Achilles' heel.

More than ten years after Rafsanjani's articulation of Iran's interests, Iran still won't tolerate having anyone trying to exploit its internal ethnic and sectarian divisions. Meaning, if car bombs start going off in Tehran, we can count on the Iranians setting off responding ones in Iraq and Saudi Arabia. Iran would undoubtedly return to international terrorism if it thought foreign support of Iran's *takfiris* was seriously weakening its regime.

The Iranians want us to stop dealing with three Iranian terrorist groups responsible for killing Iranians: the Party for the Free Life of Kurdistan (PEJAK), an Iranian Kurdish separatist organization that has taken refuge in northern Iraq; the Mujahidin-e Khalq, which is based in Iraq; and Jundallah, an Iranian Baluch group affiliated with al Qaeda. All three groups maintain contact with American intelligence. Iran's demand is that we not help these groups, as we have asked Iran not to help al Qaeda.

Iraq. Iran is there to stay. Nothing short of a regime collapse in Tehran will change that. Empire aside, Iran does have a vital interest in putting an end to the chaos in Iraq. It also opposes having a hostile leader like Saddam, whether Sunni or Shia, taking power there.

Energy. Iran wants a better price for its oil, modern technology to more efficiently lift it, and alternative energy sources for the day it runs out of oil. This would include nuclear power plants.

In spite of Iran's threat to close Hormuz and make the United States suffer economically, Iran has no long-term interest in undermining international energy markets, driving up energy prices to the point of forcing the West into a depression, or in any other way damaging the world's economy. Iran wants order in oil markets, not chaos.

An Iranian empire. Short of drastic action, Iran won't cede its dominion in Lebanon, Iraq, Syria, the Gulf, and Gaza. Iran will insist on dominion in the Gulf after the United States leaves. It will hold itself out as the protectors of the Shia as well as the Palestinians.

At the same time, Iran understands that duties come along with empire. Iran may feel responsible for the Shia in Saudi Arabia's Eastern Province, but that doesn't mean it will push Saudi Arabia's Shia into a civil war. Iran will not attempt to create Shia Islamic republics in any country where it exerts influence, knowing that Sunni-Shia civil war would be the result.

Control of Mecca. Iran wants control of Mecca. For 1300 years, the Shia have been second-class Muslims. With Iran's newfound military predominance, there's no longer any reason to accept the status quo. It's unclear what precisely Iran's mullahs will demand, but it will probably be co-administering both Mecca and Medina along with Saudi Arabia.

Recognition/equality. At the bottom of it all, the Iranians want to be treated fairly. Iran wants to be recognized for what it is: a stable country that has lived within the same borders for thousands of years, the most powerful country in the Gulf, OPEC's second-largest producer, a regional economic power, and a major influence in Islam.

Iran wants to live under a fair international system. Why, for example, does the world ignore UN Resolution 242, which calls for Israel to withdraw to its pre–June 5, 1967, borders but not UN resolutions against Iran? And why should Iran be put under an International Atomic Energy Agency nuclear inspection regime and not Israel?

A sense of unfairness pierces the core of the Iranians' basic beliefs. Not only is justice a guiding principle in itself, it is a manifestation of God as well. It's a defining precept of Khomeini's revolution. But it's also deeper than that, as expressed in the writings of Ali Shariati, the man who helped establish the foundation for Khomeini's revolution.

Shariati was born in a small village in Khorasan, a province on Afghanistan's border. His father was a popular Friday prayer leader.

At university, Shariati supported Mosaddeq and was imprisoned after the coup. After his release, he went to study in Paris. There he fell under the spell of the Algerian war of liberation against France. He was particularly influenced by Frantz Fanon's *The Wretched of the Earth*, a scorching condemnation of colonialism.

Shariati returned to Iran with not only a doctorate but also a life-long hatred of colonialism. He was influenced by liberalism and Marxism but was also convinced that they alone were inadequate to mobilize the Muslim world. Some hybrid was needed—something combining Islam with socialism that would liberate Iran and other Muslim countries.

Shariati was convinced that faith was the bond that held Muslims together and inspired them to revolt. He referenced the lives of Shia Islam's early martyrs, Ali and Husayn, and built his political theories around their defiance and sacrifice. The first principle was that the leader of the faithful had to be an imam. But it's the second that the West must understand if we are to understand what Iran wants.

Justice, for Shariati, is elevated to the rank of a theological principle, part of an Iranian's cosmological view. It is as simple as "God equals justice." So not only can a believing Muslim not tolerate tyranny in his own country, he cannot tolerate it anywhere.

Shia Islam—or really, Islam in general—is therefore a progressive political movement, an ongoing struggle between justice and injustice. It is tied to action, which is why Shariati disregarded "quietist" Shia clerics like Ayatollah Sistani. To Shariati's mind, a cleric who stays out of politics has abandoned the quest for divine justice.

Again, we see in Iran a hybrid—a hegemon seeking justice. Iran has a divine obligation to render justice, to overthrow the grotesquely corrupt regimes on the Arab side of the Gulf. It's very similar to America's "manifest destiny," or even our commitment to spreading democracy and free trade. Grand values like this are never attainable, and indeed Iran has fallen far short, but nonetheless they drive the Iranians at a very basic level. Shariati's political philosophy, it should also be noted, is deeply rooted in Zoroastrian notions of good and evil.

Shariati turns the seventh-century Husayn myth—the death of the lone, abandoned martyr—on its head. You don't simply let yourself be slaughtered in the desert like a lamb. You don't simply wait for end times, the Mahdi's return. Instead, you fight. As if in a modern-day Husayn myth, Iran has now cast America in the role of the ancient Umayyids—as a decadent, corrupt force doomed to lose. Just as the Iranians are doomed to sacrifice.

Above all, in the way the Iranian regime has cast the conflict, the United States represents injustice. The longer we prop up failing regimes in Saudi Arabia and Pakistan, and the longer we don't force the Israelis to comply with UN Resolution 242, the longer the Iranian regime can count on the support of the Iranian people. When Blackwater contractors murder seventeen unarmed civilians in downtown Baghdad, or when Israel shells Gaza, killing civilians—these are the things that keep the Iranian revolution alive and win over converts to Iran's hegemony. As long as Iran has a convincing case that the West is unjust, it will continue to successfully contest us for dominion in the Middle East.

None of Iran's six core interests are impracticable or excessive. But meeting them would globally shift the balance of power. How should the West respond? With nine defined negotiating points, as outlined in the Epilogue.

EPILOGUE

In the Middle East, as everywhere, there are no moral absolutes, only lesser evils. My hope for this book was to sort them out, to choose what is practicable and what isn't. And to set the facts straight.

For too long now, the West has looked at Iran through a prism that distorts the country beyond recognition. During the thirty-year war between Iran and the United States, we overlooked Iran's worst transgressions—kidnappings, bombings, and assassinations. At the same time, we missed Iran's transformation into a rational, calculating state.

It's time we finally recognize Iran for what it is today, rather than what it was in February 1979. It doesn't matter what we call Iran—a regional power, a hegemon, or a superpower—we have to do something about it. We have three broad options:

Contain Iran. This would mean indefinitely staying in Iraq. Iraq can be held together only by sheer armed force. The same is true of Afghanistan. With the amount of territory NATO already has lost to the Taliban, we would need another 200,000 troops to take it back. Before long, we'd match the size of the Soviet Union's onetime occupation force in that country.

In all, we would need to position roughly 500,000 troops on Iran's borders to restore order in Iraq and Afghanistan and stop Iran from spreading its influence. And for how long? Optimistically, this would be the start of a new thirty-year war. Pessimistically, it's a hundred-year war. Keeping two armies of this size in the Middle East would necessitate bringing back the draft and raising trillions of dollars in additional taxes. And still, it would be only a standoff, with no chance of victory. America's will to indefinitely sacrifice young men and women and empty its treasury wouldn't last ten years, much less thirty or a hundred.

The United States could go to war with Iran, but the outcome is uncertain. As President Bush's secretary of defense, Robert Gates, said in a 2008 *New York Times* interview, taking on Iran is not an option.

"The last thing the Middle East needs now is another war," he said.

Given the advances the Iranians have made in asymmetrical warfare, and their continued fostering of a cult of death, invading Iran would be nothing like invading Iraq. And holding on to Iran would be a nightmare. The result would be hundreds of thousands of American casualties.

Finally, the United States could undertake a long open-ended bombing campaign, the same thing we used to contain Saddam from 1991 to 2003. But that won't work either, according to Gates.

"I think there's a risk that an attack would strengthen Ahmadinejad and solidify the Iranian people's support for their regime," he told the *New York Times*.

Not only should we count on bombing Iran having the opposite of the intended effect, we should also count on Iran's retaliating by either shutting down Hormuz or rocketing the Gulf's oil facilities.

Provoke a Sunni-Shia civil war. The *Mad Max* option is to provoke Muslims to kill one another rather than us. Already there are neocons in Washington who are thinking about this. One scenario is to restart the civil war in Lebanon by arming Sunni *takfiris* to attack Hezbollah. The idea is that Hezbollah, plunged into a sectarian war, would no longer be able to rocket Israel, ending its leadership of the resistance. Iran couldn't help but support the Shia in Lebanon, and would lose its anticolonial credentials in the process.

But the last time anyone tried something like this was when the

Saudis supported the Sunni *takfiris* in 1979—which ended up doing more damage than good, culminating in the rise of al Qaeda and the 9/11 attacks. And that's not to mention that if the West sets Lebanon on fire, we'd be setting fire to the roof of the Arab Gulf states. Could those six very dysfunctional sheikhdoms—Bahrain, Oman, Kuwait, Qatar, Saudi Arabia, and the United Arab Emirates—not collapse in civil war themselves, taking the world's reserve tank with them?

Settle with Iran. Alternatively, America could take its medicine and sit down at the negotiating table with Iran, treat it like the power it has become, and see what it has to offer. This would be a bitter pill, acknowledging Iran's predominance in the Middle East—declaring Iran a superpower if that's what it wants to be called. But we would finally find out if there's truly a confluence of interests, as I suspect there is. We would answer the question: As an ally, would Iran be more reliable and more reasonable than the Sunnis, the sect we've so long placed such blind trust in?

The only real option for the United States—if we admit we're not prepared to enter a hundred-year war, with a determined enemy, on the other side of the world—is the last one. Yes, it would be wrenching, with consequences as profound as the British walking away from their empire after World War II or the French theirs in Southeast Asia. But the first two alternatives are much worse.

It's difficult to admit that we failed in Iraq and now need Iran's help. And it's even more difficult to face the truth: that Iraq must be partitioned. We would need Iran's help in dividing up Iraq along ethnic lines—into Sunni Kurdistan, Sunni Anbar Province, Shia Baghdad, and the Shia south. Washington and London won't want to acknowledge they made a strategic blunder. But then again, Iraq is halfway to being partitioned already.

Why not allow the Iranians to take a more direct control of the parts of Iraq they already influence through proxies? This would be more efficient, and there would be less violence. Let the Iranians take direct responsibility for the cities of Najaf, Karbala, and Basra, which would force Iran to be more cautious and less the spoiler. Anyhow, Iran stands a better chance of putting an end to the chaos in those cities. The Iranians have shown a better ability to create order out of chaos than anyone in the Middle East. They have the troops to occupy Iraq. So why not let them shoulder the costs of occupation along with us?

Turning any part of Iraq over to Iran would be a Gulf Arab nightmare. But an even worse one would be to allow Iraq's chaos and sectarian divisions to spill across its borders. If cooperation between Iran and the United States were to work in Iraq, and expand to other parts of the Middle East, in the long run it would have a reassuring effect on the Arabs. It would mitigate the possibility of, for instance, Saudi Arabia and Iran fighting a war in Iraq.

Anyway, what really is the alternative? How many lives and how much money is the United States prepared to spend to prop up the Persian Gulf, keep the corrupt Al Saud family in power, keep Dubai's fancy hotels open? If the Congressional Budget Office estimate is right, and we're spending $2.4 trillion a decade to fight in Iraq and Afghanistan, how long can that go on? That figure would go much higher, of course, if it included the defense of the rest of the Gulf and massive arms packages to Israel.

We're talking about spending the country's wealth on a part of the world where we barely understand *who* we're fighting, much less *why* we're fighting. We could take that same money, spend it on alternative energy resources, and let the Middle East work out its own problems.

Effective sanctioning of Iran is a dream. Iran's regime is still standing after thirty years of sanctions—still able to buy anything it wants from China and Russia. Some of America's closest allies, such as Turkey and Japan, trade with Iran as if there were no sanctions at all.

A January 2008 Government Accountability Office report put it like this: "U.S. officials and experts report that U.S. sanctions have specific impacts on Iran; however, the extent of such impacts is difficult to determine." More to the point, as long as the price of oil is high, and the world is running out of oil, Iran will be able to buy what it needs to remain a regional power. An airtight embargo, if it were possible to enforce, would only take us back to war.

Willingly turning any part of the Gulf over to Iran would be decried as a capitulation, the equivalent of granting Osama bin Laden amnesty and accrediting him as Saudi Arabia's ambassador to the UN. But that, of course, completely mischaracterizes Iran.

To borrow a French diplomatic term, Iran is the Middle East's only *interlocuteur valable*—the only country that can and will deliver. The others sit on foundations of sticks, bound to fail us, bound to collapse. Pakistan is on its way to collapsing, Saudi Arabia teeters on the edge, the Emirates are little more than a giant high-end shopping mall, Qatar has the population of a large hotel. Algeria is still in the middle of a vicious, no-quarter-given civil war—yet another failed Sunni state. Iran is the only stable, enduring state in the Gulf.

If we ignore their words and focus on their actions, Iran and its proxy Hezbollah are rational actors. They're willing to talk to the West. They're willing to set bounds. They have fixed, reasonable demands. It is time the United States stops standing on pride and principles it can no longer afford.

In the interest of realpolitik, we should explore the possibility of cooperating with Iran in policing the Gulf. After all, Iran already allows 17 million barrels of oil to pass through the Strait of Hormuz daily, unimpeded and untaxed. In contrast, given the means, a Sunni *takfiri* such as bin Laden would have tried to choke off that oil flow long ago, whatever the consequences. Sunni *takfiris* already tried to blow up a tanker off the coast of Yemen in 2002. And Saudi *takfiris* have twice tried to blow up their country's own main Abqaiq oil facility, in hopes of causing global havoc.

We share with the Iranians a common interest in keeping the Gulf open. Iran has the navy to do it, and the United States can keep fewer aircraft carrier groups there while still maintaining a presence.

Working with Iran will narrow the opportunities for conflict and accidents.

Engaging Iran would also slow or put a stop to its drift toward Russia and China. Those two countries have been arming Iran for years, and America's continuing to isolate Iran only pushes it closer to them. If we do nothing, Russia and China will sell Iran even more sophisticated submarines, surface-to-air missiles, and tanks, all of which will sharply increase the price of a settlement later. Also, with Russia and Iran being the number-one and number-two producers of natural gas, they could easily form a monopoly that would decide whether Europe goes to bed cold or warm. And none of this is to mention that China and Russia are happy to continue helping Iran develop a nuclear weapon.

Russia is a wild card in Middle East poker; even the Saudis are trying to play it. In February 2008, Saudi foreign minister Prince Saud Al Faisal flew to Moscow to meet with then-president Vladimir Putin and propose a bilateral cooperation agreement, including $50 billion in investments between the Russians and the Saudis. The Saudis see the way the wind is blowing in the Gulf, and they're doing anything they can to undercut a Russian-Iranian alliance. The Saudis are doing what the United States should be doing—balancing their strategic alliances.

Not surprisingly, one of the Saudis' worst fears is that an Iranian-American pairing is inevitable.

"Every time I go to Riyadh," a State Department officer told me, "the Saudis ask, What happens to us when you come to your senses and reconcile with Iran?"

But to put it bluntly: Do we really care what happens to Saudi Arabia if Iran is able to guarantee Saudi oil fields?

The Shia ascendancy is unmistakable, the arc from Shia defeat to Shia victory almost complete. The Shia truly sense they've entered a century that is theirs.

For 1300 years, the Shia looked at Husayn's seventh-century martyrdom at Karbala as a metaphor for eternal suffering—and a metaphor that they'd have to wait until the hereafter for justice. But that all changed in October 1983, in Nabatiyah, Lebanon, when an Israeli patrol shot two Ashura celebrants dead. From that day on, the Shia stopped accepting suffering in silence and fought back. Over the next eighteen years, the Shia in Lebanon erased centuries of humiliation, figuring out that justice could be obtained in the here and now, setting the first pillar of new Persian empire.

America's choice is whether we attempt to hold back the Shia, force Iran to kneel, and submit to a destiny we intend to choose for them, or whether we find a way to ride the tide.

In January 2008, during Ashura demonstrations in Lebanon, Hassan Nasrallah declared, "Oh Zionists, your army is lying to you. . . . Your army has left the body parts of your soldiers in our villages and fields. . . . I'm not talking about just body parts. I tell the Israelis, we have the heads of your soldiers in our villages and fields, we have hands, we have legs."

Nasrallah's gruesome imagery was not a cruel taunt; it was a message: Hezbollah's victory over Israel in 2006 was a military one. Hezbollah had stopped the Israeli juggernaut. It wasn't just slaughter for slaughter's sake: Hezbollah's intention was to take ground, to kill Israeli soldiers rather than civilians. Hezbollah's fight wasn't against the West as a whole but against an occupying colonialist force.

So Nasrallah's words were aimed not only at his followers but also at the Egyptians, the Jordanians—at anyone in the Middle East who would willingly turn away from the random, rage-filled slaughter of bin Laden, toward a gruesome but conventional war.

We're in a military struggle with Iran, and military struggles can be negotiated. The Iranians aren't demanding surrender; they're ready to negotiate. And it won't be the first time Iran has negotiated with a Western country and reached a satisfactory outcome for both sides—the negotiations after the Paris bombings in the mid-eighties followed the same pattern.

When the Iranian-backed terrorists set off their bombs in Paris, the French had to make a decision. Would they continue to send arms to the Iraqi army? Or would they make a deal with Iran? And if they did reach an agreement with Iran, how could they be sure Iran would stick to it? It's not as if a country that sets off bombs in a European capital can exactly be trusted. Talks took place in complete secrecy, and a step-by-step solution was agreed to: As soon as France initiated an arms-and-financial package for Iran, the Iranians released French hostages held by the Revolutionary Guards in Lebanon.

We can look at this in one of two ways: Either the Iranians are good blackmailers or they're trustworthy negotiators. In either case, the Iranians kept their promises to the French in spite of ups and downs in their relations. In the early nineties, when Imad Mughniyah proposed resuming attacks in Europe, the Revolutionary Guards refused. A deal was a deal.

The evidence we have now points to an Iran that we can deal with—so unlike the Sunni *takfiris* whom we can't even find, much less talk to. We just have to overcome our prejudices rooted in the past.

Détente between the United States and Iran should be another step-by-step process, establishing a list of quid pro quos that must be met for the process to continue.

1. **Guarantee Iranian internal security.** The United States would immediately stop calling for regime change in Iran. Iranian opposition groups in Iraq would be expelled. U.S. contacts with Iranian resistance groups, from the Baluch to the Iranian Kurds, would be halted. And the Shah's son would be stopped from using U.S. soil to call for regime change in Tehran.

Why shouldn't the Americans grant the Iranians what we're asking them to grant us? Besides, a stable Iran makes its leadership less paranoid, less susceptible to listening to radical factions, less prone to stumble into confrontation with the West. The more stable Iran is, the more rationally it acts.

In return, Iran would stop sending arms and money to Hamas and the Palestinian Islamic Jihad.

2. **Joint patrols in the Persian Gulf.** The worst fear of the U.S. military and State Department is that there will be an accidental confrontation between our ships and Iranian ships. As we did during the Cold War between Moscow and Washington, we need to establish a hotline between Tehran and Washington, as well as direct military-to-military communications in the Persian Gulf. This would be the first step in acknowledging Iran's security role in the Gulf.

In return, Iran would stop challenging our ships.

3. **Ease the embargo on Iran.** Western oil companies would be allowed to invest in Iranian fields—providing an immediate benefit to Iran's economy as well as a global benefit, by making Iran's oil fields more efficient. Iran would be allowed to import spare parts for its passenger airplanes.

In return, Iran would put a moratorium on arms shipments to Hezbollah.

4. **Grant Iran a defined security role in Iraq and Afghanistan.** Iran should take a direct role in stabilizing Basra and the Iraqi south. The United States would announce a timetable for its withdrawal, and negotiations for an international peacekeeping force would start. In Afghanistan, Iran and the United States should coordinate operations against the Taliban. Iran has already demonstrated that it's willing to work with the United States in

Afghanistan. The Northern Alliance was both an American and an Iranian ally. Iran encouraged the Northern Alliance, an Iranian proxy, to help the Americans recapture Kabul in 2001.

There's also no reason the United States shouldn't recognize Iran's predominant interest in Iraq and Afghanistan—the same kind of interests we have in Canada and Mexico. As long as Iraq remains in a state of civil war, or at the very least civil unrest, Iran's security is far more threatened than ours. We shouldn't expect Iran to contentedly place its security in our hands, based on our promises and failing record. Especially when we've been calling for the Iranian regime's overthrow for the last thirty years.

5. **UN Resolution 242.** In return for negotiating an Israeli-Palestinian settlement based on UN Resolution 242, which calls for Israel to withdraw to its pre-June 5, 1967 boundaries, Iran should be expected to help impose an immediate cease-fire on Hamas and the Palestinian Islamic Jihad.

Iran cannot guarantee a cease-fire, but basing a Palestinian settlement on international law will stand a lot better chance of succeeding with the Palestinians. At the same time, this would convince Iran that the international system was impartial.

So what can the Palestinians accept? In 1965, when the PLO was founded at the first session of the Palestine National Council, it adopted a charter to eliminate "Zionism in Palestine"—in other words, to destroy Israel. But in 1988, the PLO repudiated that part of the charter. It also reiterated that repudiation several times afterward, including in Oslo in 1993. Offering UN Resolution 242 might just be a deal the Palestinians can't refuse.

What we also would be achieving would be to separate Iran from the Palestinian issue, taking it away from Iran as a rallying cry. We want to get Iran out of the anti-Crusader business.

6. **Incorporate Hezbollah's militia into the Lebanese army.** Lebanon may in fact be hopeless, a country destined to break up into its ethnic pieces. Having Iran take part in Lebanon's dismemberment, if indeed it comes to that, would be essential. Hezbollah will never willingly disarm, but under Iranian guidance it would be more likely to accept a peaceful solution.

7. **Mecca.** We cannot and should not try to stand in the way of Iran's quest to dominate Islam. This is an issue the West has little interest in. We shouldn't care who administers Islam's two holy places, Medina and Mecca, just as long as they don't become a bank for terrorism or a recruiting station for jihadis.

   We should support Iran in demanding equal rights for the Gulf's Shia. Saudi Arabia's treating its Shia minority as chattel serves no one's interest.

   We should also join with Iran in eliminating *takfiri* movements. Working together, we should sanction Pakistan and Saudi Arabia whenever they support *takfiri* groups.

8. **Put Middle East nuclear arms under international supervision, including Israel's.** Once again, this speaks to the core issue of fairness in applying international laws. At the same time, by this step, Iran will have had to fully join the comity of nations.

9. **Establish an international body to audit oil supplies and set the price for oil.** It is in Iran's interest as much as ours to know how much oil is left. Vast swings in the price of oil don't serve Iran's interests. Iran's interests would be served by a regime to set the world price of oil.

The United States' allying with Iran would be one of the most momentous policy shifts in modern history—as significant as Nixon flying to China in 1972. But there isn't another choice.

We could stay with the status quo, try to force the mullahs out, continue to embargo Iran, or even try to bomb it into submission, but Iran will still be there, with its enduring interests, the same threat to the Gulf. The longer we fool ourselves about how we're making progress in Iraq and Afghanistan, the more costly it will be trying to reach a settlement later. Afghanistan, Iraq, Lebanon, Syria, Bahrain—they will all fall into Iran's hands, not so much like dominos but like water flooding a valley through a broken dam. The new world order, with the United States the sole superpower, cannot last, whether we launch a war against Iran or not.

It's time not to surrender but rather to deal. America can accommodate many parts of Iran's quest for empire without ceding any of its core vital national interests. Recognizing Iran for the regional power it is will avoid much of the violence that goes with the creation of empire. We avoided a nuclear confrontation with Russia during the Cold War because we established red lines neither country crossed, and in fact worked together to dampen down conflict in the Middle East. Why can't Iran play the same role?

The United States shares with Iran a common enemy in the Sunni *takfiris*. Both Iran and the West suffer from their random violence, but also would suffer from the collapse of Sunni states like Saudi Arabia and Pakistan. When it comes time to do something about a lost nuclear weapon in Pakistan, for example, we'll want Iran on our side—just as we will if the Taliban make a grab for Kabul.

And it wouldn't be as if we were completely siding with Iran, supporting the Shia against the Sunni. Rather, it would be working with the one Mideast power that can produce results, unlike the Saudis. Who knows, an alliance with Iran might make the Sunni sit up and pay attention, do something about their *takfiris*, in order to return to being a responsible, trusted player.

Few thought Mao's China would ever become the United States' partner in East Asia, or even one of our main trade partners, or that it would be our two countries who eventually drove a wedge into the Soviet Union. Blindly confronting Chinese Communism resulted in the deaths of tens of thousands of Americans in Korea and Vietnam—far more than the Iranians have ever caused. But we were ultimately able to ignore the recent past in the interests of balance-of-power politics.

And that's precisely what we could accomplish with Iran. Having Iran on our side would counter Russia and China. Whenever Russia threatened to shut off natural gas to Europe, we'd have Iran to step in to make up shortfalls from the Persian Gulf. If the UAE dissolved into a civil war, we'd have Iran to restore the peace.

We've come this far, so why not speculate on redrawing the Middle East's borders? National demarcation lines between the Tigris and Nile rivers are artificial, drawn for colonial expediency rather than the interests of the people who live within them. The 1916 Sykes-Picot Agreement that divided up the Middle East was kept a secret, because the British and the French knew that the borders were arbitrary and likely to please almost no one. And in fact Sykes-Picot proved to be an unqualified catastrophe. There's no reason to keep it.

The question would be whether to redraw the lines in Israel's favor or Iran's. The neocons believe that if the West gives Jordan to the Palestinians, the Middle East's problems will evaporate. That, of course, would solve only a small part of the problem. The Iran-Iraq War had nothing to do with the Palestinians, and neither do the current Iraq-Afghan wars.

But why not redraw borders in both Iran's *and* Israel's favor? They're the two most politically stable countries. Their combined militaries dwarf those of the Arab states. And many of their vital national interests intersect.

Yes, redrawing borders is messy. We're in the situation we are in today because the Ottoman Empire collapsed in a messy way. On the other hand, the Soviet borders were dissolved with relatively little violence, because Moscow concurred and helped the breakup.

Moreover, we must consider that, in effect, we've already started the process of rewriting Sykes-Picot in Iraq and Lebanon. Why not smooth out the turmoil through formal negotiations?

Holding on to Sykes-Picot, holding together the Middle East through blunt military force, can only lead to more war. Shouldn't we get on as quickly as we can with the partition of Iraq? The Shia already control 80 percent to 90 percent of Baghdad. The Kurds have rearmed and are ready to fight for their independence. Can we really stop them, fight valley by valley to keep Kurdistan part of Iraq?

There's no harm in leaving Anbar to the Sunni and encouraging them to federate with Saudi Arabia; strong tribal links already exist. As for Jordan, there's no reason we should be bound by our emotional ties to the ruling Hashemite family. We should bow to demographics and turn Jordan into a Palestinian state, federated with the West Bank, or for that matter give Gaza back to Egypt. Finally, why not hold a referendum in Bahrain to determine whether it stays as is or returns to its old status as an Iranian island?

The Middle East we grew up with has already vanished, in all but name. Anticipating the consequences rather than futilely trying to stop them is the easiest—and ultimately surest—path forward.

GLOSSARY

abaya, chador, hijab Women's head covers, intended to protect their propriety.

Al Saud The ruling dynasty in Saudi Arabia.

Amal A Lebanese Shia political party.

Arba'in Fortieth day of mourning for Imam Husayn, a descendant of the prophet Muhammad who was killed at Karbala on December 10, 680.

Ashura A day of mourning for Imam Husayn.

ayatollah A high rank awarded to Shia clerics. A grand ayatollah, *a marja'al-taqlid,* is the highest rank for a Shia. Worldwide, there are only about twenty grand ayatollahs, including Ali Sistani in Iraq and Ali Khamenei in Iran.

Ba'th Arab Socialist Party that ruled in Iraq under Saddam and still rules in Syria.

Basij Reserves of the Islamic Revolutionary Guard Corps.

Coalition Provisional Authority The U.S.-led transitional government in Iraq, which governed the country from April 21, 2003, to June 28, 2004.

Da'wa An Islamic party, founded in the 1950s, that was formed by Iraqi Shia clerics to promote Islamic values. Da'wa was ruthlessly put down by Saddam Hussein.

Expediency Council An advisory body to Iran's Supreme Leader that resolves disputes over legislation. In October 2005, the Expediency Council was given "supervisory" authority over all branches of government, which significantly strengthened the hand of its chairman, the former Iranian president Hashemi Rafsanjani.

Fatah A Palestinian resistance organization founded by Yasser Arafat in 1955. It is the largest organization within the Palestine Liberation Organization.

Hama Syria's third-largest city. In February 1982, the Syrian army put down a Muslim Brotherhood revolt there, killing an estimated 25,000 people in what became known as the "Hama Massacre."

Hamas A branch of the Muslim Brotherhood located in the Palestinian Gaza strip.

Hezbollah In Arabic, literally "party of god." Lebanese Hezbollah was officially founded in 1985 to bring together in one organization Iranian-allied militant groups and clerics. The Islamic Revolutionary Guard Corps supervises and funds Hezbollah. Other Shia and Sunni groups going by the name Hezbollah were subsequently established by Iran in other countries.

ijtihad A process of arriving at a legal decision using independent judgment based on the Koran, the sayings of the prophet, and other sources of Islamic law. This concept is rarely used by Sunni Muslims, who instead look to tradition and precedent in issuing legal edicts.

imam In Arabic, literally "in front." Imam refers to a cleric who leads prayer in a mosque. For Shia, an imam has a wider connotation in that a Shia imam is an intermediary between Allah and a believer, giving the Shia imam more authority and generally more respect than a Sunni imam. The divinely appointed successors to the prophet are also called imams.

Imam Husayn The grandson of the prophet Muhammad and the son of Ali, the fourth caliph. Husayn was killed at the battle of Karbala in A.D. 680.

Iran-Contra A controversial arms-for-hostages deal undertaken during the Reagan administration.

Iraqi National Congress An Iraqi umbrella group formed in 1992, headed by Ahmed Chalabi.

Islamic Amal A breakaway faction from Lebanon's Amal Party. It is financed by Iran.

Islamic Jihad Organization The name of a front group, under the Jerusalem Force, used to claim terrorist attacks.

Islamic resistance The name used by Hezbollah for its eighteen-year war against Israel in Lebanon (1982–2000).

Islamic Revolutionary Guard Corps (IRGC) Formed in May 1979, the Revolutionary Guards were originally organized to protect Khomeini's revolution. During the Iran-Iraq War, they were integrated into Iran's armed forces. Today, they are a force roughly equivalent to U.S. Special Forces, but in addition they maintain their own air force and navy. They also command Iran's rocket forces.

Jerusalem Force (Quds Force) A secretive Revolutionary Guard unit responsible for overseas operations, including intelligence collection, assassinations, coups, and training of foreign guerrilla forces. In the eighties and early nineties it was involved in kidnappings, hijackings, and the murder of civilians.

Karbala The site of the battle of Karbala in A.D. 680 in which the prophet's grandson, Imam Husayn, was killed.

Mahdi Army An Iraqi Shia paramilitary force formed by Muqtada al-Sadr in June 2003.

Majlis Iran's parliament.

Maronite Christians Members of an Eastern Catholic sect, one of the largest religious minorities in Lebanon.

mujtahid A Shia scholar qualified to issue legal edicts using independent judgment.

Muslim Brotherhood An Islamic revival movement founded in Egypt in 1928. It later splintered into factions, some of which retained the name the Muslim Brotherhood while dozens of others took different names.

Najaf, Iraq Twelver Shia Islam's holiest city, the site of a renowned Shia seminary and mosque.

Oslo Accords The first time Israel and the Palestinians negotiated directly. The Accords, signed on September 13, 1993, were intended to establish an independent Palestinian state in return for the Palestinians' recognition of Israel.

platter charge An explosive device that propels a flat or curved metal plate. One variety is an "explosive-formed projectile" (EFP), now commonly found in Iraq.

Qum, Iran The largest center for Shia theological scholarship in the world.

SCIRI Supreme Council for the Islamic Resistance in Iraq, founded in 1982 under the tutelage of the Revolutionary Guards. SCIRI's headquarters was in Tehran until April 2003, when it relocated to Baghdad. In May 2007, SCIRI changed its name to the Supreme Islamic Iraqi Council.

shaped charge An explosive charge formed in the shape of a cone in order to more deeply penetrate the armor of a tank.

T-72 Iraq's main battle tank, designed with Soviet-era technology from the sixties.

takfiri A dualistic Sunni militant who strictly divides the world into believers and nonbelievers. Nonbelievers are beyond the pale of the law, and the *takfiri* believes it is licit to destroy them.

taqqiyah A tenet of Shia Islam that allows a believer to lie or obfuscate in order to conceal his faith.

Twelver Shia Twelvers are the largest denomination in Shia Islam. The term derives from the Twelver Shia's belief in twelve divinely ordained imams who followed the prophet. Twelvers are a majority in Azerbaijan, Bahrain, and Iran. They are a significant minority in Lebanon, Kuwait, Saudi Arabia, Pakistan, and Afghanistan.

Umayyid Caliphate A seventh- to eighth-century Sunni ruling dynasty based in Damascus.

velayat-e faqih Literally, in Farsi, "the rule of the jurisprudent." Ayatollah Khomeini, who introduced the concept into modern Iran, believed that the cleric with the highest level of Islamic scholarship should rule.

ACKNOWLEDGMENTS

This book could not have been written without Lisa Dickey, editor, book doctor, skeptic, and invaluable scold. Every morning I turned on my computer to find an e-mail from her challenging one thing or another. "Why should the reader care?" she'd ask. Lisa made sure that irrelevant trivia, which so often find their way into books written by people who spend their lives in the Middle East, stayed out, and she put everything neatly in order.

I also could not have written this book without Kevin Toolis, Many Rivers Films, and Britain's Channel 4, which allowed me to tag along in their filming of documentaries on suicide and car bombers. I am deeply indebted to Nikki Keddie's *Modern Iran,* Vali Nasr's *The Shia Revival,* and Roy Mottahedeh's *The Mantle of the Prophet,* essential reading for understanding modern Iran. Finally, I thank my editor at Crown, Rick Horgan, who gave me the idea for the book—and kept it on track. In the end, any failings in this book are entirely mine.

INDEX

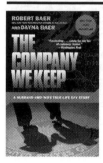

Printed in the United States
by Baker & Taylor Publisher Services